W9-CBZ-268

Historical Anthology
of Music by Women

Historical Anthology of Music by Women

EDITED BY

James R. Briscoe

INDIANA UNIVERSITY PRESS

Bloomington and Indianapolis

© 1987 by Indiana University Press

All rights reserved
No part of this book may be reproduced or utilized in any form
or by any means, electronic or mechanical, including photocopying
and recording, or by any information storage and retrieval system,
without permission in writing from the publisher. The Association
of American University Presses' Resolution on Permissions constitutes
the only exception to this prohibition.

Manufactured in the United States of America

Library of Congress Cataloging-in-Publication Data

Historical anthology of music by women.

English, French, German, Italian, and Latin words;
includes English translations printed as texts for
non-English-language works.
Principally reprints.
Contains vocal and instrumental music from the
Middle Ages to the present, with introductory
essays on each composer.
1. Music—Scores.   2. Women composers—Biography.
I. Briscoe, James R., 1949–
M1.H664   1986   85-45987
ISBN 0-253-21296-0 (pbk.)

1   2   3   4   5   91   90   89   88   87

Contents

Foreword

This historical anthology of music by women makes an important contribution to the growing literature about women composers. While many of the composers whose works it presents have been discussed in a variety of recent studies, and recordings of a number of the works already exist, without the scores presented here our understanding of these composers would remain limited. Teachers and students who wish to focus primarily on women's history as composers will find this anthology indispensable, but all teachers of traditional music history and literature courses should avail themselves of it and include examples from it in the courses they teach. Performers and students of performance wishing to broaden their repertoire will also find it valuable.

The anthology is especially useful since it presents works from all the traditional periods of Western music history, although because of the loss of many early works by women as well as women's slow entrance in significant numbers into musical composition, the earlier periods are less richly represented. But more than merely offering a chronology of women's works in the Western tradition, this anthology illustrates the development of the varied spheres in which women were active as composers—first convent and court, then home and private concert, then opera stage, public concert, ballet theater, and church. It also traces women's increasing embracement of wider genres of musical composition, moving from solo song to multivoiced vocal works, to solo instrumental and chamber music, and from there to symphony, opera, ballet, and, finally, experimental composition. Since this widening compositional realm was made possible by the expansion of music education opportunities for women and was accompanied by a shift from largely amateur to largely professional status, the anthology also illustrates these matters. Let me explain my claims.

The opening compositions by the nuns Kassia and Hildegard call attention to the earliest sphere we know that provided women with the kinds of musical training necessary for learning to compose—the convent. The work of Anne Boleyn represents the other early sphere in which we know women composed—the court. There, aristocratic women had access to private music training and, if especially gifted, learned to write words and music. Of course, neither nuns nor noblewomen were professional musicians.

With Maddalena Casulana a new level of women's participation in music was reached. Although she remains a shadowy figure, Casulana must have had access to a rather extensive musical education in order to master the composition of multivoiced madrigals, and she was also the first woman, in 1566, to seek the publication of her works. With the early seventeenth-century Francesca Caccini, we witness another step forward: just shortly before she was born, women began to achieve professional singing careers in northern Italian courts, and Caccini's appointment as a singer to the Florentine court gave her the opportunity not only to perform her own music but also to put forward works of larger scope. Just slightly later, Isabella Leonarda exemplifies the effect expanded opportunities for performing polyphony in Italian convents had on nun composers— at least in those places where nuns' music making was not interfered with by bishops and before convents themselves were suppressed.

Although the influence of the court was still strong at the turn of the eighteenth century, the city was soon to offer women new opportunities for music making because of the growth of private concerts. In early eighteenth-century Paris, harpsichordist

Elizabeth-Claude Jacquet de la Guerre became famous for concerts in her own home, thus becoming the first woman to achieve widespread distinction as an instrumentalist. Active over many years as a composer of most of the leading genres of her day, La Guerre was one of the first women to publish instrumental works and the first to write a complete opera. Her range as a composer exceeded that of any woman before her. Clearly a professional musician in every sense, she nevertheless did not hold an institutional position, as many of her male contemporaries did.

Other eighteenth-century women represented in the anthology illustrate the continued importance to women's musical creativity of belonging to a privileged class. Among them, Marianne von Martinez, considered very fine as both a singer and a keyboard player and the composer of numerous large and small works, described herself as a "dilettante at Vienna," thus distinguishing herself from those who worked in music professionally at a time when being a dilettante was still a mark of distinction.

The musical activities of her younger Viennese contemporary, Maria Theresia von Paradis, however, as well as those of the later figures Maria Szymanowska, Clara Schumann, and Cécile Chaminade, signal an important new influence on the development of women's music making—the public concert. With the rise of public concerts, women could and did promote themselves as vocalists and soloists on a variety of instruments—although it is revealing that all four of these women were pianists. At the same time, the domestic sphere became increasingly important for women's music making, and songs for voice and piano, such as those in this anthology by Fanny Mendelssohn Hensel, Schumann, Josephine Lang, and Pauline Viardot-Garcia, were one of the chief genres cultivated there. The work of Viardot-Garcia, however, also represents the continuing relationship between performing and composing, for she was an outstanding opera singer.

With Louise Farrenc, another new stage in the development of the woman musician arrived. Not only was Farrenc the first woman to hold a permanent professorship of piano at the Paris Conservatoire, but also she produced a steady stream of compositions throughout much of her life, feeling none of the uncertainties about her powers as a composer that Clara Schumann did, for example. Then in the late nineteenth and early twentieth centuries, Amy Marcy Beach and Ethel Smyth focused their musical energies primarily on composition. It was with their generation that women finally "came of age" as composers, even though Beach was entirely self taught in composition.

With the remaining women represented in the anthology, a variety of approaches to career and composition can be observed. Many of these women were trained in conservatories or universities, and a number of them also held or hold significant professional positions. Their work demonstrates the wide range of work women in this century have considered themselves capable of undertaking as well as the greater number of opportunities they have had. This is not to say, of course, that some of them have not been affected by their biology in ways men have not been and that marriage and motherhood have not brought about peculiarly female deflections of life courses and careers.

Still, this anthology reflects women's slow progress toward full participation in all spheres of musical life, along with offering some remarkable examples of their work. While I cannot begin to mention all the compositions I am moved by or find wonderful, I want to call particular attention to the magnificent first movement of Amy Beach's Symphony and to the scene from Ethel Smyth's finest opera, *The Wreckers.* But users of the collection should explore and sample a variety of works on their own, and in that way get to know many voices of women, not just one or two.

University of Wisconsin—Milwaukee   JANE BOWERS

Preface

> Throughout history the more complex activities have been
> defined and redefined, now as male, now as female,
> sometimes drawing equally on the gifts of both sexes. When
> an activity to which each could have contributed . . . is
> limited to one sex, a rich differentiated quality is lost from
> the activity itself.
>
> —Margaret Mead

The *Historical Anthology of Music by Women* aims above all to provide a single, accessible source of compositions by women suitable for mainstream music history teaching. It aims secondarily to show performers that a panoply of scores is available to them. If teaching and performance thus may be enriched with women's works from many eras, we might move a step further toward that differentiated quality of which anthropologist Margaret Mead spoke but which has not yet been realized. Furthermore, the presence of women's compositions in our classes and performances projects essential role models of women composers. Since education in music frequently omits such models from professional training, who can say how many young women have been discouraged from pursuing composition? As psychologist Grace Rubin-Rabson has noted:

> Women appear so impressed by the dismal picture history has so far given of
> their contribution to the arts that they picture creativity as an enduring character-
> istic of the male role. So long as they retain this picture of themselves, it is likely
> that relatively few will . . . put forth the effort essential to sustained creativity.

Only by impressing a full spectrum of future professionals and nonprofessionals alike with the image of successful women composers can debilitating habits of thought be broken. The *Historical Anthology of Music by Women* intends to set women composers apart only momentarily, only long enough to point out their essential contribution and thereby encourage the full integration that they deserve and that our contemporary culture requires.

The compositions in this anthology have been chosen above all because they are vital artworks that heretofore have received less attention than they merit. They also happen to meet criteria that are important for the classroom and the concert hall: they are drawn from all style periods of Western music; their idioms are compelling and hold students' and listeners' attention; they represent virtually all important genres and are in the forefront of contemporaneous musical thought; they are available on recordings or are readily performed in class; and their composers' lives highlight important aspects of period and society. The anthology thus is pertinent to survey courses in music history, where it may supplement standard anthologies, as well as to seminars on women composers. Because main styles and formal structures are represented, the anthology may also serve in theory and analysis courses.

The compositions span twelve centuries, from Byzantine chant by Kassia to the Symphony No. 1 by Ellen Zwilich, the recipient of the Pulitzer Prize in Music for

1983. These compositions can create an awareness of women's achievements as composers throughout Western history. Such an awareness is not merely fashionable: it is just, it encourages depth perspective in our view of music history, and it is necessary as we educate audiences and students.

The essay introducing each composer has been written by an established authority or, in some cases, by the composer herself. Each essay provides an overview of the composer's life and major works, traces main aspects of her style, and points out salient characteristics of the composition at hand. The essays include translations for vocal works that are not in English and suggest additional readings and recordings wherever pertinent.

The editor gratefully acknowledges the advisory role of the Committee on the Status of Women of the College Music Society. The particular counsel of Nancy B. Reich, chair, Adrienne Fried Block, past chair, and Karin Pendle has been most valuable. The idea for an anthology of women's scores grew out of a paper session during the 1983 national conference of the College Music Society in Dearborn, Michigan. So collegial was the experience of the session, and so supportive of the initial idea were the scholars just named, that the anthology became a happy inevitability.

The editor also wishes to thank the publishers of works under copyright and private holders of copyright; they have permitted the reprint of complete segments and even whole works for a modest fee or no fee at all. Full acknowledgment of their support is indicated on the first page of each score. The editor and the publisher are particularly honored to present first and first modern editions of several important works: Sinfonia from *Pallade e Marte* by Maria Grimani, the cantata *Semelé* by Elizabeth-Claude Jacquet de la Guerre, Prelude No. 2 for piano by Ruth Crawford Seeger, and the choral work *La Corona* by Louise Talma.

Along the way the support of Marcia J. Citron, chair of the Committee on the Status of Women of the American Musicological Society; Phillip Rhodes, president of the College Music Society; Bea Friedland, of Da Capo Press; and Barbara Garvey Jackson has proven of considerable importance. The editor extends his deep appreciation to the authors of the introductory essays, who have given generously of their time and expertise in the interest of a wider understanding; and he is sincerely grateful to the composers, living and past, for the enlightenment their work has brought. The editor reserves his highest appreciation for his wife, Anna, whose musicality first proved the heights to which women could soar and to whom he dedicates this edition.

Butler University   JAMES R. BRISCOE

xii

Historical Anthology
of Music by Women

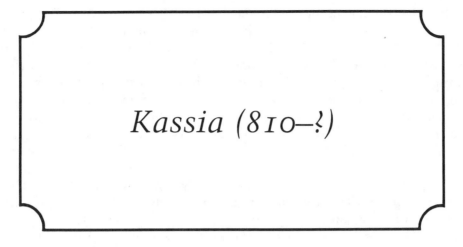

Kassia (810–?)

DIANE TOULIATOS-BANKER

The most important woman composer of medieval Byzantine chant is Kassia, who is also identified in manuscripts by other forms of her name (Κασία, Κασσία, Ε'ικασία, and Ἰκασία). Besides being a gifted composer and poet, she is an important historical figure. According to the chronicles of the Byzantine empire, Kassia, a beautiful and highly educated woman, was brought to the brideshow of Emperor Theophilos, where he would select his bride-to-be with the token of a golden apple. Theophilos first screened his candidates by testing their intelligence and wit. Kassia's response to his question displayed a mind far superior to his, which displeased and embarrassed the proud Emperor. Although Kassia captured Theophilos' heart, her greater wisdom lost her the opportunity to become empress, and she spent the rest of her life in a convent.

Kassia is mostly known as a composer of sacred poems, although she also wrote secular epigrams and moral sayings. She is credited with having written 49 liturgical compositions; however, 26 are of doubtful authorship, and the authenticity of some of her melodies has been questioned. Specifically, it has been debated whether Kassia wrote the music as well as the text for her liturgical poetry; but according to the tradition of the period, early hymnographers composed both text and music. Kassia also composed music to the text of other writers of the period.

The majority of Kassia's music falls under the category of the Sticheron, a lengthy verse chanted in various parts of the morning and evening office throughout the liturgical year. In one of her most popular melodies, the Sticheron "Augustus, the Monarch," Kassia compares the rule of Augustus with that of Christ. Besides the parallelism of textual themes, the metrical rhyming scheme corresponds to the parallelism in the music, for the melody consists of three phrases, each immediately repeated and followed by a fourth unrepeated phrase. This melodic structure, *aabbccd*, is one of several sequence forms. Although it is difficult to prove that the sequence is of Eastern origins, at least Kassia's composition substantiates the use of the sequence form in Byzantium as well as in the West.

Kassia's most famous composition is her Troparion "The Fallen Woman," which is sung in the morning office of Holy Wednesday. It was written after Kassia entered the convent and is considered autobiographical in part. Having regretted not choosing Kassia for his bride, Emperor Theophilos later attempted to meet her to express his sorrow and love. Although Kassia avoided the Emperor, in her heart she felt she had returned his love and had become a "fallen woman." With the exception of verse eight of the poem, which is attributed to Theophilos, the melody and text are Kassia's. According to legend and documentation, Kassia was in the process of writing this composition when Theophilos made one of his state visits to her monastery. On seeing him unexpectedly, Kassia fled and left the unfinished poem on her desk. Her departure inspired Theophilos to write the verse "Thy feet, whereof when Eve in Paradise heard the sound, she hid herself for fear." Although this line is not consistent with the theme of a fallen woman, it was retained. It is perhaps this incident that made the hymn so well known.

The setting of this chant is primarily syllabic with a few neumatic sections. The melody has an unusually wide ambitus of an octave and a fourth: c' to f". The linking device throughout this lengthy hymn is the motive B–A–G and its variants, which occur throughout the chant and are marked with brackets in the score. No recordings exist of Kassia's works, but because of its fame, "The Fallen Woman" has been arranged by many composers during Byzantine times as well as recently.

Further Reading

Touliatos-Banker, Diane. "Women Composers of Medieval Byzantine Chant," *College Music Symposium* XXIV/1 (1984):62–80.
———. "Medieval Women Composers in Byzantium and the West," *Acta Scientifica "Musica Antiqua"* 1982:687–712.
These articles contain a complete catalogue of Kassia's compositions, including types, incipits, modes, and occasions on which the chants were performed.

Augustus, the Monarch

Kassia

Mode II Authentic

Transcription from Athens MS. 883, f.97r
by D. Touliatos-Banker

"When Augustus became monarch upon earth,
    The multitude of kingdoms among men was ended.
And when Thou wast incarnate of the Holy One,
    The multitude of divinities among the idols was put down.
Beneath one universal empire have the cities come,
    And in one divine dominion the nations believed.
The folk were enrolled by the decrees of the emperor,
    We, the faithful, have been inscribed in the name of Deity.
        Oh, Thou our incarnate Lord,
        Great is Thy mercy, to Thee be glory."

Translation: H. J. W. Tillyard

"Augustus, the Monarch" and "The Fallen Woman" reprinted by permission of the publisher, The College Music Symposium.

3

The Fallen Woman

Kassia

Transcription from Athens MS. 883, f. 261v
by D. Touliatos-Banker

Mode IV Plagal

Κύ- ρι- ε ἡ ἐν πολ- λαῖς ἁ- μαρ- τί- αις πε- ρι- πε- σοῦ- σα

γυ- νὴ τὴν σὴν αἰ- σθο- μέ- νη Θε- ό- τη- τα.

μυ- ρο- φό- ρου ἀ- να- λα- βοῦ- σα τά- ξιν ὀ- δυ- ρο- μέ- νη

μύ- ρον σοι προ του ἐν- τα- φι- α- σμου κο- μί- ζει Οἴ- μοι

λέ- γου- σα ὅ- τι νύξ μοι ὑ- πάρ- χει οἶ- στρος ἀ- κο- λα- σί- ας

ζο- φώ- δης τε καὶ ἀ- σέ- λη- νος ἔ- ρως τῆς ἁ- μαρ- τί- ας

δέ- ξαι μου τὰς πη- γὰς τῶν δα- κρύ- ων ὁ νε- φέ- λαις δι-

εξ- ἀ- γων τῆς θα- λάσ- σης τὸ ὕ- δωρ κάμ- φθη- τί μοι

πρὸς τοὺς στε- ναγ- μοὺς τῆς καρ- δί- ας ὁ κλί- νας τοὺς οὐ- ρα- νοὺς

τῇ ἀ- φρά- στω σου κε- νώ- σει κα- τα- φι- λή- σω

τοὺς ἀ- χράν- τους σου πό- δας ἀ- πο- σμή- ξω τού- τους

δὲ πά- λιν τοῖς τῆς κε- φα- λῆς μου βο- στρύ- χοις ὧν ἐν τῷ Πα-

ρα- δεί- σῳ Εὖ- α τὸν δει- λι- νὸν κρό- τον τοῖς ὠ-

σὶν ἠ- χη- θεῖ- σα τῷ φό- βῳ ἐ- κρύ- βη ἁ- μαρ- τι- ῶν

μου τὰ πλή- θη καὶ κρι- μά- των σου ἀ- βύσ- σους τίς ἐξ-

ι- χνι- ά- σει ψυ- χο- σῶ- στα Σω- τήρ μου μή με τὴν

σὴν δού- λην παρ- ί- δῃς ὁ ἀ- μέ- τρη- τον ἔ- χων τὸ ἔ- λε- ος.

Mode III cadence

"Lord, the woman fallen in many sins, seeing Thy Divinity,
  Taking the part of myrrh-bearer, wailing bringeth to Thee myrrh
    against Thy burial.
Alas, she crieth, for that night is to me the wildness of sin, dusky
    and moonless, even the love of transgression.
Accept the springs of my tears, who with clouds partest the
    waters of the sea:
Bend to the groanings of my heart, who hast brought down Heaven
    by Thine ineffable humiliation.
I will kiss again Thy stainless feet,
I will wipe them then with the hair of my head—

Thy feet, whereof when Eve in Paradise heard the sound, she
    hid herself for fear.
The multitude of my sins, and the depths of Thy judgment who
    shall explore, Savior of souls, my Redeemer.
Forget not me Thy servant, Thou, whose mercy is infinite."

Translation: H. J. W. Tillyard

5

Hildegard von Bingen (1098–1179)

BARBARA JEAN JESKALIAN

A woman of the Middle Ages did not have many ways in which to distinguish herself. She could contract an expedient marriage; she could enter the church and rise to some degree in its hierarchy; or she could develop renown in the healing and occult arts. If we count the spiritual marriage of a nun as a Bride of Christ, Hildegard von Bingen distinguished herself in all three of these areas and more.

In her middle and late years, Hildegard was the abbess of a Benedictine monastery in the Rhineland. The Benedictines—the musicians of the Roman Catholic church—provided the rich atmosphere for her creativity and were the community that performed her compositions on festal days. Her many gifts included prophecy, the composition of the first morality play in the Western world (*Ordo Virtutum*, or *Order of Virtues*), correspondence with such notables of the time as Frederick Barbarossa and St. Bernard of Clairvaux, the writing of poetry and philosophy, and the compilation of a compendium of herbals for healing. Significantly, her musical compositions are among the most precious of her gifts to the world.

Her compositions do not conform to the linguistic and musical designs of her time. Hildegard used free texts and did not adhere strictly to the strophic form, in which all the stanzas of the text are sung to the same music rather than to a different melody for each verse. What distinguished her use of strophes was the elasticity and freedom with which she elaborated them. Inclined often toward melismatic style, she used as many as eleven notes to a syllable.

Hildegard's antiphons to the Virgin Mary give us some insight into the depth of her musical vision. "De Sancta Maria," #13 in the modern edition of her music cited below, is a chant sequence. It is both syllabic and neumatic and is written in the Aeolian mode. At "guttis pluviae" the change in clefs is especially notable and is possibly necessitated by a register change. It has certain strophic elements, but it is not written in a clear strophic form.

> O virgin, as well, the diadem of the crimson royal purple of the king who in your gate like as a breastplate
> You, becoming verdant, bloomed through all the changes which Adam brought forth in every race of man.
> Hail, hail, from your womb all life proceeded which Adam had stripped from his sons.

O flower, you were not to put forth from the dew, neither from the drops of rain, nor from the air which flowed from above, but the divine clarity brought you forth a most noble virgin.

O virgin, God foresaw your flowering in the first day of his creatures. And from the Word, he made your golden matter.

O most noble virgin, o how great it is, in his •trength from the side of man God produced the form of woman, which he made a mirror of all to his adornment and an honor to all of his creatures.

For that, the heavenly sounds celebrate and all the earth wonders, O most laudable Mary, whom God has certainly loved.

O how certainly it is to be bewailed and lamented because the sorrow from the guilt through the craftiness of the serpent has flowed in women.

But now, a woman alone whom God has made Mother of all, has expelled through her womb the disaster of ignorance and has manifested the full grief of her race.

But, O morning star, from your womb a new sun has exploded, banishing every guilt of Eve and has brought through you a greater blessing because Eve harmed man.

Whence, O Salvatrix, you have brought forward a new human light, gather together the limbs of your son to heavenly harmony.

[Translated from the Latin by Clifford Johnson.]

"In Evangelium," #44, is written in the Dorian mode with a frequently flatted B, suggesting the Aeolian mode. It is syllabic but does have some melismatic elements.

O redness of blood, Thou which has flowed down from the highest, which the Godhead has touched, Thou art the flower that the winter chill from out of the breath of the serpent surely has not wounded.

[Translated from the Latin by Clifford Johnson.]

Hildegard was consecrated to her religious order by her parents, Hildebert and Mathilde, as a tithe because she was their tenth and last child. To her, serving God was foremost; one of Hildegard's most striking ways of doing so was through writing music. (In the *Ordo Virtutum*, Diabolus has no musical lines to sing, but only shouts his words. This is Hildegard's way of expressing the Devil's separation from God.) Like the mystics who preceded and followed her—Tauler, Meister Eckhart, and Jakob Boehme—Hildegard moved toward unity with God by the mystic's path. Her compositions—musical, medical, theological, philosophical—were all part of that path. For the twelfth century she was a truly remarkable woman; she is also a model for the century in which we live.

Recordings

A Feather on the Breath of God. MHS 4889 M.

Hymns and Sequences. Gothic Voices Ensemble. Hyperion A66039 (same recorded performance as above).

Music for the Mass by Nun Composers. "Kyrie." University of Arkansas Schola Cantorum. Leonarda LPI-115, 1982.

Further Reading

Hildegard von Bingen. *Lieder,* edited by Prudentia Barth, Immaculata Ritscher, and Joseph Schmidt-Görg. Salzburg: Otto Müller Verlag, 1969. (Includes extensive textual and musical commentary and all extant scores.)

De Sancta Maria

Hildegard von Bingen

Sequ.

The musical notation (neumes on staves) with the following text underlay:

virga ac di-adema purpu- / ræ Regis, quæ es in clausura tua sic / ut lorica. Tu frondens floru-isti in / ali-a viciositudine, quam Adam o- / mne genus humanum produceret. / Ave, ave, de tuo ventre ali-a vita / processit, qua Adam fi-li-os suos de- / nudaverat. O flos, tu non germinasti / de rore nec de guttis pluviæ, nec / a-er desuper te volavit, sed di-vi-na / claritas in nobilissima virga te pro-

du-xit. O virga, floriditatem tu-am / De-us in prima di-e creaturæ su-æ / præ-vi-derat. Et de Verbo su-o aume- / am materiam, o laudabilis Virgo, / fecit. O quam magnum est in viri- / bus su-is la-tus viri, de quo De-us / formam muli-eris produxit, quam fe- / cit speculum omnis orna-menti / su-i et amplexi-o-nem omnis cre- / aturæ su-æ. Inde conci-nunt / cælesti-a organa, et mi-ratur o-

"De Sancta Maria," "In Evangelium," and "Kyrie" reprinted by permission of the publisher from Hildegard von Bingen, *Lieder*, edited by Prudentia Barth, Immaculata Ritscher, and Joseph Schmidt-Görg (Salzburg: Otto Müller Verlag, 1969).

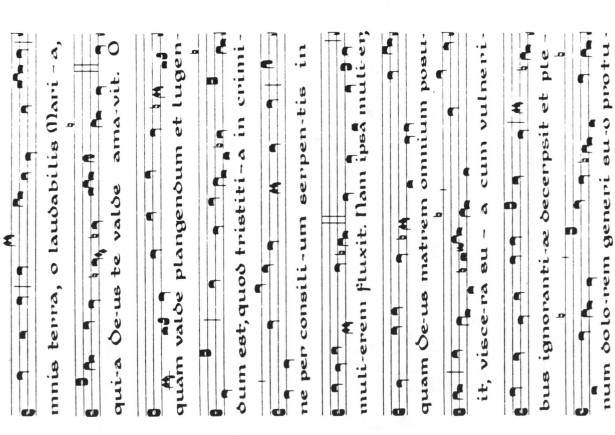

In Evangelium

Kyrie

Hildegard von Bingen

BEVERLY J. EVANS

"The Countess of Dia, a beautiful and good woman, was the wife of Guillaume de Poitiers. She fell in love with Raimbaut d'Orange, in whose honor she wrote many good songs." So reads the entire *vida,* or medieval biographical sketch, of the trobairitz whose "A Chantar" is presented here. Even this meager information needs to be regarded with skepticism, for it has never been proven that any Guillaume de Poitiers was ever married to a woman with a claim to the title of the county of Die. Be that as it may, lack of documentation has not deterred the popular imagination from formulating an intriguing genealogy based on sparse historical evidence and tantalizing legend.

One possible identification of the Countess of Dia proposes that the trobairitz, whom tradition has referred to as "Beatritz," was really Isoarde (d. 1212 or 1214), daughter of Isoard, Count of Die. The Raimbaut of the *vida* (d. 1218) would be the grandnephew of the troubadour Raimbaut d'Orange. A related story suggests that a certain Guillaume, an illegitimate son of the house of Poitiers, was married to a woman whose son bore the title Count of Die. This marriage produced twin daughters, born around 1140, one of whom would eventually marry another Guillaume and fall in love with Raimbaut d'Orange, the troubadour. Whatever the case, it would be a mistake to assume that any twelfth-century *canso,* or love song, was intended to reflect the details of anyone's personal life.

It is difficult to say very much about the Countess of Dia as a composer. "A Chantar" is the only one of the four or five poems attributed to her that has survived with its melody. This single melody, which is also the only one by a trobairitz to have been identified, is preserved in only one thirteenth-century manuscript, and it includes only the first *cobla,* or stanza. The melody "A Chantar" is characterized by the same supple style that is associated with troubadour lyric in general. As there is some evidence that the musical meter of troubadour song may not have been precisely measured, it is possible that, in practice, individual notes were of more or less equal duration. The overall form of the piece can be classified as a "rounded" chanson, since the B section returns at the end. The formal schema of "A Chantar" follows.

musical scheme:	A	B		C	D	B
rhyme scheme:	a	a		b	a	b
syllables per line:	10˘	10˘		10	10˘	10

It is worth noting that "rounded" songs would enjoy widespread popularity in the thirteenth through the fifteenth centuries, for composers and poets would develop a fascination with the sense of closure inherent to this form. The five *coblas* are made up of seven ten-syllable lines, with lines 2, 4, and 7 sharing the same melodic contour.

A striking difference can be seen in the first stanza of "A Chantar" as it occurs in manuscripts written in Occitan, the language of the Countess of Dia, which was spoken in southern France, and as it appears in the manuscript containing the only extant melody. It is clear from the Occitan text that the person who feels moved to sing of the pain of love is a woman, an "amia." This identification thus connects the twelfth-century text with the tradition of the "chanson de femme," a well-established mode of love lyric expressed in the feminine voice. Nevertheless, it is revealing to notice that the scribe who produced the thirteenth-century copy of the text, as given in the musical score below, must have assumed that the composer was a male, as was more often the case for the troubadour lyric. This later version of the piece, whose language reflects a mixture of Occitan and Old French, shows changes from "lui" to "cele" ("him" to "her") and from "amia" to "amigs" ("female lover" to "male lover")— in spite of the fact that the latter modification is inappropriate to the meter and music of line 2. The normal pattern of versification would require the feminine "amie," a form ending in "-e," in order to fit both the rhyme scheme of the first four lines ("deu-ri-*e*," "si-*e*," "cur-te-si-*e*") and the melodic figure with which these lines end. One can only speculate as to why such modifications occur in the transmission of a text. Perhaps they were due to prejudice against women composers or to the scribe's habit of thinking only in terms of male composers. For the purposes of studying "A Chantar," it is sufficient to note that only a "male" version exists, even when "female" versions of the text predate the "male" one that accompanies the extant music.

Recording

Chansons der Troubadours. "A Chantar." Studio de frühen Musik, Thomas Binkley, director. Telefunken SAWT 9567-B.

Further Reading

Bogin, Meg. *The Women Troubadours.* New York: Pendragon, 1976.

A Chantar

La Comtessa de Dia

I must sing of that which I would rather not, so embittered am I toward her whose lover I am, for I love her more than anything. My good looks, courtly bearing, virtue, merit, and intelligence are worthless, for I have been tricked and betrayed as if I were unpleasing.

Reprinted from *The Extant Troubadour Melodies*, 1984, by permission of the author and publisher, Hendrik van der Werf.

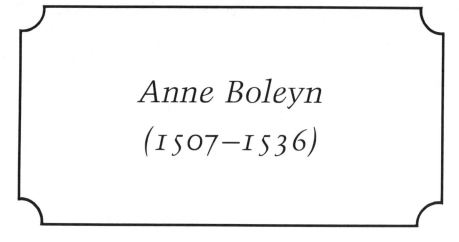

Anne Boleyn
(1507–1536)

EDITH BORROFF

Anne Boleyn well represents the type and class of woman who was likely to compose in the sixteenth century. The medieval era had been a good one for professional women, but their numbers shrank in the Renaissance, which was an era of hu*man*ism, conveying the notion of male preeminence in the arts and sciences. (That this was in fact a change from earlier days is perhaps difficult to recognize from the distance of modern times.) However, the cultural climate in England was relatively favorable to women, for social structures based on Roman law, which was male-dominated, did not affect the northern countries as much as they did life on the Continent.

Anne Boleyn reflects the Tudor love of music, which was characteristic not only of Henry VIII as an individual but also of his Welsh heritage, the court in general, and the kind of scholarship for which Henry was famous. All learned persons were expected to study the Quadrivium, of which theoretical (acoustical) music was a vital element, and the Trivium, in which music was regarded as an aspect of Rhetoric (a singer was called a rhetorician well into the seventeenth century). It is thus no wonder that Henry had one of the most impressive musical establishments of the world: at the end of his reign he had 60 musicians on his payroll in addition to those in the Chapel Royal.

Anne Boleyn, who was certainly one of the great passions of Henry's life, was of relatively humble stock. Even so, her father achieved a high position under the young Henry and spent some years as Ambassador to France. Anne lived at the French court from her twelfth to her sixteenth year; a Frenchman wrote in 1522 that "she was such a graceful maiden that no one would have believed she was in fact English." Specific mention was made of her skills in dancing, "all games fashionable at Courts," and, of course, music. In any case, her style of composition was very English, as was her choice of instruments (she owned a virginals and was known to play the lute). She was mainly influenced by Spanish and Italian, rather than French, sources. She was known as an intelligent and vivacious woman (rather than as a beautiful one) with a good reputation as a performer and a composer.

"O Deathe, rock me asleepe," for voice and keyboard or lute, represents a compendium of the certainties and also the probabilities of Anne's life as a musician. Although the authenticity of this work has not been established, it comes down to us as a piece written in the Tower of London as Anne faced execution. The poem is literate and effective, with a pun on "dye" against "remedye" (the syllable "dye" having the same pronunciation in both words, like the modern "die") and a reference to bells, which the ostinato (or ground) evokes. Grounds were newly appreciated, having been brought to English attention in modern form by such Spanish lutenists as Enriquez de Valderrabano and Diego Ortiz, and were doubtless improvised in great numbers.

The improvisatory quality of "O Deathe" and the extreme brevity of the ground figure give the piece a certain immediate sadness. The shift in the ground, to the more steeply descending figure that takes over from the "bell" ground, is a French feature, for the French never felt obliged to continue an ostinato figure beyond its artistic usefulness. The abrasions of the chromatic semitone (B against B flat and F against F sharp) are a British trait, beloved throughout the Renaissance and after; but the restricted range of the melody and the rhythm is not typical of music of the time and must be seen as a means of conveying the terrible constrictions of sorrow. Thus the song, with its combination of English, Spanish, French, and purely individual elements, comes off as extremely personal, high in exigency and low in energy; in short, it well bespeaks the grief of the condemned queen. Even its excessive final phrase, the six consecutive statements of "I dye," suggests the terrible final moments of her remarkable life.

Recording

"O Death," in *Songs in Shakespeare's Plays.* James Bowman, counter-tenor, and James Tyler, lute. Archiv Produktion Stereo, 2533 407.

O Deathe, rock me asleepe

Anne Boleyn (attributed)

O Deathe, O death, rock me a - sleepe, bring me to qui-et rest, let passe my wear-ye gilt - les ghost out of my_ care-full brest. Tole on thou passe-ing bell, ringe out _ my dole-full knell, Lett thye sound my deathe tell,

* original has B♭ A in left hand

Reprinted from *Royal Collection* by permission of Novello and Company, Ltd.

2

My paynes who can expres,
Alas they are so stronge;
My dolor will not suffer strength
My lyfe for to prolonge.
Toll on, *etc.*

3

Alone in prison stronge
I wayle my destenye;
Wo worth this cruel hap that I
Should taste this miserye.
Toll on, *etc.*

4

Farewell my pleasures past,
Welcum my present payne,
I fele my torments so increse
That lyfe cannot remayne.
Cease now the passing bell,
Rong is my doleful knell,
For the sound my deth doth tell,
Deth doth draw nye,
Sound my end dolefully,
For now I dye.

Maddalena Casulana
(ca. 1540–ca. 1590)

BEATRICE PESCERELLI

Maddalena, called Casulana probably because she was born at Casola d'Elsa (Casula) near Siena, received her earliest musical education and experiences in Florence. She began her career as a composer in 1566, when she published four madrigals in four voices in the first book of the anthology *Il Desiderio* and a fifth madrigal in four voices in the third book of *Il Desiderio.* In Florence Maddalena Casulana had connections with Isabella de' Medici, daughter of the Grand Duke of Tuscany Cosimo I. She dedicated her first book of madrigals *a 4* to Isabella in 1568, a publication that appears to be the first printed work by a woman in the history of European music. In the same year the renowned composer Orlando di Lasso conducted her five-voice composition *Nil mage iucundum* during the festivities in Monaco surrounding the marriage of Wilhelm IV of Bavaria to Renée of Lorraine. Casulana's music for this work has not survived, but the text, by Nicholas Stopius, is extant.

In 1570 Casulana published a second book of madrigals *a 4,* dedicating it to Antonio Londonio, a magistrate of the city-state of Milan. Of all her known madrigals, this set alone survives intact. In the following years Maddalena lived in northern Italy, where she seems to have married one Mezari: in the publication of her first book of madrigals *a 5,* which appeared in 1583, the composer's name is shown as Maddalena Mezari "detta Casulana."

The last of Casulana's known works is a madrigal in three voices, which appeared in the 1586 anthology *Il Gaudio.* However, the catalogue of the Venetian editor Giacomo Vincenti, in a publication of 1591, mentions another collection presently unknown: a first and second book of *madrigali spirituali* (sacred, devotional madrigals) in four voices.

Maddalena Casulana was fully aware of her exceptional position as a woman composer in the sixteenth century. In the dedication of her first book of madrigals to another woman, Isabella de' Medici, she declared proudly the desire "also to show to the world (as much as is possible in the profession of music) the vain error of men that they alone possess intellectual gifts, and who appear to believe that the same gifts are not possible for women." According to various witnesses Maddalena was a talented singer and an able lutenist. Her talents as a composer and performer were appreciated by such contemporary poets and musicians as Antonio Molino, Giambattista Maganza, Orlando di Lasso, and Filippo di Monte. It was di Monte to whom she dedicated her 1586 madrigal in three voices.

The madrigal presented here, "Morte—Che vôi?" is the sixth work in the second book of madrigals *a 4*, published in Venice by Gerolamo Scotto in 1570. The words are by Serafino Aquilano, whose texts had been set to music beginning earlier in the century. Casulana's choice of Aquilano (an esteemed friend of Josquin Desprez) as a poet testifies to her uncommon literary interests.

The composer seems to have been attracted to the dramatic form of the dialogue, which she exploits ably in the musical structure by distributing the questions and answers throughout the several voices. She alternates the voices polyphonically in the first section, bringing them together only in the final verse. The exclamations "Sì fa!" and "Non fa!" inspired a musical interpretation using the corresponding notes B (si) and F (fa).

> Death, you whom I call, behold, for I draw near.
> Take me and complete thereby all that remains of my sorrow.
> You cannot do so?
> Since, in you, no longer shall my heart reign,
> Yes . . . no . . . have done!
> Then restore that which life can no longer destroy.

Further Reading

Bridges, Thomas W. "Casulana, Maddalena." *The New Grove Dictionary of Music and Musicians* IV:1–2.

Pescerelli, Beatrice, ed. Preface to *I madrigali di Maddalena Casulana*. Florence: Olschki, 1979.

Madrigal VI.
Morte—Che vôi?—Te chiamo

Text by Serafino Aquilano   *Maddalena Casulana*

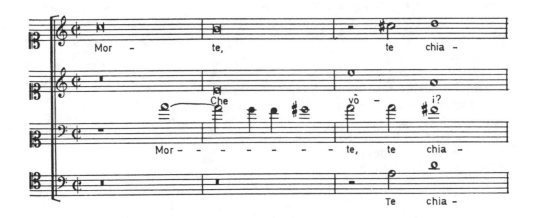

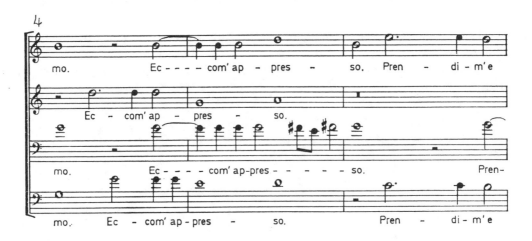

Reproduced from *I madrigali di Maddalena Casulana* by permission of the publisher, Leo S. Olschki.

Francesca Caccini
(1587–c.1630)

CAROLYN RANEY

Francesca Caccini of Florence was the composer of the first Italian opera to be given outside Italy. She was also the chief musical ornament (and highest paid composer) at the Court of Tuscany under three Grand Dukes: Ferdinando I, Cosimo II, and Ferdinando II. When the consort of family singers organized by her father visited France in 1604, Henry IV said, "She is the best singer ever heard in France." He asked the Grand Duke to let her enter the service of the French court, but Ferdinando I would not let her go.

Monteverdi heard her play three different instruments and sing, "all very well," in 1610, when he visited her father, Giulio Romano Caccini. Giulio, a member of the Florentine *Camerata*, and Jacopo Peri are generally credited with devising the first opera. Peri sang in Francesca's opera performances as time went on. The poet Chiabrera reported her as "a marvel" when he heard her in 1615. Even long after her death, Pietro della Valle wrote that he had heard Francesca in his youth and that she had been admired for many years for her composing, her singing, and her poetry in both Latin and Tuscan.

It was as a composer, however, that Francesca was most valued at court. During her late teens, she began composing major "entertainments" with Michelangelo Buonaroti the Younger (grandnephew of the artist) as lyricist. She continued to sing in public until her success as a singing teacher produced a whole school of disciples whom she trained for private performances for the ailing Cosimo II, for special services for the court during sacred festivals, and for public performances in opera. Francesca was married in 1607 to another singer of the *Camerata*, Giovanni Battista Signorini. Their daughter Marguerita, born in 1621, was also a singer. At an early age she entered the Convent of San Girolamo in Florence.

Francesca Caccini's major compositions include five operas, which she called "ballettos," written with official court dramatists, and a large volume of sacred and secular songs, set to her own poetry. Only one opera, *La liberazione di Ruggiero d'al isola d'Alcina* of 1625, and her *Primo Libro* of 1618 have survived.

The question of ornamentation of solo songs and arias has long been a controversial subject. In general, Francesca Caccini the singer has made sure that posterity would use the ornamentation that Francesca Caccini the composer wanted in her works. She notated the ornaments in all her published works exactly as they appear here, including the final *trillo*, which was printed only when and if she wanted it in the cadence.

22

Il primo libro, a collection of short vocal works for one or two voices with *basso continuo*, includes nineteen sacred solos, thirteen secular solo songs, and four duets for soprano and bass. The songs are indexed by the composer according to the first line and also by the form of the poems, most of which she wrote herself. "Laudate Dominum" is based on the current Latin version of Psalm 150. It appears as follows in the King James version of the Bible.

> Praise God in His sanctuary.
> Praise Him in the firmament of His power.
> Praise Him for His mighty acts.
> Praise Him according to His excellent greatness.
> Praise Him with the sound of trumpet.
> Praise Him with the psaltery and harp.
> Praise Him with the timbrel and dance.
> Praise Him with stringed instruments and organs.
> Praise Him upon the loud cymbals.
> Let everything that hath breath praise the Lord.

Francesca designates this work as a *mottetto*, a sacred Latin text set to music in sections. She usually inserts an *alleluia* between the sections and always adds one as an extended coda. The irregular phrase lengths in this song are characteristic of Francesca's style in general and are particularly appropriate to the irregularity of the psalm lines.

Placed as she was between the words of modality and functional tonality, Caccini had an unusual tonal sense and an individual style. She employed curved melody lines with double peaks, strong walking-bass lines (*Il Primo Libro* contains six examples of melodies written above a *romanesca* bass), displaced rhythmic accents, unprepared dissonances, extensive melodic and rhythmic variations, musical word-painting and other special emotional or descriptive effects, and a tonal momentum even with modal material. The melodic variations exploit the brilliance and warmth of the center of the human voice, in large and small melismas using changing rhythmic groupings.

"Maria, dolce Maria" is described in *Il Primo Libro* as a *madrigale.* The Italian *madrigali* of 1600 were composed of poetic lines of eleven syllables and seven syllables, variously arranged for six lines but always ending in a rhyming couplet: *abc abc dd.* The composer changes harmony under such expressive words as "dolce" and "serena" and introduces gentle turns in the melody itself as the words "soave" and "celeste" are sung. And since Francesca herself was famous for her "ravishing roulades," she has written a long melisma for the words "canto" and "alma." The entire song seems to express her joy and serenity on contemplating the character of Mary, mother of Jesus.

> Mary, sweet Mary,
> A name so gentle
> That whoever pronounces it learns to speak from the heart,
> Sacred name and holy
> That inflames my heart with heavenly love.
> Mary, never would I know how to sing
> Nor my tongue
> Draw out from my breast ever
> A more felicitous word than to say Mary.
> Name that lessens and consoles
> Every grief.
> Tranquil voice that quiets every breathless agitation,

That makes every heart serene
And every spirit light.

The instrumentation for the *ritornello* of "Aria of the Shepherd" originally included three recorders, two tenor and one alto. Printed instructions indicate that the *ritornello* is to be played as an introduction and again at the end of the strophe. The aria itself was accompanied by a keyboard instrument, probably a gravicembalo, a wing-shaped harpsichord. Francesca wrote the opera for the state visit of the Prince of Poland, "Ladisloa Sigismondo" (later King Ladislaus IV), to Florence in 1625. This aria was not mentioned in reports of the first performance, although it is included in the index of the 1625 edition and in a Polish publication that appeared after a production in Warsaw in 1628. That performance was the first of an Italian opera outside Italy. The text of the aria can be translated as follows:

> My heart used to burn for the prettiest and most beautiful earthly star that today obscures the golden rays of Phoebus. Love used to laugh, longing to report on my torment.
>
> But having been sneered at, deeply repentant, your piety healed my breast. Therefore I keep faith with whoever does not believe that Love is the only God of every delight.

In other words, the shepherd is beyond the temptation of Love. The hero, Ruggiero, envies him!

Although the two strophes of the song show the same harmonic plan, each presentation varies subtly in melody, rhythmic pattern, and especially in the placement of the *trillo*. This particular excerpt shows fewer melismas than do the other arias of the opera, in keeping with the simple character of the shepherd himself.

Further Reading

Raney, Carolyn. "Francesca Caccini, Musician to the Medici, and her *Primo Libro.*" Ph. D. diss., New York University, 1971.

Laudate Dominum, from *Il Primo Libro*

Francesca Caccini, transcribed by Carolyn Raney

16

-um se - cun - dum mul-ti-tu- di - nem ma-gni

19

tu - di-nis e - ius. Lau-da-te e - um in

[#]

23

so - - - - - - - - no - tu - ba.

25

Lau- da-te e - um in psal-te - - - - - - - rio

[b]

26

27

30

Maria, dolce Maria, from *Il Primo Libro*

Francesca Caccini, transcribed by Carolyn Raney

mai sepr'io can . . . . to ne pùo _____ la lin-gua mi . a più fe-li - ce par-

o - - - - - - - - - - - - la. _____ Tror- mi dal sen gio mai che dir

che dir _____ Ma - ri . . a No - me ch'og-ni do-lor _____

32

35

tem·prae con·so·la, ro·co tran·quil·la ___ ch'ogni af·fan ___ no acque-

39

ta ch'ogni cor fa se·re ___ no, ch'ogni cor fa se·ren' ___

43

___ ogn'al ___ ma liet·ta, ch'ogni cor fa se·re ___

47

___ no, ch'ogni cor fa se·re ___ no ogn'al ___ ma, ogn'

33

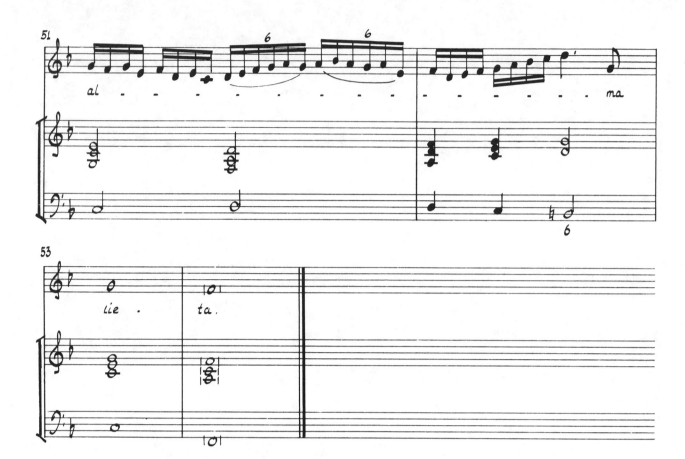

al - - - - - - - - - - - - - - - - - - ma

lie . ta .

Aria of the Shepherd

Francesca Caccini

From *La Liberazione di Ruggiero*, edited by Doris Silbert; Smith College Archives. Reprinted by permission of The Trustees of Smith College.

Ritornello, di flauti come sopra [meas. 1] Segue il medesimo Pastore. [meas. 42]

Ma d'ha- ver-mi scher-ni- to to- sto pen- ti- to,

Con la pie- tà di lei mi sa na'il pet-

to, ond' io fò fe- de, A chi nol

cre- de, ch'a- mo- re à so- lo'il Dio

d'o- gni di- let- to ond' io' fò

fe- de, A chi nol cre- de, Ch'a- mo- re

è so- lo'il Dio d'o- gni di- let- to

Ritornello di flauti come sopra [meas.1]
Ruggiero

O fe- li- ce Pa- sto- re Chi non

Isabella Leonarda
(1620–1704)

BARBARA GARVEY JACKSON

Isabella Leonarda was born in Novara, Italy, into a family of minor nobility. Little is known of her early life or her musical studies. Isabella took her vows at age sixteen, and she and some of her sisters were nuns in the convent of Sant'Orsola in Novara. Isabella may have been a student of Gasparo Casati, chapelmaster of the Novara cathedral, since her earliest known compositions appeared in a volume of Casati's *sacri concenti* in 1640.

From the prefaces and title pages of the twenty volumes of music she subsequently published, it appears that Isabella served her order as an administrator—*madre* (Mother Superior) by 1686, *madre vicaria* in 1693, and *consigliera* (Counselor) in her last years. Since the Ursulines were a teaching order, it is possible that there was a school attached to the convent, but little is known of either the institution or its musical life. Many records were probably lost when the convent was closed in 1811. Two motets by Isabella Leonarda were dedicated to musical nuns of her own convent and two to nuns of other congregations. These nuns were probably singers, and the works may reflect their singing skills.

Leonarda's publications include over 200 works, all for Church use, although only about a quarter of them are settings of liturgical texts. Her first published Mass was in Opus 4 (1674), together with several psalm settings. Opus 18 (1696), from which the following Kyrie and Crucifixus are drawn, contains three Masses. Leonarda also set litanies, Magnificats, Marian antiphons (she had a special devotion to the Virgin and used a double dedication for each volume of her works—to the Virgin and to a human patron), responsories, a hymn, and a sequence. Most of her works were settings for one to four voices (often with *concertato* violins) of nonliturgical religious texts, many of which she may have written. They express a passionate religious devotion, usually to the Virgin. Opus 16 (1693) is entirely devoted to *sonate da chiesa* ("church sonatas")—eleven trio sonatas and one solo sonata for violin and organ continuo. It is the first known publication of instrumental sonatas composed by a woman.

In accordance with regional practice, Leonarda set only the Kyrie, Gloria, and Credo in her Masses, and not the Eucharistic portions of the Ordinary. Her style, which is similar to that of other north Italian contemporaries, is marked by an intense personal identification with the religious text. For example, in the Crucifixus portion of the Credo she marks a change of tempo or character in the middle of the sentence "Crucifixus etiam pro nobis." The word "Crucifixus" is *adagio* and mournful in spirit, but the phrase "etiam pro nobis" is abruptly marked *spiritoso*, joyfully responding to the thought that the sacrifice was *for us.* The alternation continues, with text repetitions of the joyful phrase. Leonarda sometimes indicates dynamics—"et sepultus est" is marked *piano.* After the concluding words there is a meditative *adagio* Sinfonia, the last phrase of which is also marked *piano.*

Kyrie eleison.	Lord have mercy on us.
Christe eleison.	Christ have mercy on us.
Kyrie eleison.	Lord have mercy on us.
Crucifuxus etiam pro nobis	He was crucified also for us,
sub Pontio Pilato passus	under Pontius Pilate suffered
et sepultus est.	and was buried.

Recording

Music for the Mass by Nun Composers. Messa Prima from Opus 18, Isabella Leonarda. Schola Cantorum of the University of Arkansas, Jack Groh, conductor. Leonarda LPI-115, 1982.

Modern Editions

"Ave Regina Caelorum" for SAT soli, mixed chorus (SATB), and continuo, edited by Stewart Carter. In *Nine Centuries of Music by Women* series. New York: Broude Bros., 1980.
Messa Prima from Opus 18 a 4 voci con violini (1696), edited by Barbara Garvey Jackson. Fayetteville, AR: ClarNan Editions, 1981.
Sonata Duodecima from Opus 16 (1693) for violin and continuo, edited by Barbara Garvey Jackson. *Baroque Chamber Music Series,* no. 16. Ottawa: Dovehouse Editions, 1983.
Selected Compositions, edited by Stewart Carter. *Recent Research in Music of the Baroque.* Madison: A-R Editions, forthcoming. Includes two concerted liturgical settings, four motets, and two sonatas.

Further Reading

Carter, Stewart Arlen. "The Music of Isabella Leonarda (1620–1704)." Ph.D. diss., Stanford University, 1981.
Giegling, Franz. "Leonarda, Isabella," *Die Musik in Geschichte und Gegenwart* VIII: 634.
Roberts, Rosemary. "Isabella Leonarda," *The New Grove Dictionary of Music and Musicians* X: 337. Alphabetized under "Isabella."

Messa Prima

Isabella Leonarda

Reprinted by permission of the publisher, Barbara Garvey Jackson, ClarNan Editions. 1981.

43

46

Spiritoso

47

48

53

from the 𝕮redo

54

56

Elizabeth-Claude Jacquet de la Guerre (1666 or 1667–1729)

SUSAN ERICKSON

The French composer Elizabeth-Claude Jacquet de la Guerre achieved recognition at an early age as a harpsichord virtuoso, celebrated for her improvisations. She attracted the notice of Louis XIV, enjoyed his continued protection, and dedicated most of her compositions to him. Her early education was closely supervised by Mme de Montespan, the king's mistress. She was descended from a noted family of harpsichord builders and was married to the organist Marin de la Guerre. Her husband and her son died in 1704, and thereafter she was active as a public performer until her retirement in 1717.

La Guerre is a remarkable figure in several ways: She wrote and published works in almost every form then popular, and she was instrumental in introducing the new Italian style to France. She was one of the first women to compose in such a wide variety of genres and to be fully recognized for her achievements in a field generally reserved for men. One of her earliest works was the five-act opera *Céphale et Procris*, published in 1694. Some early trio and solo sonatas, from around 1695, were among the first of that genre composed in France. La Guerre was equally a pioneer in the new French cantata. Her two books of biblical cantatas, published by Ballard in 1708 and 1711, are noteworthy for their unusual subject matter and Italianate style. Other works, now lost, include a ballet, *Les Jeux à l'honneur de la victoire* of 1691, and a *Te Deum*, written to celebrate the recovery of Louis XV from smallpox in 1721.

La Guerre published a set of harpsichord pieces as early as 1687. In 1707 she published a set of six sonatas for violin and figured bass, along with fourteen movements for harpsichord solo. These harpsichord pieces make up two suites, in D and G. "La Flamande et son double" in D minor, reproduced below, is actually an allemande with a varied repeat of each section. Its broad compass and abundant ornamentation follow the great tradition of the French *clavecinistes*, established by Chambonnières and developed by François Couperin and others. The concluding Chaconne is an expansive and virtuosic set of variations.

La Guerre also wrote a volume of cantatas on traditional mythological subjects; it was dedicated to the Elector of Bavaria and published by Foucault, probably after 1715. (Her previous works had been dedicated to Louis XIV, who had died in that year.) A short comic duet for soprano and bass, "Le Raccommodement comique de Nicole et Pierrot," is included in the collection. La Guerre explains in the score that there are just three cantatas (rather than the customary six), because each one is longer than usual. All three cantatas are scored for soprano and continuo, with *symphonie.*

Semelé is the first of the three cantatas and is included here in its first modern edition. It is based on the Greek myth of Semele, mistress of Zeus and mother of Dionysus. When Semele insists on knowing the identity of her lover, Zeus appears in the form of a thunderbolt, and Semele dies. She is later rescued from Hades by her son, and her return to Earth is associated with the yearly return of Spring. The three airs of *Semelé,* all in da capo form, are on a larger scale than those typically found in the cantatas of La Guerre's contemporaries. The composer explains in her preface that they may be performed separately, if desired. The recitatives are typically French, in that there are frequent meter changes to accommodate the rhythm of the speech. The instruments, violin and continuo (with the suggestion of flute in the second air, "Quel triomphe"), are used in independent instrumental numbers and interludes. In certain recitatives and one air they provide contrast and intensify the expression of the text.

NARRATOR: Jupiter had made an indiscreet oath, to grant any wish to a faithful lover. Semele doubts the rank of her lover, and this doubt torments her; she aspires to see him in his immortal glory; but Love, out of pity for her, averts the moment of so fatal a pleasure! Semele however laments, frets. She complains of waiting overlong.

SEMELE: Can one not live in your bonds without suffering the pains of a mortal? Love, you promise a thousand gifts, but one finds none at all in your chains. A heart which has let itself be charmed must sacrifice all to its flame. My lover, if he were able to love, would forsee the desires of my soul.

NARRATOR: But what astonishing noise bursts forth in the air. What devastation; the thunderbolt roars, the sky opens; and the lightning flashes announce to me the master of the world.

SEMELE: What a great display, what a spectacle for me; forgive me, I was wrong to doubt your faithfulness. What triumph, what victory flatters my ambitious heart, is anything equal to my glory, I will enjoy the fate of the gods. I do not wish mystery to hide the happiness of my fetters; Let all know that I was able to please the greatest God of the universe. Ah! what sudden conflagration terrifies me, I see this palace catch fire; Ah! heaven! I feel myself consumed; Jupiter, what is the fate of your mistress! One desire has led me to the final misfortune. What horrible torment, I succumb, I die."

NARRATOR: When Love binds us in his most engaging knots, let us not mix with his fires the ardour of a vain glory, let us not divide his desires; Splendour, supreme grandeur, were never a blessing. It is in a tender bond that one finds supreme happiness. Splendour, supreme grandeur are of no importance.

Recordings (of Suite in D minor)

Complete Harpsichord Works of Elisabeth Jacquet de la Guerre. Thurston Dart, harpsichord. London Edition of L'Oiseau-Lyre. OL 50183, 1959.
Keyboard Works by Women Composers. Nancy Fierro, piano. Avant Records, AV 1012.

Further Reading

Bates, Carol Henry. "The Instrumental Music of Elizabeth-Claude Jacquet de la Guerre." Ph.D. diss., Indiana University, 1978.
Borroff, Edith. *An Introduction to Elisabeth-Claude Jacquet de la Guerre.* Brooklyn, N. Y.: Institute of Mediaeval Music, 1966.

Pièces de Clavecin

Elizabeth Jacquet de la Guerre

La Flamande

© 1965 by J. B. Hanson, Editions de l'Oiseau Lyre, Les Remparts, Monaco. Reprinted by permission.

(*) ♭♯♮ dans l'original

Chaconne

5.ᵉ Couplet

On reprend le 1.ᵉʳ Couplet 𝄋

65

Semelé, Cantate avec Simphonie

Elizabeth Jacquet de la Guerre

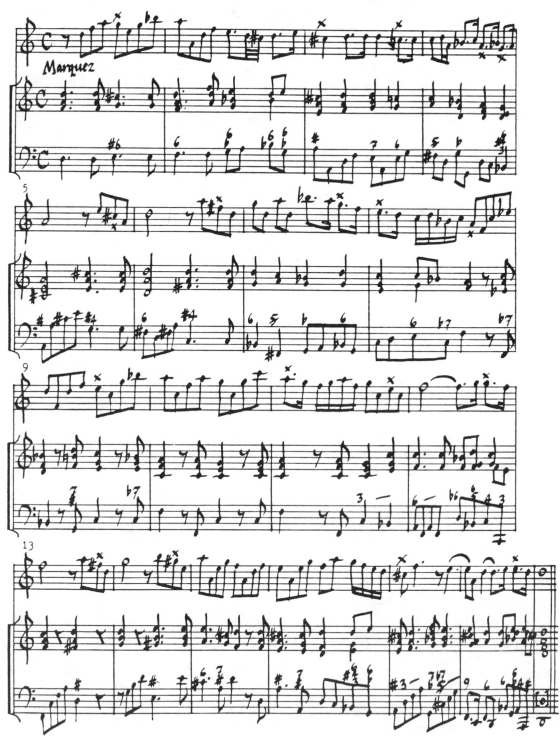

Source: *Cantates françoises.* Paris: Foucault, n.d. (PN Vm7. 161.) Printed by permission of Bibliothèque nationale, Paris. First modern edition by Susan Erickson and Robert Bloch. Continuo realization by Robert Bloch.

67

68

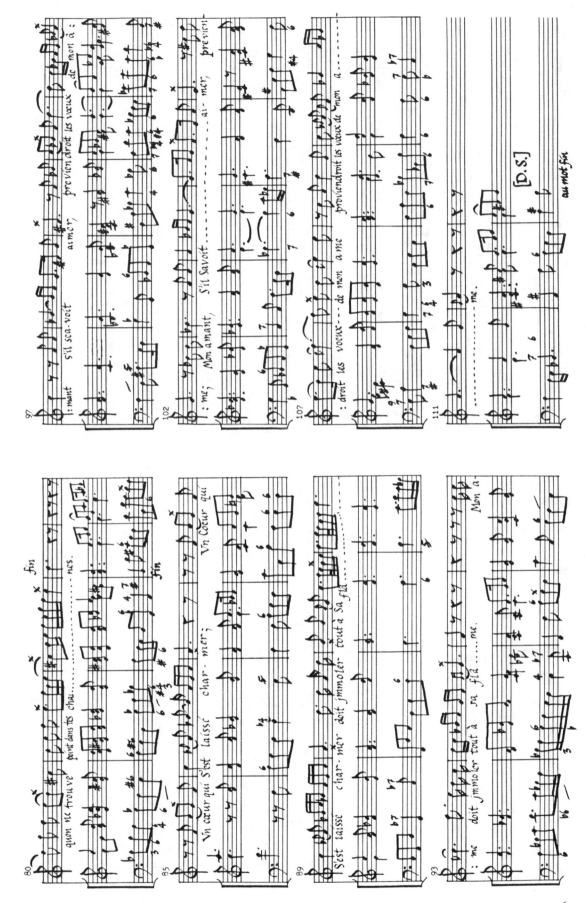

69

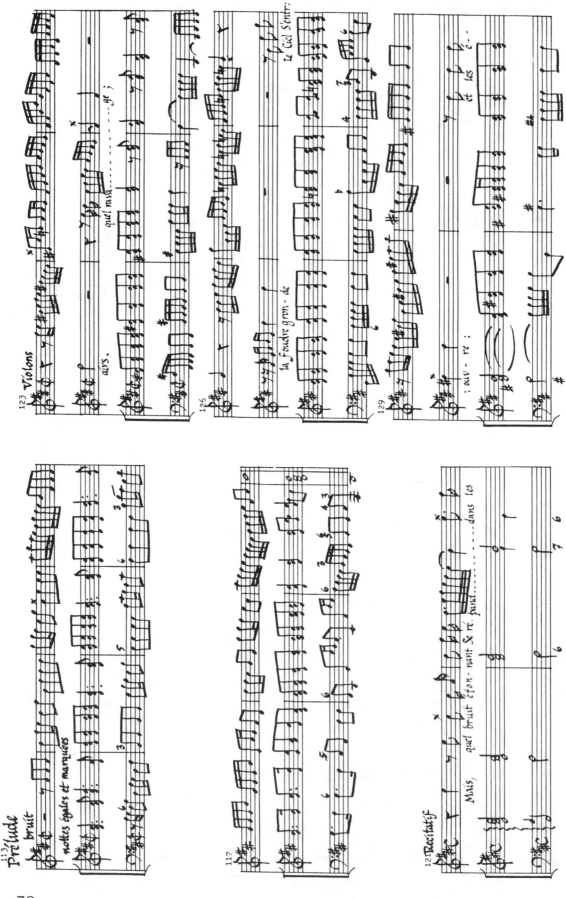

70

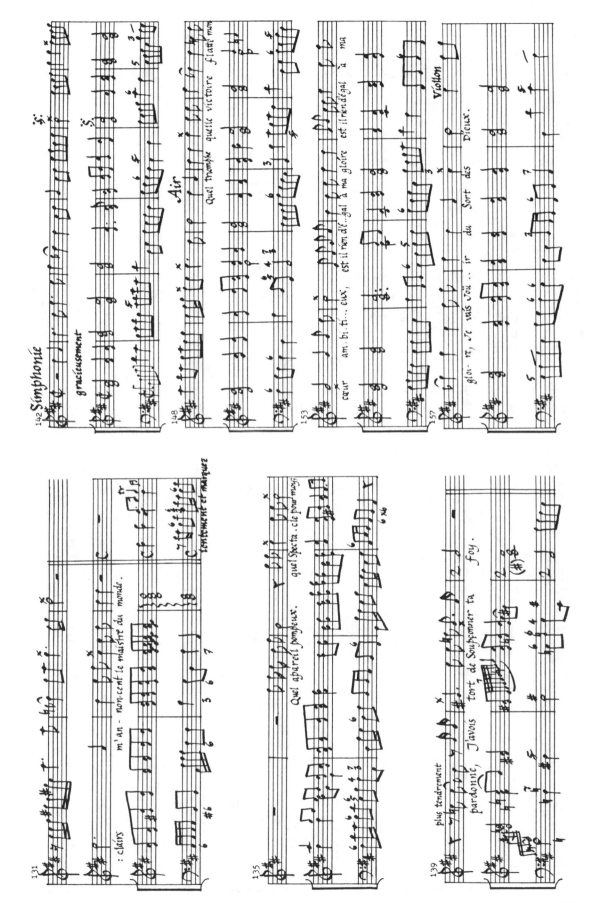

71

72

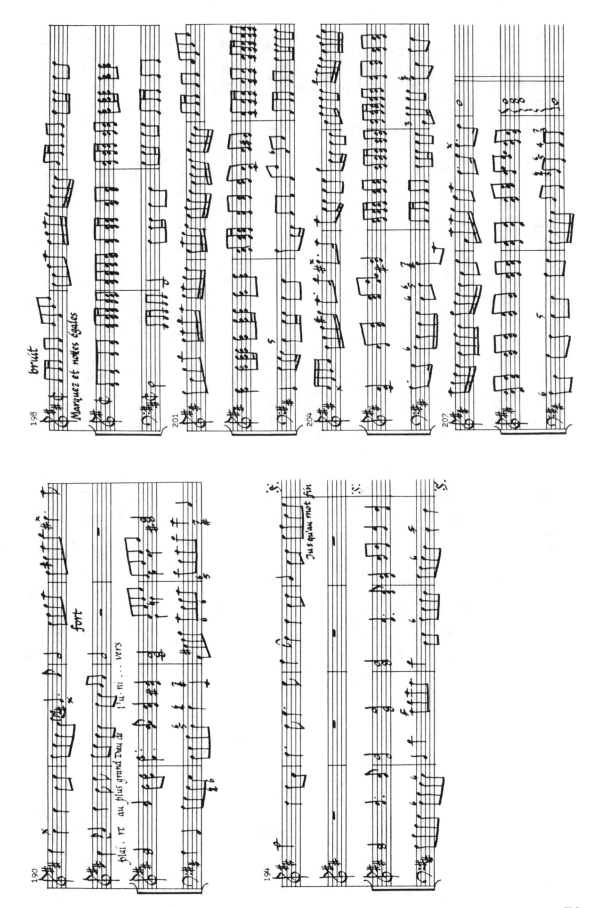

73

74

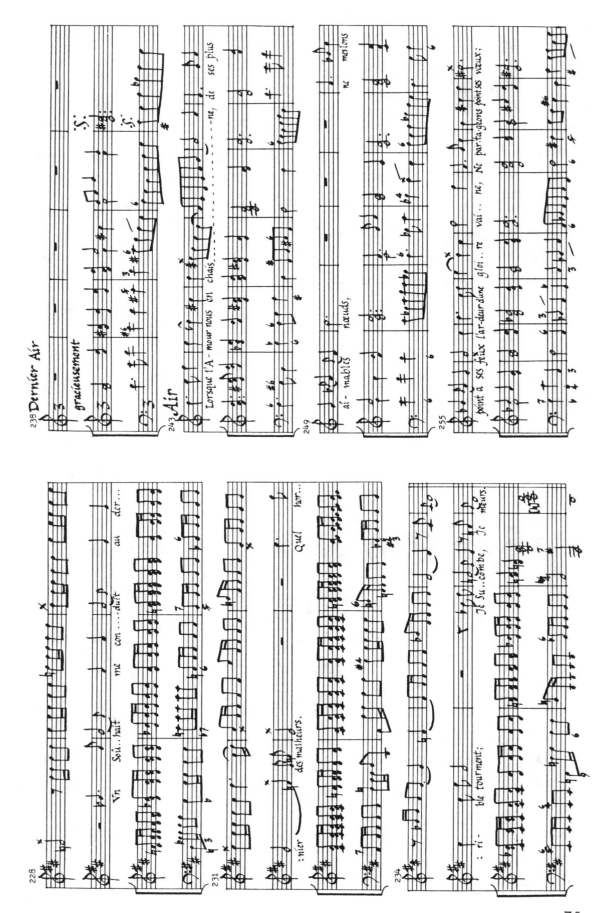

75

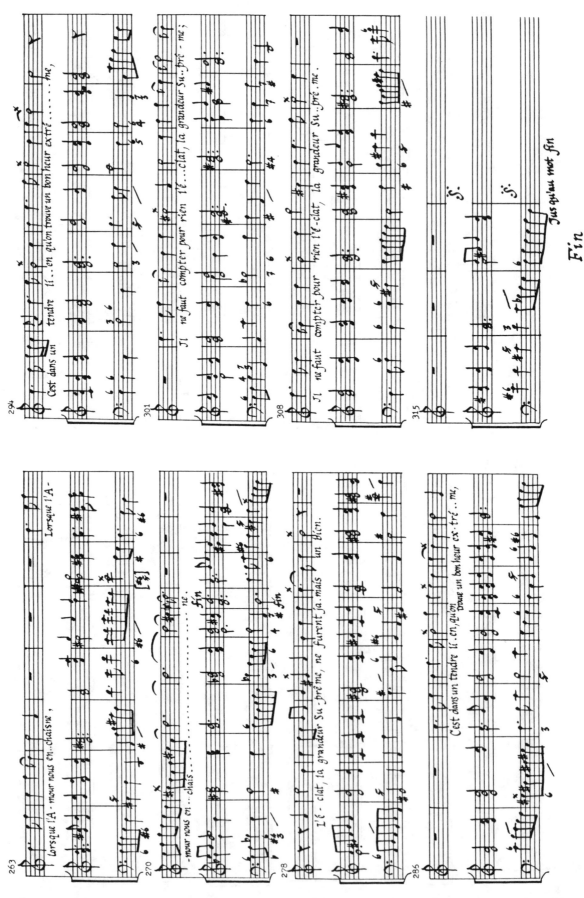

Fin

76

Maria Margherita Grimani (fl. ca. 1713–1718)

BARBARA GARVEY JACKSON

Seven women are known to have composed oratorios and other dramatic works that were performed in northern Italy or Vienna between 1670 and 1724. Among the works performed at court in Vienna were two oratorios and a dramatic work (which may have been staged) by Maria Margherita Grimani.

Nothing is known of Grimani's life except the dates of these performances. It is not even certain that she was ever resident in Vienna; the manuscript score of *Pallade e Marte* is inscribed "April 5, 1713, Bologna." Perhaps she lived there. An important family of Venetian aristocrats bears the name Grimani, but it has not been possible to establish a definite relationship between them and the composer. It may be significant that one Pietro Grimani was the ambassador negotiating an alliance with Emperor Charles VI in 1713, the very year the composer's works began appearing in Vienna. We do not even know whether Maria Margherita was a nun or whether Grimani was her maiden name or her married name.

Pallade e Marte, an "opus dramaticum" for two singers, was performed on the name day of the emperor in Vienna on November 6, 1713. Later the same year Grimani's oratorio *La Visitazione di Santa Elisabetta* appeared, and two years later her *La Decollazione di S. Giovanni Battista* was heard. *La Visitazione* was revived in 1718, the last time her name appears in Vienna.

All Grimani's surviving works are for soloists and orchestra. As in other oratorios and similar works of the early eighteenth century, they used da capo arias, often followed (if they are continuo arias) by short orchestral *ritornelli* as interludes. The recitatives are all *secco*, that is, with only a figured bass accompaniment. Several arias are performed with concertante instruments, and some are accompanied by string orchestra. The works open with *sinfonie* in several movements, as in the example presented here. An ensemble of soloists often appears at the conclusion; typically, there is a vocal duet at the end of *Pallade e Marte*.

Pallade e Marte, from which the following three-movement Sinfonia is drawn, is the shortest of Grimani's works (65 pages of manuscript). It is set for soprano and alto, with solo cello, oboe, theorbo, strings, and continuo, the same scoring (except for the theorbo) as in *La decollazione*. The vocal soloists sing alternate arias: Pallas is accompanied by the strings; and Marte responds along with cello obbligato, theorbo, and continuo. Pallas then answers with strings, a continuo aria with orchestral ritornello for Mars follows, Pallade sings with oboe obbligato, and then comes the closing duet. The aria types are typical of the Italian and Viennese oratorios of the period, as cultivated by Alessandro Scarlatti and others, and they are similar to those used by the other contemporary women composers whose music survives. The movements of the opening sinfonia are appropriately short for a work of this scale.

Recording

Women's Orchestral Works, Performed by The New England Women's Symphony. Sinfonie [*sic*] (1713) by Maria Grimani. Concertmaster, Jean Lamon. Galaxia Women's Enterprises, 1980. The jacket notes incorrectly state that the longer work that the Sinfonia introduced has been lost and that no figured bass is indicated.

Further Reading

Eitner, Robert. "Grimani, Maria Margherita," *Quellen-Lexikon* IV:378–79.
Klein, Rudolph. "Grimani, Maria Margherita," *Die Musik in Geschichte und Gegenwart* V:922–23.
———. "Grimani, Maria Margherita," *The New Grove Dictionary of Music and Musicians* VII:733.

Pallade e Marte

Maria Margherita Grimani

Sinfonia.

Source: Oesterreische Nationalbibliothek, Musiksammlung, Vienna. Sign.: Mus.Hs.17.741.
Reprinted by permission.

Segue l'Allegro. Subito.

82

83

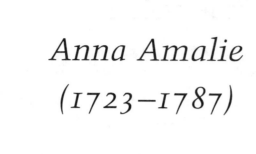

Anna Amalie
(1723–1787)

JANE P. AMBROSE

Anna Amalie was the twelfth child and sixth daughter of Frederick Wilhelm I of Prussia and the youngest sister of Frederick the Great. She studied first with her brother Frederick and then with Gottlieb Hayne, a Berlin cellist and cathedral organist. She became an accomplished performer on keyboard instruments, flute, and violin. In 1758, Amalie appointed J. P. Kirnberger, one of Bach's most distinguished students, as her Kapellmeister and studied with him until 1783. Her choice of Kirnberger is an indication of her rejection of the prevalent Berlin style of composition in favor of the highly contrapuntal style of the late Baroque. She shared this taste with her brother, some of whose compositions were even more reactionary than her own.

Although the general assessment is that her music was inferior to her brother's, that judgment is not borne out by an examination of her music. Kirnberger thought well enough of Amalie's work to include an excerpt from her setting of *Der Tod Jesu* (which pre-dates Carl Heinrich Graun's famous one) in his *Kunst des reinen Satzes*, one of the classics of eighteenth-century compositional technique. Her compositions also include sonatas, chorales and arias in the old style, and marches and songs (some of which were published in a modern edition in Berlin in 1927/28). Amalie became more reactionary as she grew older; for example, she denounced Gluck in a letter to Kirnberger, but she remained supportive of C. P. E. Bach, perhaps because of her devotion to his father's work.

Amalie's most important contribution to music was the founding of a superb music library, now known as the Amalien-Bibliothek and housed partly in East Berlin and partly in West Berlin. Begun under Hayne and nurtured by Kirnberger, the library assembled one of the truly great collections of eighteenth-century and earlier music. It is particularly rich in manuscripts and early printed editions of Bach, including the Brandenburg Concertos, St. Matthew Passion, B-minor Mass, most of the harpsichord concertos, and many cantatas. It also contains compositions by earlier composers, such as Hans Leo Hassler and Palestrina; work of other late Baroque composers, including Handel and Telemann; and works by Amalie's contemporaries Johann Adolph Hasse, Carl Heinrich Graun, Johann Gottlieb Graun, and C. P. E. Bach. Three eighteenth-century catalogs list the contents of the collection—approximately 3,000 books and over 600 volumes of music. The catalog was continued by Johann Friedrich Reichardt and Carl Friedrich Zelter, who added many Bach items. The contents of the library provided much of the material for Johann Nikolaus Forkel's study of Bach

(1802) and was the inspiration for the Berlin Bach movement led by Zelter. It became one of the central points for the collection of Bach manuscripts and was a major source for the complete edition of Bach's works.

The style of the Sonata for Flute in F major suggests an early date of composition, before Amalie began to adhere to the counterpoint of the late Baroque. Only the first movement, Adagio, is presented here. The entire sonata compares favorably with the sonatas of Amalie's brother and of C. P. E. Bach, both of whom were extraordinarily prolific in this genre. The gracious "affective" style of the melody and the simplicity of the harmony are very much in keeping with the sonatas composed for Frederick's evening performances at his palace Sans Souci. Perhaps this sonata was composed for one of these soirées.

Further Reading

Blechschmidt, Eva Renate. *Die Amalien-Bibliothek*. Berliner Studien zur Musikwissenschaft. Berlin: Verlag Merseburger, 1965.

Sachs, Curt. "Prinzessin Amalie von Preussen als Musikerin," *Hohenzollern Jahrbuch* XIV (1910):181–91.

Sonata for Flute

Amalie, Princess of Prussia,
edited by Gustav Lenzewski

© 1975 by Chr. Friedrich Vieweg, Music Publishers, Munich, Germany. Reprinted by permission.

Marianne von Martinez
(1744–1812)

KARIN PENDLE

Vienna-born Marianne von Martinez was only nine years old when the poet and librettist Pietro Metastasio discovered her great musical talents and undertook to supervise her training. To this end he called on Niccolò Porpora and the then-unknown Franz Joseph Haydn to give the young girl lessons in singing, playing keyboard instruments, and composition, while Metastasio himself provided her general education. In addition, Martinez studied counterpoint with Giuseppe Bonno and probably received informal suggestions and guidance from Johann Adolph Hasse.

Marianne was quick to attract the attention of the Viennese court because of her abilities as a performer, and she was only in her teens when an early Mass of her own composition was performed at St. Michael's, the court chapel. Other works soon followed—oratorios, cantatas, sacred choral compositions, arias, piano concertos, piano sonatas, and a symphony among them. Though her music was performed and much admired, most of Martinez's compositions remained unpublished; they exist only in the manuscript copies owned by the Gesellschaft der Musikfreunde in Vienna.

Charles Burney's account of the time he spent with Marianne von Martinez during his visit to Vienna in 1772 remains the most extended and enthusiastic appreciation of her skills as a singer, keyboard artist, and composer. It is also a testimony to her intelligence and refinement. Mozart sought Martinez out to perform with him in his piano duets, and singer Michael Kelly paid tribute to her in his memoirs. In 1773 she was made an honorary member of Bologna's Accademia Filarmonica, which cited the nobility of expression and the amazing precision exhibited in her works. About the same time, she may also have received an honorary doctorate from the University of Pavia.

Though Marianne von Martinez was never a professional musician in the technical sense of the term, she devoted her life to music and the arts. After the death of Metastasio, who left her and her siblings large sums of money, Martinez's home became a center of artistic life during a truly Golden Age of Viennese music. During the 1790s, when Martinez had apparently ceased to be an active composer, she turned to teaching, and the singing school she opened in her home turned out many fine pupils.

The Sonata in A is one of two piano sonatas by Marianne von Martinez published in 1765 by Johann Ulrich Haffner of Nürnberg. She was only 21 at the time the sonata was printed, but she had learned her lessons well. The three-movement work is written with a sure hand in a style that reveals Martinez's own facility at the keyboard and the influence of her teacher Haydn. The first movement, a sprightly Allegro, is reproduced here.

At the opening, thematic ideas are stated, expanded upon, then recalled in a different order and a more concise manner than in their original presentation. The dotted rhythm that marks the initial A-major theme soon gives way to triplet figuration as the music moves to the dominant. Here, several identifiable ideas emerge (see mm.4, 6, 8, 9, and 12). Though each of these themes has a different shape, they are similar in character and are unified by the recurrence of scalar fragments in 64th notes that lend a feeling of energy and forward motion to this section of the work.

The second half of the movement presents the themes of the first in new combinations, in a working-out that is largely sequential. At m.25, material from mm.6–8 returns, this time in the tonic. A restatement of the movement's opening theme (m.29) is followed by ideas from mm.9–13, but in A rather than E. The transparent texture and the highly ornamented melody of the first movement create a sunny atmosphere that is clouded over only slightly in the second, a rather melancholy Adagio in A minor. This middle movement features a melody that is clearly in the popular *empfindsamer Stil* of the time. An appealing minuet in A major concludes the sonata.

Recording

The Romance of Women's Music. Sonata in A major, Nancy Fierro. Pelican LP 2017 (1979).

Further Reading

Biographical articles in *The New Grove Dictionary of Music and Musicians* and in *Die Musik in Geschichte und Gegenwart.*

Burney, Charles. *The Present State of Music in Germany, the Netherlands and United Provinces.* 2 vols. 2d ed., corrected. London: T. Becket, J. Robson, and G. Robinson, 1775.

Geiringer, Karl. *Haydn, a Creative Life in Music.* Rev. ed. Berkeley and Los Angeles: University of California Press, 1968.

Newman, William S. *The Sonata in the Classic Era.* 3d ed. Chapel Hill: University of North Carolina Press, 1983.

Scholes, Percy, ed. *An Eighteenth Century Musical Tour in Central Europe and the Netherlands.* Dr. Burney's Musical Tours in Europe, vol. 2. London: Oxford University Press, 1959.

Sonata

Marianne von Martinez

Reprinted from *Alte Meister, Sammlung wertvoller Klavierstücke des 17. und 18. Jahrhunderts.*
No. 60. Edited by E. Pauer. Leipzig: Breitkopf & Härtel [1868-85]. By permission of G. Schirmer–Associated
Music Publishers.

93

Maria Theresia von Paradis (1759–1824)

KARIN PENDLE

Maria Theresia von Paradis was born in Vienna, the daughter of Imperial Court Secretary Josef von Paradis and goddaughter of Empress Maria Theresa, for whom she was named. Although she lost her sight at an early age, Paradis acquired the education necessary for a career in music, studying with some of the most prominent musicians of her day. Piano lessons from Leopold Kozeluch, vocal training with Vincenzo Righini and Antonio Salieri, and instruction in theory and composition from Salieri, Abbé Vogler, and Carl Friberth prepared her for her long career as a virtuoso pianist, singer, composer, and teacher. After performing in Vienna at public concerts and private musicales, in 1783 Paradis began an extended European tour that took her to such major musical centers as Paris, London, Hamburg, Berlin, Prague, and Salzburg. Mozart was so impressed with her playing that he undertook to write a piano concerto for one of her Paris concerts. Unfortunately, the work—the Concerto in B-flat major, K.456—did not reach her in time, and Paradis apparently never had the pleasure of performing it.

Paradis ended her concert tour in 1786 and returned to Vienna. Although she continued to perform until she was nearly 50, she never undertook so long and strenuous a journey again. Instead, she turned increasingly to composition, using a peg-board system invented for her by her friend and librettist Johann Riedinger. In addition to the songs she began producing during the years of her grand tour, Paradis wrote operas, cantatas, choral pieces, piano concertos, and chamber and keyboard works. (Two piano sonatas, labeled Opus 1 and 2 and mistakenly ascribed to her, are actually by Pietro Domenico Paradisi, an older contemporary.) Paradis's works were performed publicly in Vienna and elsewhere, but only some of her songs and a fantasy for piano were published during her lifetime. Manuscripts of several unpublished works, including two of her theater pieces and the piano concertos, are no longer extant.

In 1808 Paradis founded a music school for girls, whose Sunday concerts drew many members of Viennese society. Though she continued to compose until at least 1813, teaching had become her primary musical activity. Intelligent, well educated, fluent in several languages, Maria Theresia von Paradis well represents the culture of eighteenth-century Vienna.

Paradis wrote "Morgenlied eines armen Mannes" between 1784 and 1786, while she was on her extended concert tour of Europe. It was published in 1786 by Gottlieb Emanuel Breitkopf of Leipzig as part of a collection of twelve songs that were to become their composer's best-known works. Paradis was only in her twenties when she set this rather melodramatic text, but her music shows a distinctive empathy for the sentiments expressed. The poem, by Johann Timotheus Hermes, was originally part of his popular novel *Sophiens Reise von Memel nach Sachsen* (1769–73). Paradis sets this lament strophically, an approach that leads to some problems of textual continuity in stanzas 2 and 4, when the piano interlude divides ideas that belong together. Yet strophic songs were the norm at this time, and performers and listeners doubtless took such irregularities in stride.

Although Paradis repeats some ideas exactly or sequentially, her melody is essentially through-composed and reflects the pathos of the poem in a general rather than a specific way. The opening phrases do present the broken speech of a man just awakening from a troubled sleep, but one might expect the rest in m.5 to separate the syllables of "Sehnsucht" rather than those of "meines," and the ornamental figure in m.12 might better serve to emphasize "Sorgen" than "neuen." Nevertheless, the minor mode and the numerous appoggiaturas give this Italianate vocal line an expressive quality very much in keeping with the mood of the poem.

> Do you rouse me, daylight, to more miseries
> Which reawaken all my longing,
> When, in my small room,
> My wife and baby sleep in peace?
> Ye new sorrows, strike only me;
> Spare my wife's heart.
> Let her sleep on, O painful morning,
> For ah, the last thing she viewed was grief.
>
> Now sleep peacefully; may the sorrow of life,
> My child, strike you never so late!
> You will feel how my lamentations
> Intercede for you in vain.
> Soon your naked limbe will be
> Fiercely attacked by every storm;
> Soon hunger will once more assail you,
> Hunger which even my wife cannot assuage.
>
> Slumber, beloved of my youth;
> Feel not the want that troubles me.
> It is present, for diligence and virtue
> No longer shield me as once they did.
> I can save neither child nor wife;
> Only you, merciful God, can do so.
> Make them happy, and draw more tightly
> The chains that bind me.
>
> I shall go quietly
> Along the rough path of accustomed pain,
> And pray to you today, as before,
> For bread and blessings for child and wife.
> They awaken—O, your laughter,
> Child, how it penetrates my being.
> These, the deepest pains of all,
> Surely, Lord, must move you.

The many minor triads and melodic ornaments in Paradis's popular "Sicilienne" lend it a sweetly sentimental flavor. Since neither the original manuscript nor any eighteenth-century editions of this work exist, its modern editor, Samuel Dushkin, relied on a manuscript copy of the piece found in the library of the publishing firm of B. Schott. Dushkin, who has published versions of the "Sicilienne" for violin or cello and piano, and for piano alone, has reworked and modernized the keyboard part for the version of the work printed here.

The charm of Paradis's "Sicilienne" lies in its melody, particularly in the unexpected chromatic inflections and in the irregular extensions of phrases that lend a spun-out quality not often found in music of this time (see, for example, mm.5–10 and especially mm.15–22). The simple chordal accompaniment of the "Sicilienne" merely establishes an atmosphere in which this melodic gem can work its touching magic.

Recordings (of "Sicilienne")

Version for violin and piano:

Thibaud Violin Recital. "Sicilienne," Jacques Thibaud and Tasso Janopoulo. Angel GR-2079 (197–?).

Encores. "Sicilienne," Itzhak Perlman and Samuel Sanders. Angel SZ-37560 (1979).

Greensleeves and Other Classical Favorites. "Sicilienne," Bruce Chapman and John Pawlyk. Unicorn MS 1000 (1979).

The Complete Recorded Legacy of Ginette Niveu. "Sicilienne," Ginette Niveu and Bruno Seidler-Winkler. EMI RLS 739 (1980).

Version for cello and piano:

Women's Work in Music. "Sicilienne," Evalyn Steinbock and Michael May. Gemini Hall RAP 1010 (1980).

A Jacqueline Du Pré Recital. "Sicilienne," Jacqueline Du Pre and Gerald Moore. Angel S-37900 (1982).

Version for piano solo:

Piano Works by Women Composers. "Sicilienne," Rosario Marciano. Turnabout TV 34685 (1979).

Frauen als Komponisten. "Sicilienne," Rosario Marciano. Vox FSM 53036 (1980).

Further Reading

Biographical articles in *The New Grove Dictionary of Music and Musicians* and *Die Musik in Geschichte und Gegenwart.*

Badura-Skoda, Eva. "Zur Entstehung des Klavierkonzertes in B-Dur KV. 456," *Mozart Jahrbuch* 1964:193–97.

Ullrich, Hermann. "Maria Theresia Paradis' grosse Kunstreise," *Oesterreichische Musikzeitschrift* 15 (1960):470–80; 17 (1962):11–26; 475–83; 19 (1964):430–35; 20 (1965):589–97.

———. "Maria Theresia Paradis' grosse Kunstreise (1783–1786). Die Heimkehr," *Beiträge zur Musikwissenschaft* 6 (1964):129–41.

———. "Maria Theresia Paradis. Werkverzeichnis," *Beiträge zur Musikwissenschaft* 5 (1963):117–54.

Morgenlied eines armen Mannes

Text by Johann Timotheus Hermes

Maria Theresia von Paradis

Reprinted from *Denkmäler der Tonkust in Oesterreich* 54 (1920):99-100.

3.

Schlummre, Freundin meiner Jugend,
Fühl die Not nicht, die mich schreckt,
Sie ist da, weil Fleiß und Tugend
Mich nicht mehr wie vormals deckt;
Ich kann Kind und Weib nicht retten,
|:Gott der Gnaden, das kannst du,:|
Mach sie glücklich, und zieh Ketten,
|:Die mich drücken, fester zu.:|

4.

Ich will still auf rauhen Wegen
Des gewohnten Jammers gehn
Und auch heut' um Brot und Segen
Für mein Kind und Weib dich flehn.
Sie erwachen— o dein Scherzen
|:Säugling, wie durchdringt es mich,:|
Diese allertiefsten Schmerzen
|:Wahrlich, Herr, sie jammern dich.:|

Sicilienne

Maria Theresia von Paradis

© 1931 by B. Schott's Söhne, Mainz. Arranged by Samuel Dushkin. Copyright renewed; all rights reserved. Used by permission of European American Distributors Corp., sole U.S. agent for B. Schott's Söhne.

Maria Agata Szymanowska (1789–1831)

NANCY FIERRO, CSJ

Maria Agata Szymanowska, a contemporary of Beethoven and Schubert, was the first Polish pianist of stature. Her playing won the title "Royal Pianist of the Court of Russia" and the admiration of both Liszt and Chopin in their younger years. Her many piano compositions, published during her lifetime, are significant in the history of Polish music before Chopin.

The daughter of Barbara Lanckorońska and middle-class merchant Franciscek Wolowski, Maria exhibited a precocious talent. With only scant keyboard instruction, the young girl seated at the spinet would entertain family guests with improvisations on her own themes. Between 1789 and 1802, the obscure composers Antoni Lisowski and Tomasz Gremm taught her piano; and Josef Elsner, Franciszek Lessel, John Field, and Johann Nepomuk Hummel occasionally provided her with advice about performance or prompted revisions of her compositions. Otherwise, it appears that Maria was largely self taught.

In 1810, the young pianist made her debut in Warsaw. In the same year she married a wealthy landowner, Josef Szymanowski. By 1815, she was in great demand for public concerts, but her frequent appearances were offensive to her husband. His continued disapproval caused Maria to separate from him in 1820 and take her three children with her. She earned her living through concerts and lectures on piano technique. With many performances behind her and some of her works published, she began regular appearances throughout both eastern and western Europe, returning intermittently to her beloved Warsaw.

During her successful concert career from 1810 to 1828, Szymanowska included many of her own works in her programs. She wrote more than 110 compositions: vocal music, chamber music, and a large body of piano music. In an era when society placed little value on compositions by women, it is remarkable that Szymanowska's works found immediate publication—by Breitkopf and Härtel in Leipzig and by publishers in Paris, Warsaw, St. Petersburg, Moscow, Kiev, and Odessa.

Szymanowska's piano compositions, consisting of nearly 90 miniatures, display the composer's versatility. They include nocturnes, waltzes, polonaises, minuets, marches, mazurkas, and concert etudes. Her two nocturnes exemplify early pianistic poetry. The first, "Le Murmure," in A-flat major, became one of her most popular compositions. Her second nocturne, in B-flat major, is reproduced here. It exhibits marked growth from the simple, straightforward style of Szymanowska's earlier works, with more-imaginative writing and an increase in personal expression.

The second nocturne opens with a gentle barcarolle accompaniment supporting an embellished vocal line. The tempo is slower and the idiom more reflective than in the first nocturne. Szymanowska contrasts the opening cantilena with a darker section in the parallel minor, then moves to a passage of a nationalistic character. She reinforces a reprise by a registration in octaves and closes with an extended coda.

Because the Nocturne in B flat was published (posthumously) in 1852 and differs in style from many of Szymanowska's works, doubts have been expressed about its authenticity. However, there is a plausible explanation: Between the years 1828 and 1831, when the Nocturne was composed, Szymanowska had more time to devote to personal activities. Until then, responsibility for her children, the demands of an active social life, and the exigencies of a professional career demanded most of her attention. But in her permanent home in St. Petersburg, she was free to pursue some long-delayed projects. One of these activities was collecting her compositions and copying them into one album. It is possible that for the first time she had sufficient leisure to compose a more-sophisticated piece.

On the afternoon of July 23, 1831, Maria Agata Szymanowska suddenly fell ill with cholera. She died the following morning and was buried in what is now Leningrad.

Recordings (of Nocturne in B-flat major)

Regina Smendzianaka, pianist. Muza XL0355.
Nancy Fierro, pianist. Avant 1012.
Rosario Marciano, pianist. Turnabout TV 34685.

Further Reading

Davies, Joan. "Maria Szymanowska," *The Consort* 23 (1966):167–74.
Nowak-Romanowicz, Alina. "Szymanowska, Maria," *The New Grove* 18:499.
Swaryczewska, Katarzyna. "Szymanowska, Maria," *Musik in Geschichte und Gegenwart* XIII (1966):31–32.

Nocturne

Maria Szymanowska

Published by Polskie Wydawnictwo Muzyczne, n.d. Reprinted by permission.

Josephine Lang
(1815–1880)

MARCIA J. CITRON

Josephine Lang came from a musical home in Munich, where her father was a court musician and her mother, Regina Hitzelberger, a court opera singer. Although the young Josephine started out on the piano, she soon immersed herself in song, as both interpreter and creator. Her earliest lieder date from her thirteenth year, and this genre was to occupy her compositional talents almost exclusively.

Momentous in Lang's life were her encounters with Felix Mendelssohn, in 1830 and again in 1831, when he visited Munich on his extended tour of Europe. Here was a gifted fifteen-year-old, almost entirely self-taught, whose lieder, singing, and angelic presence evoked an enraptured response from the sensitive young musician. His sisters Fanny and Rebecka must have been surprised by the intensity of his enthusiasm—they knew him as a cool, level-headed judge of the contemporary scene. In any case, such encouragement undoubtedly spurred on Lang in her compositional endeavors. From the mid-1830s to the early 1840s she was extremely prolific, producing approximately one-third of her total output of lieder. She tended to select texts that mirrored the feelings and events of her own life: "They are my diary," she wrote in 1835.

It was in this period that her music began to be published, eliciting generally favorable reviews. An assessment by Robert Schumann of "Das Traumbild," which he saw well before its publication, appeared in his journal *Neue Zeitschrift für Musik* in 1837. In 1840 Lang met her future husband, the Swabian poet Reinhard Köstlin, whose poems she would set in numerous lieder. After their marriage in 1842 they moved to Tübingen. There Lang devoted herself mainly to domestic activities, and her creative pursuits decreased markedly. Köstlin's death in 1856 left her with the heavy burden of caring and providing for their six children, and she turned to composing and publication for financial reasons. But now Lang's style was somewhat out of step with contemporary currents, and as a result she had considerable difficulty getting her music published. Through the assistance of a friend of Mendelssohn's, the influential Ferdinand Hiller, she managed to secure the publication of some lieder and thereby support her family. Her death occasioned a retrospective collection of 40 songs, many of them hitherto unpublished, by Breitkopf & Härtel in 1882.

"Frühzeitiger Frühling," based on a Goethe poem of 1801, was published for the first time in this posthumous volume. An early composition, written in 1830, when Lang was only fifteen, it was one of the songs that Mendelssohn heard during their first meeting. In its spontaneity and stunning originality it exemplifies the style that reviewers dubbed a new manner of song. The choice of the brilliant key of B major is a bold stroke. The melodic line features unusual directional turns and is often chromatic in unexpected ways. The piano part, which challenges the technical prowess of the performer, beautifully conveys the impending excitement of the poem. As in Schubert lieder, the vocal line and piano accompaniment are two distinct strata; like many of Lang's songs, the form is strophic. Brief introductory and concluding statements in the piano symmetrically enfold the dramatic core.

> Days of delight, are you here so soon?
> Are you giving me the sun, hills, and forest?
> The little brooks flow more fully,
> Is it the meadows? Is it the valley?
>
> Beneath the greenery's blooming strength
> The little bees, humming, nibble at the nectar.
> Colorful feathers rustle in the wood,
> Heavenly songs resound within!
>
> Soon a breath stirs itself more forcefully,
> But it loses itself immediately in the bush.
> But it returns in the bosom,
> Help me, you Muses, to bear this joy!
>
> Gentle movement quivers in the breeze,
> Delicious stirring, drowsy fragrance.
> Tell me, since yesterday what's happened to me,
> Dear sisters, my sweetheart is here.

Recording

Lieder of Clara Schumann, Fanny Mendelssohn, Josephine Lang and Pauline Viardot-Garcia. Leonarda LPI 107.

Further Reading

Citron, Marcia J. "Women and the Lied, 1775–1850," in *Women Making Music*, edited by Jane Bowers and Judith Tick. Urbana and Chicago: University of Illinois Press, 1986.
Tick, Judith. "Introduction" to Josephine Lang, *Selected Songs*. New York: Da Capo, 1982.

Frühzeitiger Frühling

Nº 2.

Josephine Lang

Allegro agitato.

1. Ta _ ge der Won _ ne,   kommt ihr so bald?
2. Un _ ter des Grü _ nen   blü _ hender Kraft
3. Mäch _ ti _ ger rüh _ ret   bald _ sich ein Hauch,
4. Lei _ se Be _ we _ gung   bebt _ in der Luft,

Schenkt mir die Son _ ne   Hü _ gel und Wald?   Reich _ li _ cher flie _ ssen
na _ schen die Bien _ lein   sum _ mend vom Saft.   Bun _ tes Ge _ fie _ der
doch er ver _ lie _ ret   gleich sich im Strauch.   A _ ber zum Bu _ sen
rei _ zen _ de Re _ gung   schlä _ fernder Duft.   Sa _ get seit ge _ stern

Reprinted from Josephine Lang, *Selected Songs*. Women Composers Series, Da Capo Press, 1984.
By permission.

Bäch_lein zu_mal,   sind   es die Wie _ sen?   ist __ es das Thal?
rau_schet im Hain,   himm _ li_sche Lie _ der   schal_len dar_ein!
kehrt er zu_rück,   hel _ fet ihr Mu _ sen   tra_gen das Glück!
wie__ mir geschah   lieb _ li_che Schwe_stern, Lieb_chen ist da!

sind   es die Wie_sen?   ist__ es das Thal?
himm _ li_sche Lie _ der   schal_len dar_ein!
hel _ fet ihr Mu _ sen   tra _ gen das Glück!
lieb _ li_che Schwestern, Liebchen ist da!

Fanny Mendelssohn Hensel (1805–1847)

MARCIA J. CITRON

Fanny Hensel was a prolific composer, a skilled pianist, and a respected leader of a flourishing Berlin salon. The elder sister of Felix Mendelssohn, Hensel grew up in a culturally sophisticated home, where from an early age she was exposed to the leading artistic and intellectual figures of the day. These formative contacts helped instill in her a keen discriminating mind and a knowledge and love of poetry. Heinrich Heine, the author of the text of Hensel's song "Schwanenlied," was a frequent visitor to the Mendelssohn household, and Fanny may have heard some of his poems even before they were published.

Fanny and Felix shared a common music education and developed an unusually close sibling relationship. But largely because of her sex, Fanny was not encouraged to become a professional musician. Nonetheless a prolific outpouring of pieces continued unabated throughout her life. Her husband, the Prussian court painter Wilhelm Hensel, was very supportive; and her brother, on whose good opinion she strongly depended, encouraged her composing but was opposed to her pieces being published. Largely because of Felix's negative attitude, only a very small percentage of her compositions—which number well over 400—were published.

Hensel composed almost exclusively in the genres long associated with women and their domestic environment: lieder and piano pieces. Many of these pieces, as well as her few forays into orchestral and choral works, were presented at her lively Sunday musical gatherings, or *Sonntagsmusiken*. Hensel herself was a leading participant, playing the piano as soloist or as part of the ensemble. Except for a large charity concert in 1838, Hensel did not perform in public, in accordance with her family's attitudes about woman's proper role. Thus her celebrated private gatherings provided her with a needed forum for her various musical activities.

Hensel's first published compositions, three lieder, appeared under her brother's authorship in his Opus 8 (1827); three more followed in his Opus 9 (1830). Unfortunately, we do not know the reason for this camouflage, although it was not an uncommon practice among women composers. The first piece issued under Hensel's own name was a lied in an anthology that appeared in 1837. With the exception of an isolated lied published two years later, it was not until the last year of Hensel's life that her pieces reached the public in printed form, and this time in a spate of seven publications rather than as isolated works. "Schwanenlied" is the first song in Opus 1, *Sechs Lieder für eine Stimme mit Begleitung des Pianoforte* (Six Songs for

One Voice with Piano Accompaniment). The collection appeared in the summer of 1846 and provided Hensel with the great satisfaction of finally seeing an entire volume published under her own name.

"Schwanenlied," with text by Heinrich Heine, resembles a lullaby. In its clear separation of melody and accompaniment it is akin to the style of many *Songs Without Words*, for piano solo, some composed by Hensel and some by Mendelssohn. Formally it is simple, like most Hensel settings, consisting of two strophes with the second slightly modified. That slight modification proves significant, however, for it fashions the climax of the song. Occurring in the middle of the second strophe, it is effected by an extension on the word "Fluthengrab" (depths of the river), a turning point for the carefree swan and the drama of the poem. Overall Hensel has successfully captured the bittersweet quality of Heine's text. A brief piano postlude concludes each strophe.

A star falls down
From its twinkling height,
It is the star of love
That I see falling there.
So much falls from the apple tree,
From the white leaves;
The teasing breezes come
And urge on their game.

The swan sings in the pond,
And paddles up and down,
And singing more and more gently,
He disappears into the depths of the river.
It is so quiet and dark,
Scattered is leaf and blossom,
The star has flickered into dust,
The swan song has faded away.

Recording

Fanny Hensel, Opus 1. Leonarda LPI 112.

Further Reading

Citron, Marcia J. "The Lieder of Fanny Mendelssohn Hensel," *The Musical Quarterly* 69 (1983): 570–93.
———. "Felix Mendelssohn's Influence on Fanny Hensel as a Professional Composer," *Current Musicology* 37–38 (1984): 9–17.

Schwanenlied

Fanny Hensel

Originally published by Bote und Bock, Berlin. Reprinted by the permission of the U. S. representatives, Associated Music Publishers, Inc. (G. Schirmer, Inc.).

singt der Schwan im Wei - her, und ru - dert auf und

ab, und im - mer lei - ser sin - gend,

taucht er ins Flu - then - grab. Es ist so still und

dun - kel, ver - weht ist Blatt und Blüth', der

117

Clara Schumann (1819–1896)

NANCY B. REICH

Clara Schumann, a peer of Franz Liszt and Sigismund Thalberg on the concert stage, was an exceptionally well-educated musician. As a child prodigy, she was as renowned for her compositions as much as for her celebrated virtuoso career. Her creative work was praised by the "new romantic" composers—Mendelssohn, Chopin, and Liszt—as well as by the man who later became her husband, Robert Schumann. Other admirers included Johann Wolfgang von Goethe, Louis Spohr, and Gasparo Spontini.

From her letters to friends, there is evidence that Clara Schumann found composing a source of great pleasure; and she declared more than once that only a composer could achieve true immortality. Yet she herself had grave doubts about her role as a composer and was more comfortable in the world of the interpretive artist. The ambivalence she displayed was due, in part, to the societal attitude toward women composers and was certainly influenced by her position as the wife of a creative genius.

From our vantage point, she may not rank with her husband and his friends and contemporaries, Frédéric Chopin and Felix Mendelssohn, but their esteem of her work was sincere. Both before and after their marriage, Robert Schumann encouraged and supported his wife's work: theirs was a true musical union. Robert exchanged musical ideas with her; they studied scores of Bach, Beethoven, Haydn, and Mozart together; he urged her to compose, to preserve her autographs, and to catalogue her work; he wrote to publishers on her behalf and published two of her works as supplements to *Neue Zeitschrift für Musik*, the music journal he edited. After his death, she ceased composing and devoted herself to performing piano works she respected; her time was also occupied with the supervision of her seven children, teaching, and editing the music of Robert Schumann.

Until her marriage, just before her 21st birthday, the young pianist wrote only works for performance at her own concerts, events that were carefully planned by Friedrich Wieck, her teacher–manager–father. Almost all of the 182 programs she gave between 1828 and 1840 boasted at least one work by the young Clara Wieck. But beginning in 1839, the year before Robert Schumann's "song year," she and her husband-to-be began reading poetry with an eye to eventual musical settings. Her first published works after she married Robert Schumann were three songs in a collection entitled *Zwölf Lieder aus F. Rückert's Liebesfrühling für Gesang und Pianoforte von*

Robert und Clara Schumann, brought out in Leipzig by Breitkopf & Härtel in 1841. (The collection is often referred to as Opus 37/12—Robert's Opus 37 and Clara's Opus 12.) There was no indication in the first edition as to which songs were Clara's, but Robert, who enjoyed the confusion of the critics, noted on the flyleaf of his copy that numbers 2, 4, and 11 were hers. Autographs in Zwickau and Berlin attest to her authorship.

"Liebst Du um Schönheit," with text by Friedrich Rückert, is the fourth song of the collection. The moving inner voices of the accompaniment contrast with the declamatory vocal line, which asks three simple questions then gives the answer in a moving climax. Note the way the piano part takes over the vocal line in m.16, the extension of the phrase to create the climax in mm.34–36, and the piano postlude, as it winds down from the emotional peak of "dich lieb ich immerdar."

> If you love because of beauty, then do not love me!
> Love the sun, it has golden hair!
> If you love because of youth, then do not love me!
> Love the springtime, it is young every year.
> If you love because of treasures, then do not love me,
> Love the mermaid, she has many shining pearls,
> If you love for love, O then do love me,
> Love me forever, for I love you for eternity.

The Trio for Violin, Cello, and Piano, Opus 17, composed in 1846, is decidedly different from Clara Schumann's earlier works, which were mainly character pieces and virtuoso variations. Robert Schumann, obviously proud of his wife's work, submitted the Trio to Breitkopf & Härtel and arranged to have it published and ready for her birthday in September 1847. It was her first extended composition written in the traditional four-movement form, the fruits of her studies of the chamber works of the Classical masters and her personal experience performing the trio literature of Beethoven and Schubert.

The movements of the Trio are marked Allegro moderato, Scherzo, Andante, and Allegretto. The first movement, presented here, is in clear-cut sonata form. The opening theme, a lyrical and melancholy eight-measure melody in G minor, is balanced in structure and regular in rhythm. It contrasts strongly with the second theme (m.45), a syncopated descending motive in B-flat major. In the exposition, the violin and piano dominate while the cello plays a supporting role. In the development section (after the double bar), however, the cello takes its proper place in the ensemble and, in a series of sequences and imitative episodes based on the first theme, engages in interchanges with the violin. The recapitulation, preceded by a long pedal on D, is almost literal but with the second subject in the parallel major this time.

Although the Trio was the composer's first and only published work in this style and form, it is a polished effort, eminently playable, that enriches the repertoire for this combination.

After a hiatus of seven years, Clara Schumann took up her pen again for a birthday gift for her husband. Her Variations on a Theme by Robert Schumann, Opus 20, was written in June 1853 and published in November 1854, after she had met Johannes Brahms. During the summer of 1854, the younger composer also wrote a set of variations (his Opus 9) on the same Schumann theme. Brahms quoted a theme from a childhood work by Clara Schumann (Opus 3) in his tenth variation, thus paying tribute to both husband and wife. In the coda of her Opus 20, Clara Schumann also quoted from her earlier work, and since the quotation does not appear in the 1853 autograph, it seems likely that she inserted the quotation after she heard Brahms play his Opus

9. Like Brahms and Clara herself, in Opus 20, Robert Schumann also refers to Clara's Opus 3 in his Impromptus on a Romance by Clara Wieck.

The theme of Clara Schumann's Opus 20 is based on Robert Schumann's *Bunte Blätter*, Opus 99, no. 4, a 24-measure piece in simple ternary form composed in 1841, though not published until 1852. Robert Schumann's melody, presented in its entirety but without designated repeats, appears in each of the seven variations with only slight modifications. Except for minor changes, this regularity applies to the structure and tonality as well. Only Variations 2 and 7 differ in form, and the entire set, except for Variation 3 and the Coda, is in F-sharp minor, the key of the Robert Schumann piece. Unlike Clara Schumann's earlier sets of variations, Opus 3, Opus 8, and Opus 9, which were designed to please the public by displaying her dazzling technique, this work shows balance, proportion, and control throughout. Here the composer–pianist explores the theme by skillful changes in harmony, texture, motion, articulation, dynamics, rhythmic patterns, and coloration.

Recordings

Clara Schumann, Lieder et Pièces pour Piano. "Liebst du um Schönheit," Udo Reinemann and Christian Ivaldi. Arion 38575, 1980.

Lieder, Clara Schumann, Fanny Mendelssohn, Josephine Lang, Pauline Viardot-Garcia. "Liebst du um Schönheit," Katherine Ciesinski and Rudolph Palmer. Leonarda LP1–107, 1981.

Chamber Music by Clara Wieck Schumann. Trio in G Minor. Monica von Saalfeld, Franziska Koscielny, and Gisela Reith. Oryx Romantic 1819.

Chamber Music by Women Composers. Clara Schumann, *Trio in G Minor.* Macalester Trio. Vox SvBX 5112, 1979.

Robert and Clara Schumann. The Complete Piano Trios. Beaux Arts Trio. Philips 6880 008, 1972.

Chamber Music by Clara Wieck Schumann. "7 Variations on a Theme of Robert Schumann, op.20." Monica von Saalfeld, piano. Oryx Romantic 1819.

Music by Clara Schumann and Fanny Mendelssohn. "Variations on a Theme by Robert Schumann, op.20." Judith Alstadter, piano. Musical Heritage Society 4163, 1980.

Piano Works by Women Composers. Clara Schumann, "Variations on a Theme by Robert Schumann." Rosario Marciano, piano. Turnabout TV 34685, 1979.

Clara Schumann. Two Romances, Variations, Mazurka. James Sykes, piano. Orion 75182, [1974].

Schumanniana. Variations, op.3 by Clara Schumann; Variations, op.5 by Robert Schumann; Variations, op.9 by Johannes Brahms. Musicaphon (Bärenreiter) BM30 SL 1916.

Liebst du um Schönheit

Clara Schumann

Reprinted from the edition by Breitkopf & Härtel, Leipzig, n.d. [ca. 1873].

In m.28, the second note in the vocal line should be A flat, not F.

Trio

Clara Schumann

Reprinted from the edition of 1847, by Breitkopf & Härtel, Leipzig. By permission of Verlag Walter Wollenweber, Munich, reprint 1972.

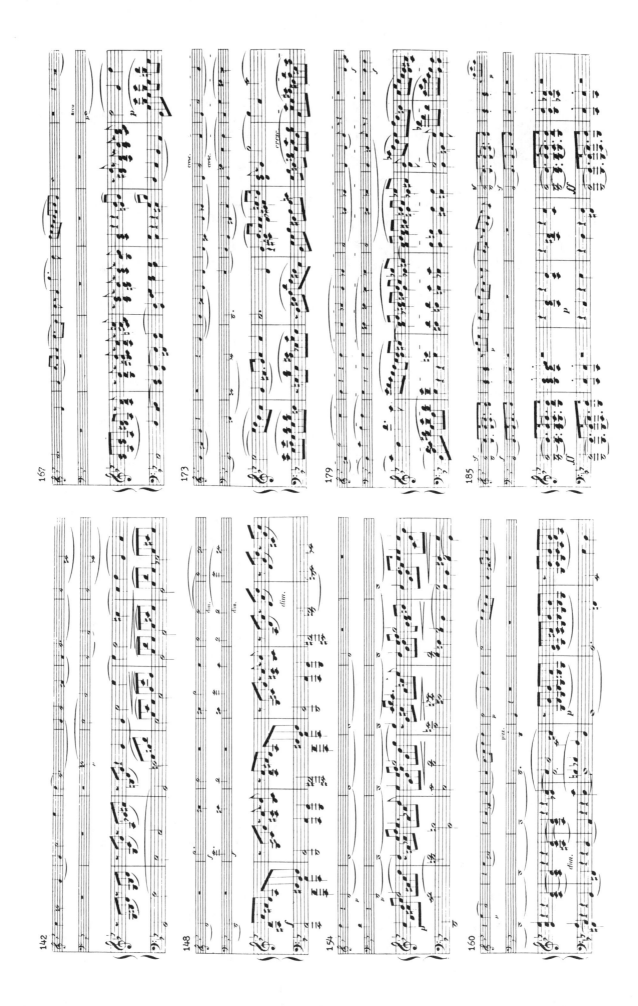

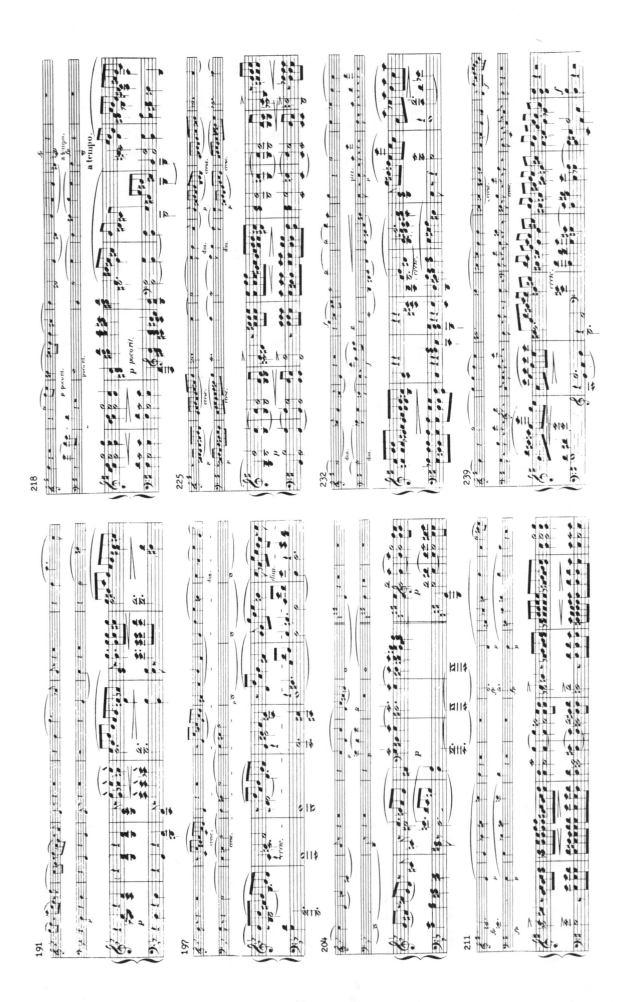

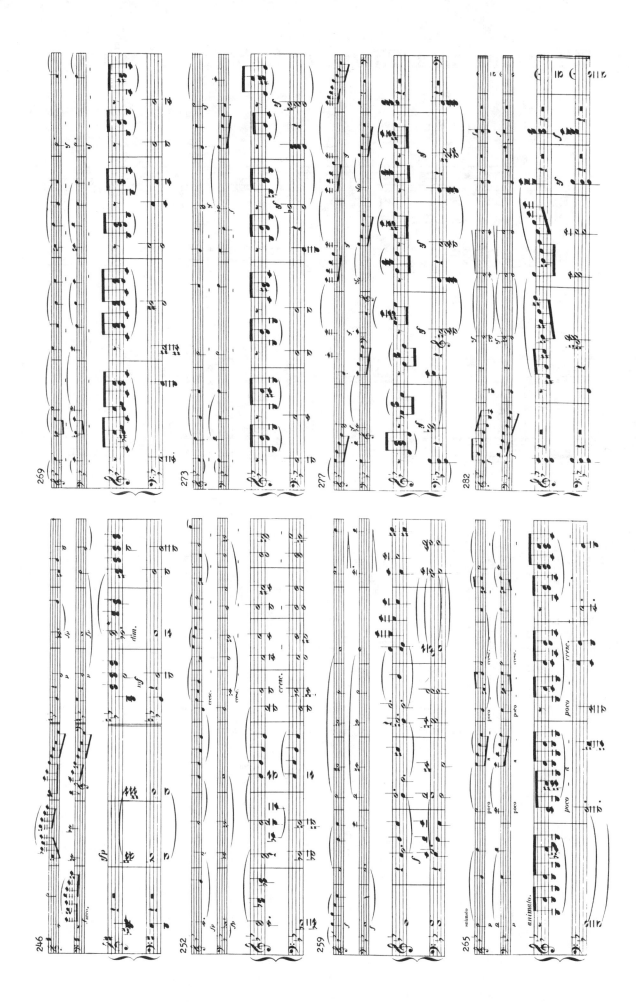

Variations on a Theme of Robert Schumann

Clara Schumann

Reprinted from the edition by Breitkopf & Härtel, Leipzig, 1854.

131

132

133

Var. III.

Var. IV.

Poco animato.

Var. V.

137

Var. VI.

138

139

molto espressivo.

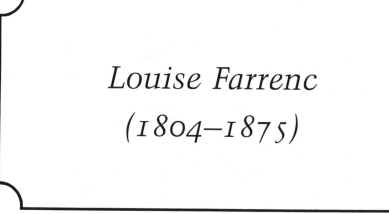

Louise Farrenc
(1804–1875)

BEA FRIEDLAND

Louise Dumont Farrenc was an unusual figure in the musical life of France during the nineteenth century: an accomplished pianist, composer of distinction, professor at the Conservatoire, and editor of early music. The quality and diversity of this achievement are best understood and evaluated when viewed not as isolated phenomena but in relation to the milieu in which she lived and worked.

In many important ways, Farrenc functioned outside the cultural mainstream of mid-century Paris, her native city and lifelong home. It was the age of the virtuoso, with superficial display pieces providing the main concert fare; she preferred to investigate and perform the little-known late sonatas of Beethoven. *La vie mondaine* revolved around the Opéra; her own predilection was for the instrumental genres. French musical aesthetics traditionally focused on the pictorial aspects of music; her creative bent favored the abstract forms of the sonata and the symphony. French women of musical ability typically sought fame and fortune on the opera stage or as composers of sentimental *romances*; Louise Farrenc quietly pursued her career as an effective teacher, composer of (mainly) chamber music, and—in the end—as a performer, editor, and champion of the largely unexplored harpsichord repertoire.

A descendant of a long line of royal artists (including several women painters) and a sister of the laureate sculptor Auguste Dumont, Louise showed artistic and musical talent of a high order at an early age. By mid-adolescence she had developed into a pianist of professional calibre as well as an exceptional theory student and a promising composer. Her studies in composition and orchestration with Anton Reicha were interrupted for a few years following her marriage in 1821 to Aristide Farrenc, a flutist and music publisher. With the resumption of work with Reicha in the mid-1820s, Louise Farrenc began to publish her compositions for piano, most notable of which are the *Air russe varié*, Opus 17 (1835), which was favorably reviewed by Schumann in *Neue Zeitschrift für Musik* a year after publication, and the Thirty Etudes in all the major and minor keys (1839 or 1840).

Farrenc's orchestral works comprise two overtures (1834) and three symphonies (completed in the 1840s). None are published, although each had more than one Paris performance, and some were heard in other major European capitals as well. Her outstanding contribution is the body of chamber music she produced between 1840 and 1860: two quintets, four trios, two violin sonatas, a cello sonata, and two unpublished pieces—a sextet and a nonet. All these works were performed many times over, and most of them were published within a few years of completion. The Institut de France twice honored Louise Farrenc for her chamber music compositions, awarding her the Prix Chartier in 1861 and 1869.

In 1842 Auber, the director of the Conservatoire, appointed Farrenc professor of piano, a post she retained until her retirement in 1873. The only woman musician at the Conservatoire in the nineteenth century to hold a permanent chair of this rank and importance, she distinguished herself by the excellence of her teaching, which has been demonstrated by the high proportion of her pupils who won competitions and went on to professional careers.

Perhaps most memorable among Louise Farrenc's musical achievements is her contribution to the 23-volume collection of early keyboard music, *Le trésor des pianistes* (1861–75). Sharing her husband's ideal of reviving the harpsichord and virginal repertory of the seventeenth and eighteenth centuries, Louise Farrenc collaborated with him (and continued alone, after his death in 1865) in preparing modern editions of old manuscripts and prints collected from France, England, Italy, and Germany. Supplementing her work as editor and publisher, she brought the music alive in a series of *séances historiques,* in which she and her pupils performed selections from *Le trésor des pianistes.* Her own compositions continued to be heard in Paris up to the time of her death in 1875—the last performance during her lifetime, appropriately enough, being the Adagio cantabile of her Third Symphony conducted by Edouard Colonne at the Concert du Châtelet, February 14, 1875.

The Trio, Opus 45, composed in 1857 and published in 1862, is the last of Louise Farrenc's compositions for three instruments. Scored for flute (or violin), cello, and piano, it is an engaging, carefully constructed piece reminiscent of Mendelssohn's Classical form and Romantic aura. The first movement, reprinted here, is illustrative of Farrenc's skill: within a traditional sonata form the composer incorporates some unexpected modulations and ingenious bits of development, producing a delightful work that "still offers performers as well as audiences an exciting experience" (so says Miriam Gideon in the Introduction to the Da Capo edition of the Trio).

Recordings

Trio in E minor, Opus 45. Katherine Hoover, flute; Carter Brey, cello; Barbara Weintraub, piano. Leonarda 104, 1979.
Trio No. 2 in D minor, Opus 34; *Five Etudes for Piano*, from Opus 26; *Air russe varié*, Opus 17. The New York Lyric Arts Trio; Gina Raps, piano. Musical Heritage Society, 3766L.

Further Reading

Farrenc, Aristide and Louise. *Le trésor des pianistes*. 23 vols. Paris, 1861–75. Reprint New York: Da Capo, 1978, with a Foreword by Bea Friedland.
Friedland, Bea. *Louise Farrenc, 1804–1875: Composer, Performer, Scholar.* Ann Arbor: UMI Research Press, 1980.

Trio

Louise Farrenc

Reprinted from Louise Farrenc, *Trio*. Women Composers Series, Da Capo Press, 1979. By permission.

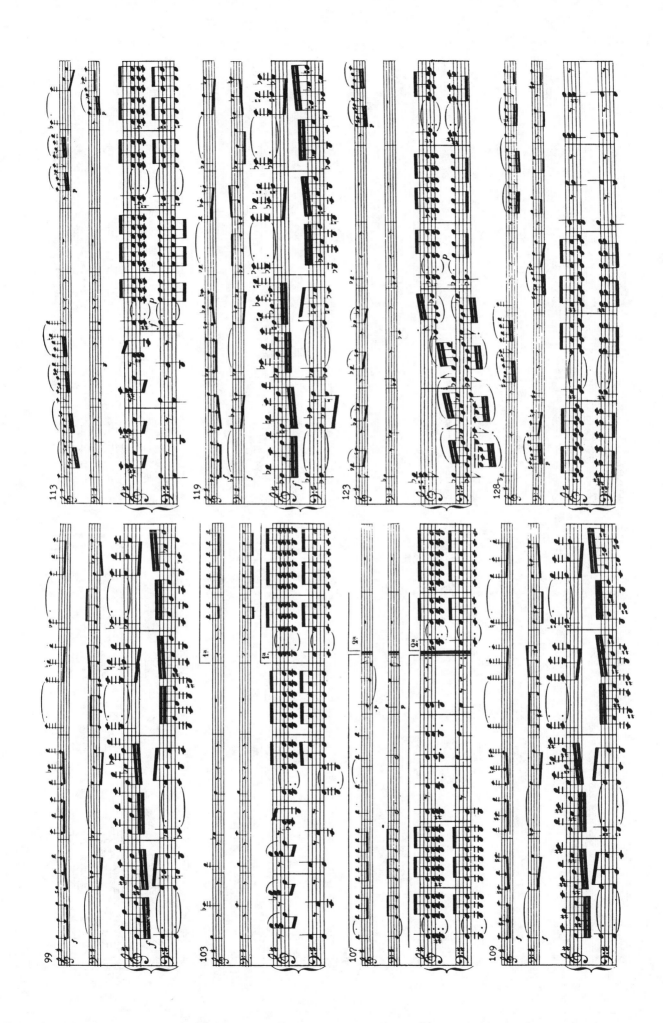

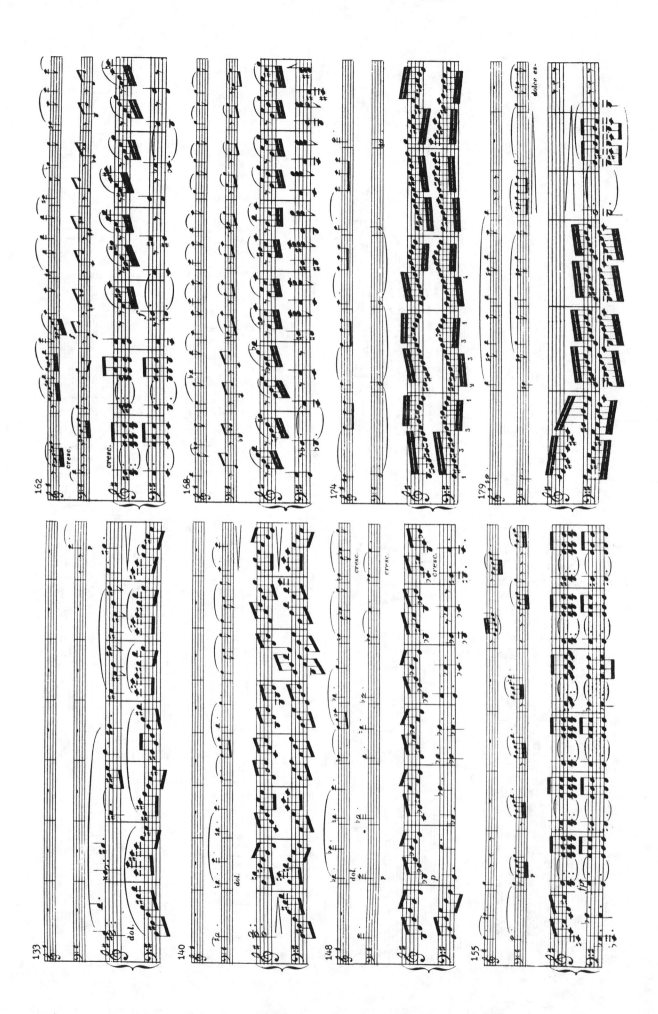

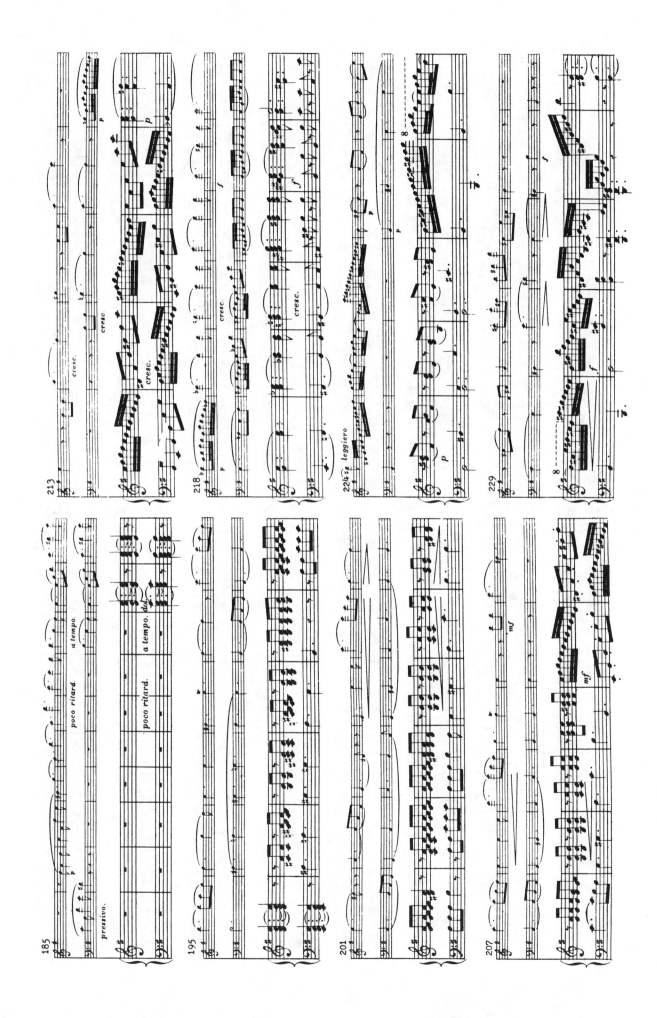

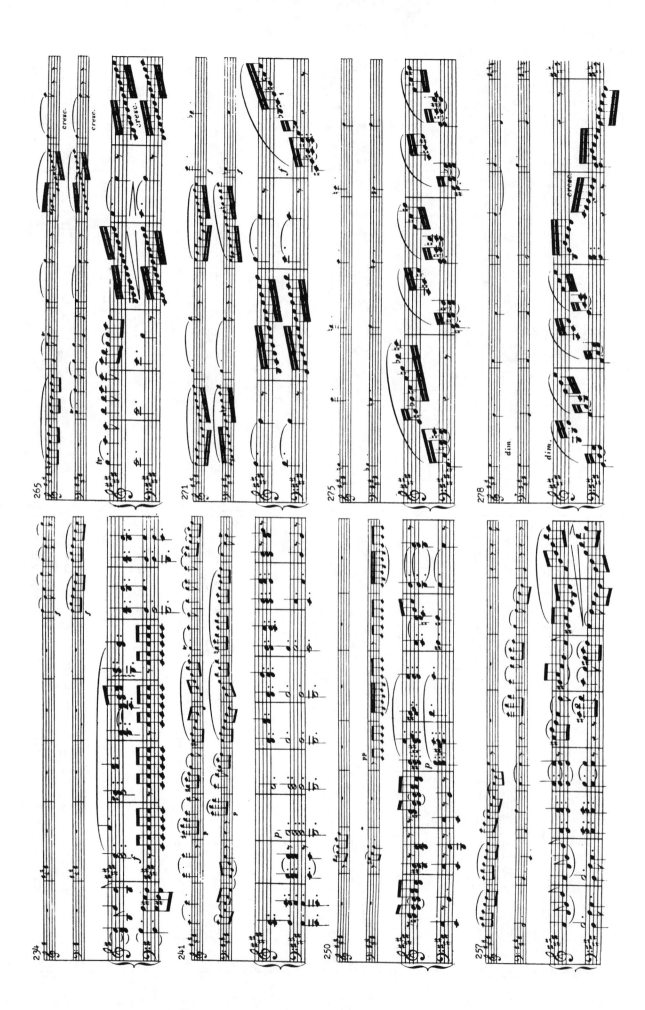

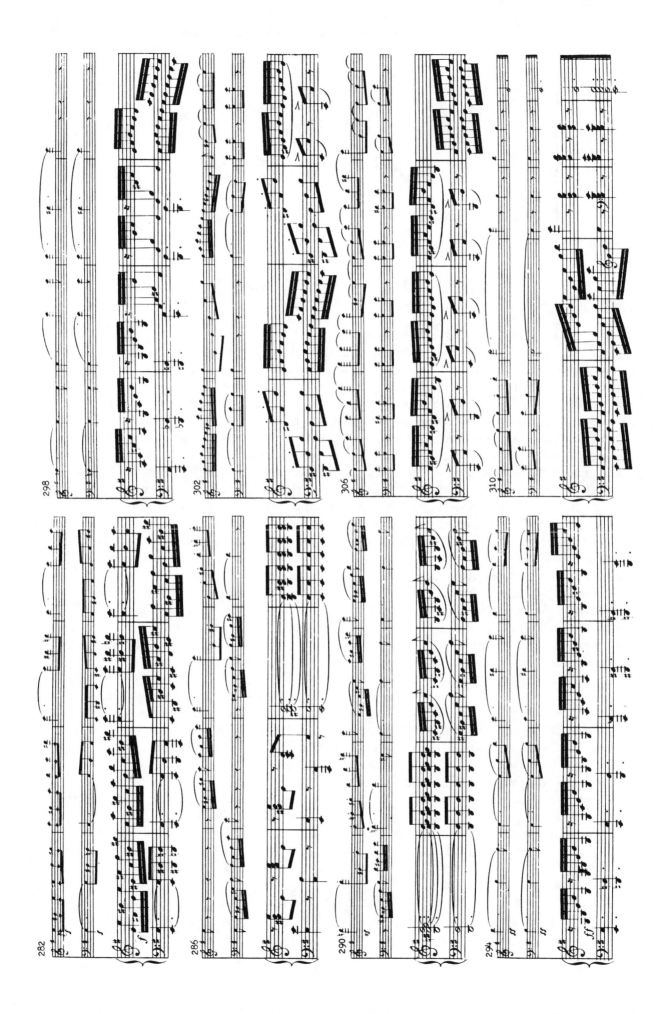

Pauline Viardot-Garcia (1821–1910)

AUSTIN B. CASWELL

Pauline Viardot-Garcia was a member of the legendary Garcia clan, which was inextricably intertwined with opera and vocal pedagogy during the nineteenth century. Her father, Manuel Garcia (1775–1832), was as famous for his family-opera-company tour of the United States and Mexico (1825–28) as for his creation of Rossini roles and the training of some of the century's most accomplished singers, among them his own children. Her mother, Joaquina Sitchez, was an accomplished actress-singer, who took over the pedagogical role at her husband's death to such an extent that Pauline claimed her mother as her only voice teacher. Pauline's brother Manuel (1805–1906), the celebrated "centenarian of song," devoted himself to pedagogy and research into vocal physiology, while Pauline and her sister Maria Malibran (1808–1836) held undisputed positions in the operatic world.

A child prodigy of diverse gifts, Pauline early and effortlessly acquired five languages, accompanied her father on the piano at age eight (she later studied with Liszt), became an accomplished portraitist, and studied composition with the reigning contrapuntist of the age, Anton Reicha. In 1839, three years after the untimely death of her sister Maria, Pauline began an operatic career that nearly matched Maria's in the Italian repertoire and surpassed all rivals in the French, performing works by Thomas, Meyerbeer, Halévy, and Gluck. She retired from the operatic stage in 1862 but gave recitals for another decade and taught at the Paris Conservatoire from 1871 to 1875.

Pauline Garcia's wide-ranging intellect made her a companion to artists, writers, and intellectuals and accords well with her marriage to the writer and critic Louis Viardot (1800–1883). The Russian novelist Ivan Turgenev fell under her influence in 1843; and she was instrumental in launching the careers of Gounod, Saint-Saëns, Fauré, and Massenet as well as of the writers Flaubert, Hugo, Sand, and Zola and the artists Doré, Ingres, and Millet. Acclaimed for her abilities as an actress, Garcia-Viardot would often treat her Thursday gatherings to monologues from Shakespeare before launching into a mélange of chansons, lieder, arias, and comic songs from current operettas, often followed by group participation in improvised farces. Testimony abounds of her ability to manipulate her admittedly limited vocal instrument and her large features to best advantage. Of her compositions, three operettas (at least one on a Turgenev libretto), many piano pieces, and around 100 songs survive in manuscript or published form.

Garcia-Viardot made repeated visits to Russia and added that country's vocal music, in Russian, to her repertoire. "Die Beschwörung" (Supplication) was published in 1865 in a set entitled *Zwölf Gedichte von Pushkin.* Both the poem and its musical setting proclaim that this is not the genteel "parlor music" usually associated with "cultivated" women composers of the nineteenth century. Pushkin's text does not deal with the timid flutterings of awakening love but with the railings of an adult against a cruel thief, Death. Similarly, neither the singer nor the pianist can be classified as genteel: The singer is not given a pretty melody to cradle, but must master rapid dramatic declamation involving extremes of pitch, tempo, and mood; while the pianist must command a technique associated with Chopin and Liszt, both of whom admired Viardot-Garcia's compositions.

Although the musical setting follows the general outlines of Pushkin's three-verse form, it allows the emotional stance of each verse to dictate the musical drama. The third verse echoes the first in key, mode, and melody, while the second makes use of contrasting material. The second verse thus presents an image of loving recollection as opposed to the firm resolve of the first and third. Especially effective are the composer's avoidance of formulaic repetition for the last-line refrain and her dramatic mastery of gradually accumulating chromatic inflections in the accompaniment.

> O, if it is true that when night
> lulls all life to sleep,
> and when only moonlight's pallid gleam
> weaves among the tombstones;
> O, if it is truly then
> that graves yield up their dead,
> It is then that I wait to embrace you
> Hear me Leila! Come to me! Come home!
>
> Emerge from your realm of shadows,
> just as you were before our parting,
> cold as a winter day,
> your face distorted with pain.
> O come back, as a distant star,
> as a breath, as a delicate sound,
> or in some more terrifying beauty,
> it makes no difference: Come to me! Come home!
>
> I cry to Leila not
> to plumb the secrets of the grave,
> nor to rebuke those
> who killed my love,
> nor even because of the bitter despair
> which tortures me.
> No, only to tell her that my
> stricken heart is still true;
> is still breathing . . . Come to me! Come home!

Recording

Lieder, Clara Schumann, Fanny Mendelssohn, Josephine Lang, Pauline Viardot-Garcia. "Die Beschwörung." John Ostendorf, baritone, and Rudolph Palmer, piano. Leonarda LP1–107.

Further Reading

Fitzlyon, April. *The Price of Genius: A Biography of Pauline Viardot.* London, 1964.
Viardot, Pierrette Jean. "Les Jeudis de Pauline Viardot," *Revue Internationale de Musique Française* 3, #8 (June 1982):87–104.

Die Beschwörung

Pauline Viardot-Garcia

Reprinted from the edition of 1865, by Breitkopf & Härtel, Leipzig.

Amy Marcy Beach
(1867–1944)

ADRIENNE FRIED BLOCK

An American-born and American-trained member of the Second New England School of composers, Amy Cheney Beach (Mrs. H. H. A. Beach) was the first woman in the United States to have a successful career as a composer of large-scale art music. She was prodigiously talented not only as a pianist and composer but also intellectually and was recognized during her lifetime as the dean of American women composers. She made her debut as a pianist in Boston at age fifteen. During the next two years she played recitals and was widely hailed as a fine pianist on her way to a brilliant performing career. In 1885, a momentous year for her, Amy Cheney played for the first time with the Boston Symphony Orchestra, began a lifetime association with the Boston publisher Arthur P. Schmidt, and married the 43-year old widower Henry Harris Aubrey Beach. Dr. Beach was a surgeon and society physician as well as an amateur singer, pianist, poet, and painter. For the next 25 years, Beach concentrated on composition, giving only occasional concerts. Leading artists and ensembles performed her works in the United States and Europe.

Dr. Beach died in 1910. A year later Beach went to Europe to rest, then to rebuild her career as a concert pianist, and not least to have her works performed and reviewed in Europe. After a highly successful three years, she returned to the United States on the eve of World War I, already booked for the 1914–15 concert season. From then until the mid-1930s, she undertook annual winter concert tours but devoted her summers to composition.

Beach was a prolific composer with 152 opus numbers to her credit. Her catalogue includes over 110 songs, piano pieces, sacred and secular choral works with and without orchestra, chamber music, a symphony, a piano concerto, a Mass with orchestra, and a one-act opera, *Cabildo*.

Beach's early works are in the late-Romantic tradition. Her harmonic vocabulary recalls that of both Brahms, in its richness, and Wagner, in its restless modulations. The energy and passion are her own, however, as is her gift for spinning out a long lyrical line. Some works composed after 1914 reveal the influence of French Impressionism along with a new leanness and restraint.

Beach set works by American, English, French, and German poets, as well as more exotic texts, such as the Scottish dialect poems of Robert Burns. As early as her very first set of songs, published in 1885, Beach's lyrical gifts and sensitivity to language are apparent. "Elle et moi" (My Sweetheart and I), composed in 1893 to a text by Félix Bovet, is in the tradition of Schubert and the lied. It has an accompaniment figure that expresses one central musical idea, possibly inspired by the idea of the flame, while the voice line, in its *fioritura*, suggests the butterfly's fluttering wings. The wonderful darkening toward D flat, the borrowed VI chord in F, and the second modulation to A flat both presage the final image of the butterfly destroyed by the flame.

On May 28, 1893, the same year that "Elle et moi" appeared in print, an article in the Boston *Herald* reported that Antonin Dvořák, visiting head of the National Conservatory of Music in New York (1892–95), recommended that American composers look to their own folk music for thematic materials for their art music. According to the article, Dvořák advocated the use of "plantation melodies and slave songs." In response, Beach wrote in a solicited statement that Negro melodies "are not fully typical of our nation. . . . We of the north should be far more likely to be influenced by old English, Scotch, or Irish songs, inherited with our literature from our ancestors." Her Symphony in E minor, subtitled "Gaelic" and completed in 1894, may well have been her thoughtful response to Dvořák's challenge.

The movements are marked Allegro con fuoco, Alla Siciliana, Lento con molto espressione, and Allegro di molto. Three of the four have themes of a distinctly Gaelic cut. Themes and motives from all four movements in this cyclical work are related but are transformed within each movement. The first movement, reproduced here, is in sonata allegro form, with motives and themes undergoing development almost immediately after their initial statements. Following an introductory chromatic passage for strings and woodwinds over an E pedal, the first heroic motive (m.17) is announced by the trumpets. The second motive (m.75), announced in the strings, is a slightly longer chromatic variation of the first. It also anticipates the dotted rhythms of the third, "Gaelic," theme in G major (m.151). This theme, presented by a solo oboe over a G drone resembling a bagpipe, is the closest to a true theme in the entire first movement. Its dotted rhythms, emphasis on modal scale degrees, and plagal cadence make it unmistakably Gaelic. Otherwise, the harmonic vocabulary is Brahmsian, and the movement's motivic underpinnings are chromatic and driving. The first performance on October 31, 1896, by the Boston Symphony Orchestra conducted by Emil Paur, had wide and mostly positive coverage by the critics. During succeeding years, leading orchestras in the United States and abroad performed the symphony.

Beach became interested in birdcalls as a child. At age eleven, when she was visiting San Francisco, the ornithologist E. R. Sill asked her to notate the song of the California lark, and he later published her transcription in a scholarly journal. Her continued interest in birdcalls can be seen in a number of works for piano and voice.

Beginning in 1921 Beach spent part of each summer as a Fellow-in-Residence at the MacDowell Colony. She produced a number of works her first summer, among them "A Hermit Thrush at Morn" and "A Hermit Thrush at Eve," which are probably her most-inspired works using birdcalls. Both are based on "exact notations of hermit thrush songs in the original keys but an octave lower, obtained at MacDowell Colony, Peterborough, N. H." Her use of the calls in this set illustrates two techniques: in the first piece, the centuries-old decorative device of imitation; in the second, a relatively new one in which the birdcalls provide the melodic material out of which the entire piece is built. The poems quoted at the head of each piece stress the immanence of God in nature and Beach's own belief in the religious content of music, which on the one hand derives from Thoreau's and Emerson's transcendentalism and on the other looks forward to Messiaen.

In "A Hermit Thrush at Eve," scalar melodies in long ascending and descending sweeps suggest flight, while the chromatic, whirring triplets may represent the beating of wings. These passages introduce the birdcalls twice, while the entire piece is framed by a passage that makes a slow three-octave ascent. Its key is the darkest E-flat minor, an appropriate setting for the bird's evensong. The complete poem quoted at the head of the piece is by an American, John Vance Cheney (1848–1922): "Holy, holy! in the hush / Hearken to the hermit thrush; / All the air / Is in prayer."

In "A Hermit Thrush at Morn," reprinted here, the song of the thrush begins in m.5 and becomes the motivic material for the Poco agitato sections, the second of which also presents the birdcall in the left hand. The descending second of the opening measure of the waltz accompaniment is also related to the song of the thrush, the principal notes of which are also a second, but ascending. This piece starts in the darker D minor and ends in the pastoral F major, suggesting the brightening at sunrise. The quotation at the head of the songs is taken from "The Thrush's Nest" by the British poet John Clare (1793–1864). It begins: "Within a thick and spreading hawthorn bush / That overhung a mole-hill large and round, / I heard from morn to morn a merry thrush / Sing hymns to sunrise, while I drank the sound / With joy. . . ."

Recordings

Amy Beach. Songs and Violin Pieces. "Elle et moi," Opus 21, no. 3. Northeastern NR 202 (1981).

Piano Music of Mrs. H. H. A. Beach. "A Hermit Thrush at Eve" and "A Hermit Thrush at Morn," Opus 92, nos. 1 and 2. Genesis GS 1054.

Symphony in E minor (Gaelic), Op. 32. Society for the Preservation of American Music, MIA 139 (1968). There are cuts in the first, third, and fourth movements. The cut in the first movement is from 32 measures after J to Q, that is, the entire recapitulation up to the Coda.

Further Reading

Apthorp, William F. "Mrs. H. H. A. Beach; Symphony in E minor, 'Gaelic,' Op. 32." In *Boston Symphony Orchestra: Programmes of the Rehearsals and Concerts, Music Hall, Boston, 1896–97.* Boston: C. A. Ellis, 1896–97, pp. 77–82.

Block, Adrienne Fried. "Why Amy Beach Succeeded as a Composer: The Early Years," *Current Musicology* 36 (1983):41–59.

Merrill, E. Lindsay. "Mrs. H. H. A. Beach. Her Life and Works." Ph.D. diss., University of Rochester, 1963.

Tuthill, Burnet Corwin. "Mrs. H. H. A. Beach," *Musical Quarterly* XXVI, no. 3 (July 1940):297–306.

Elle et moi

Mrs. H. H. A. Beach

Reprinted by permission of the MacDowell Colony, copyright holder.

Symphony in E Minor

Mrs. H. H. A. Beach

Reprinted by permission of the MacDowell Colony, copyright holder.

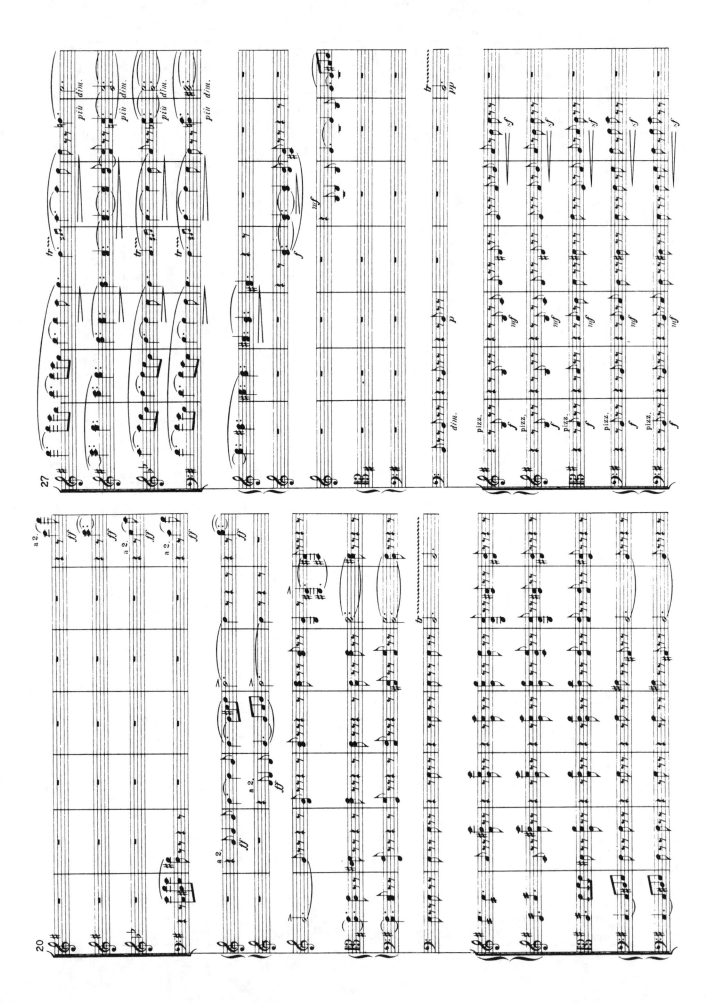

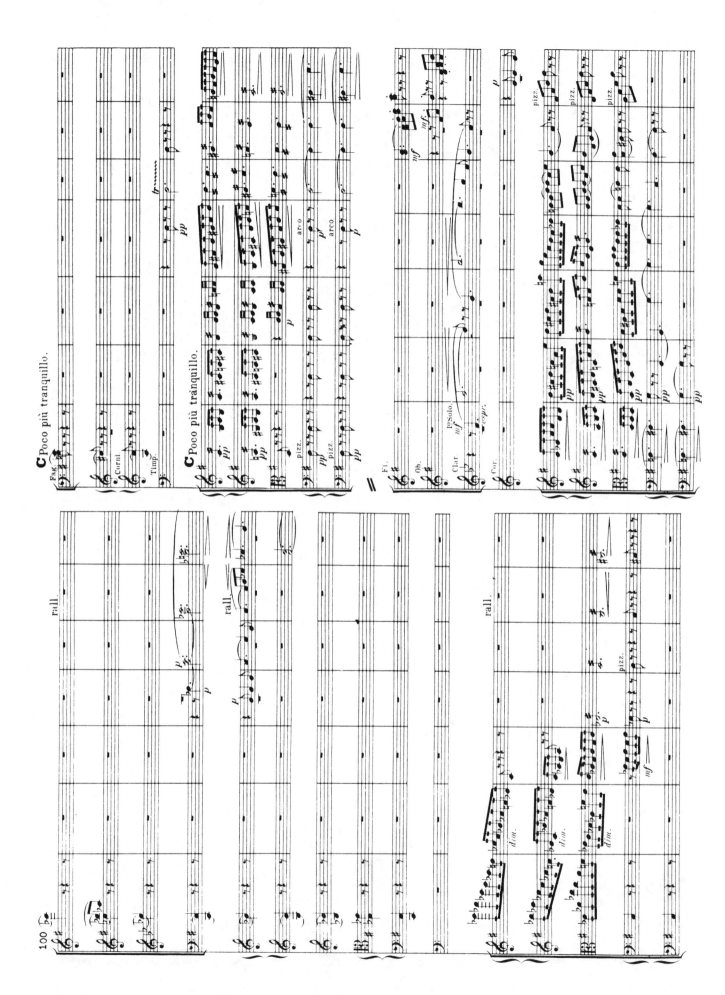

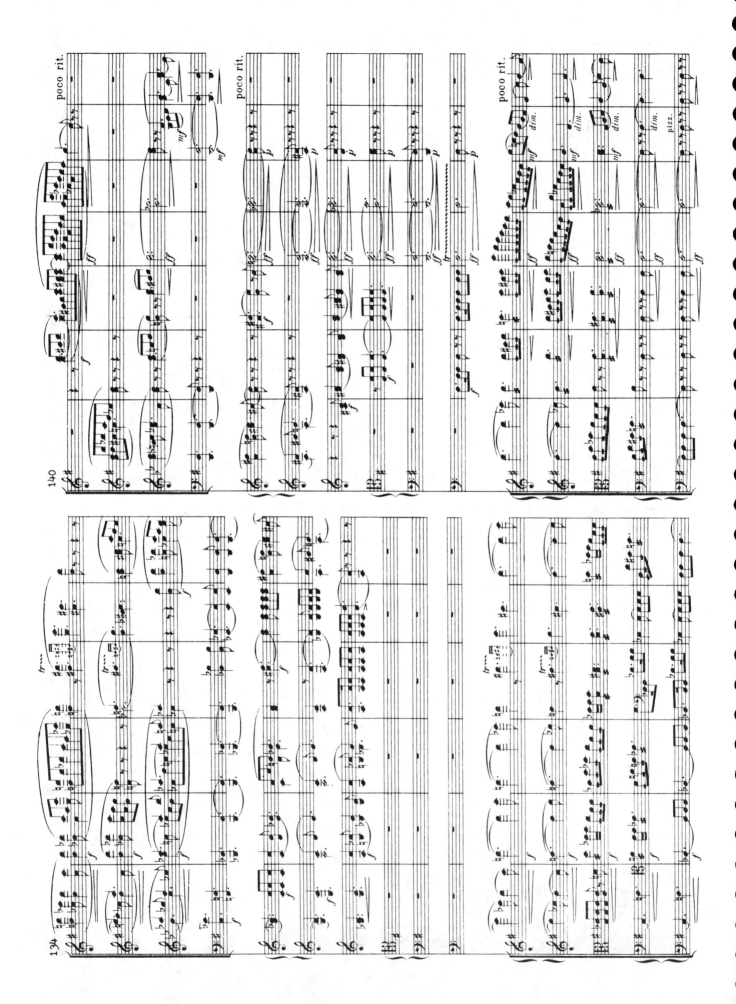

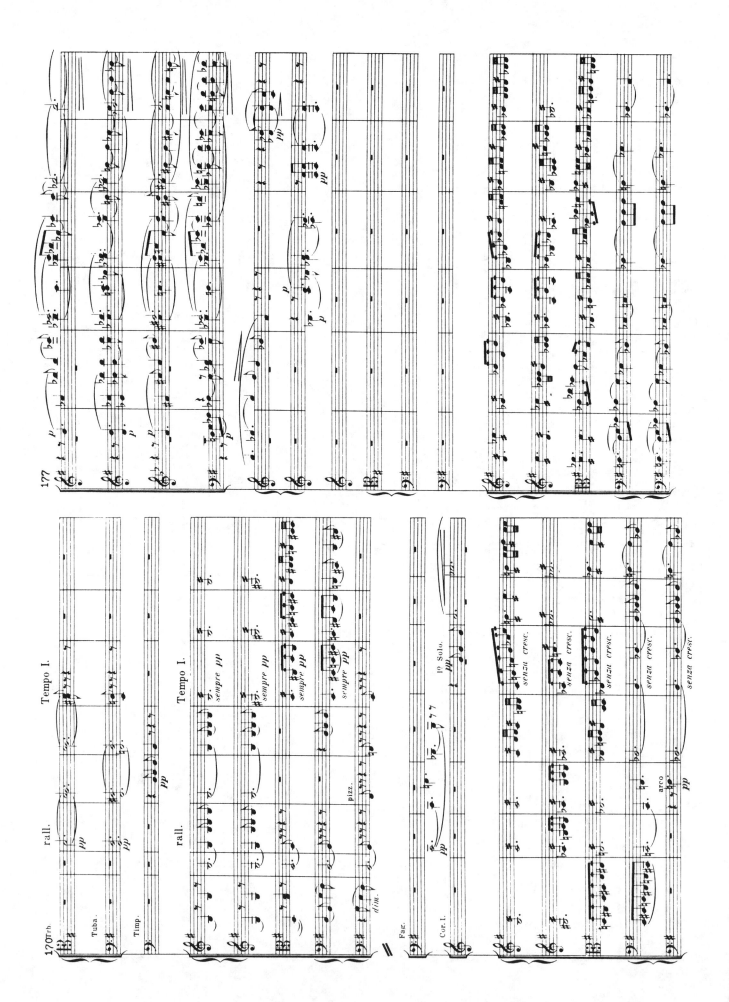

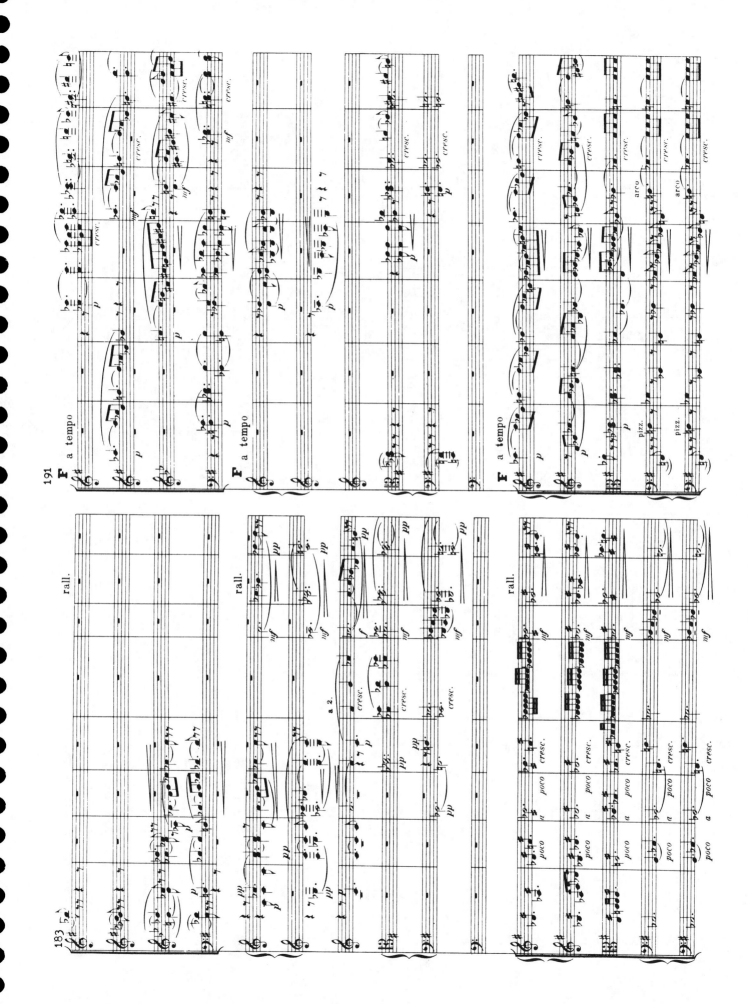

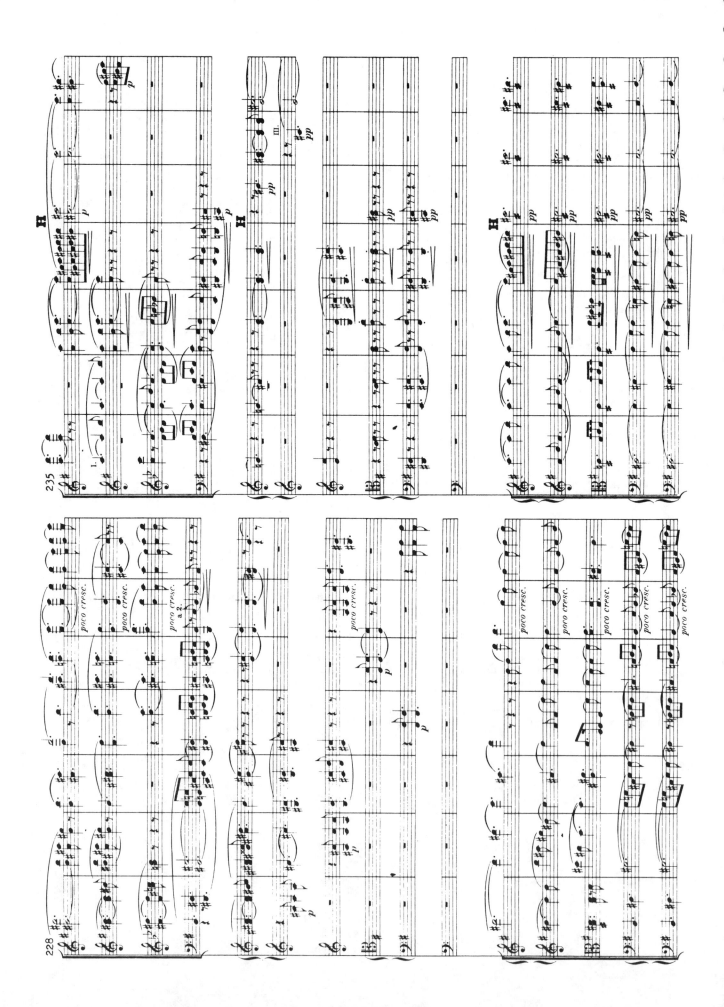

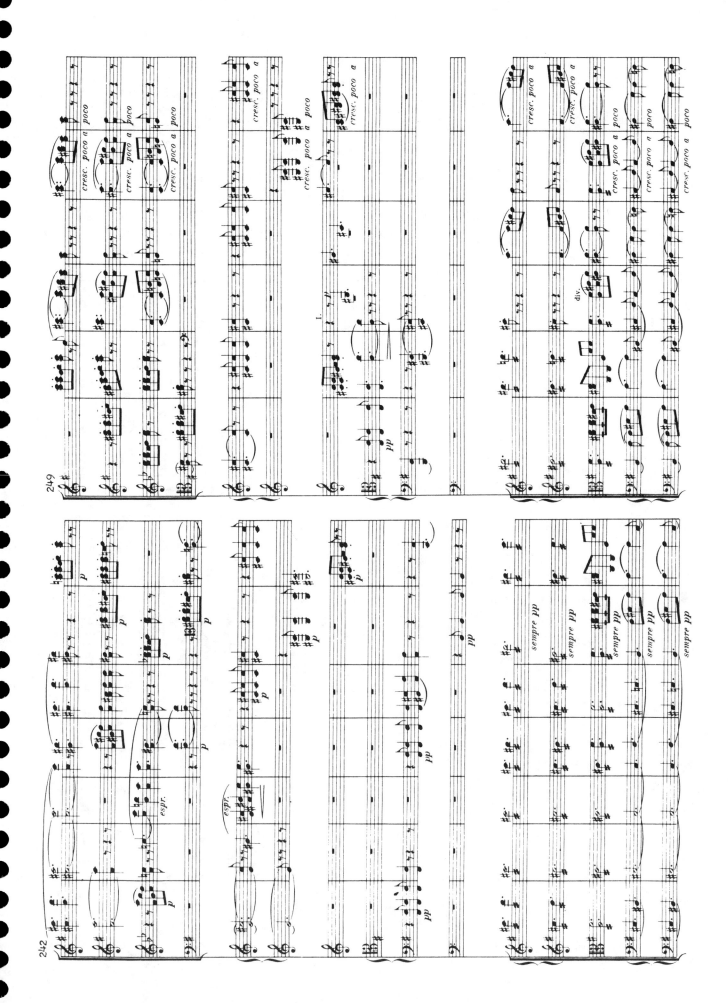

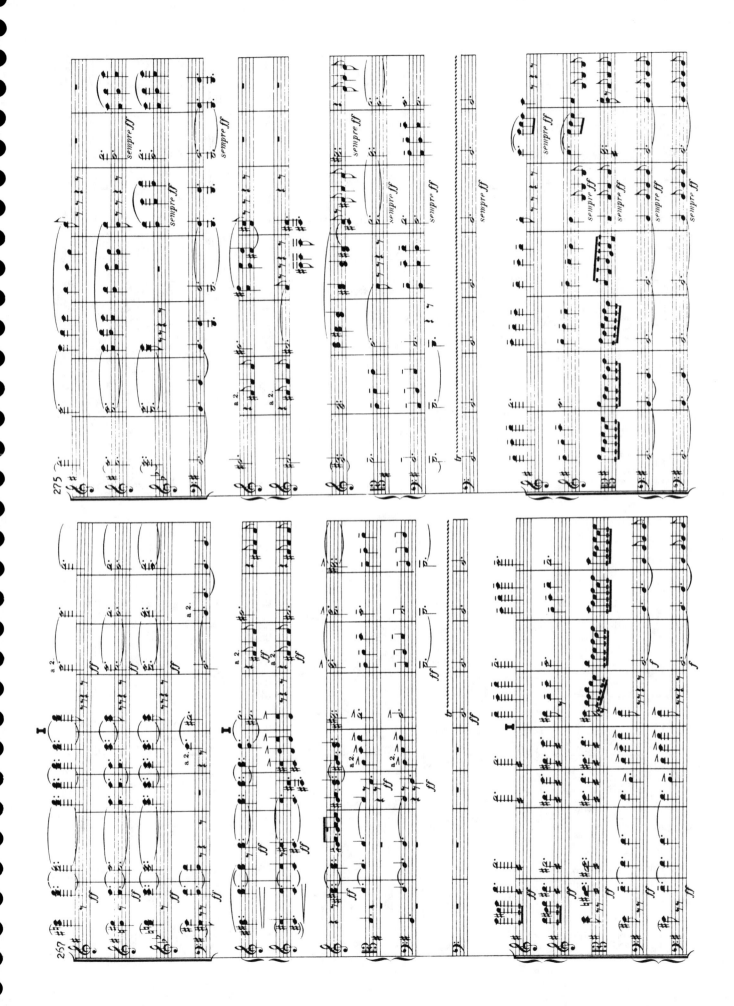

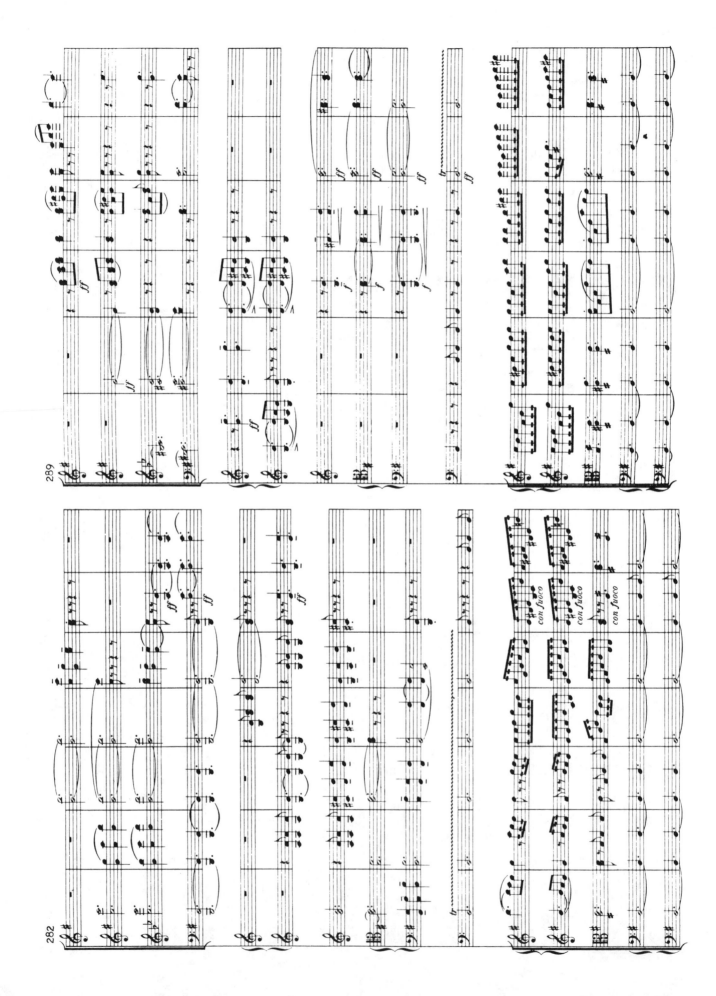

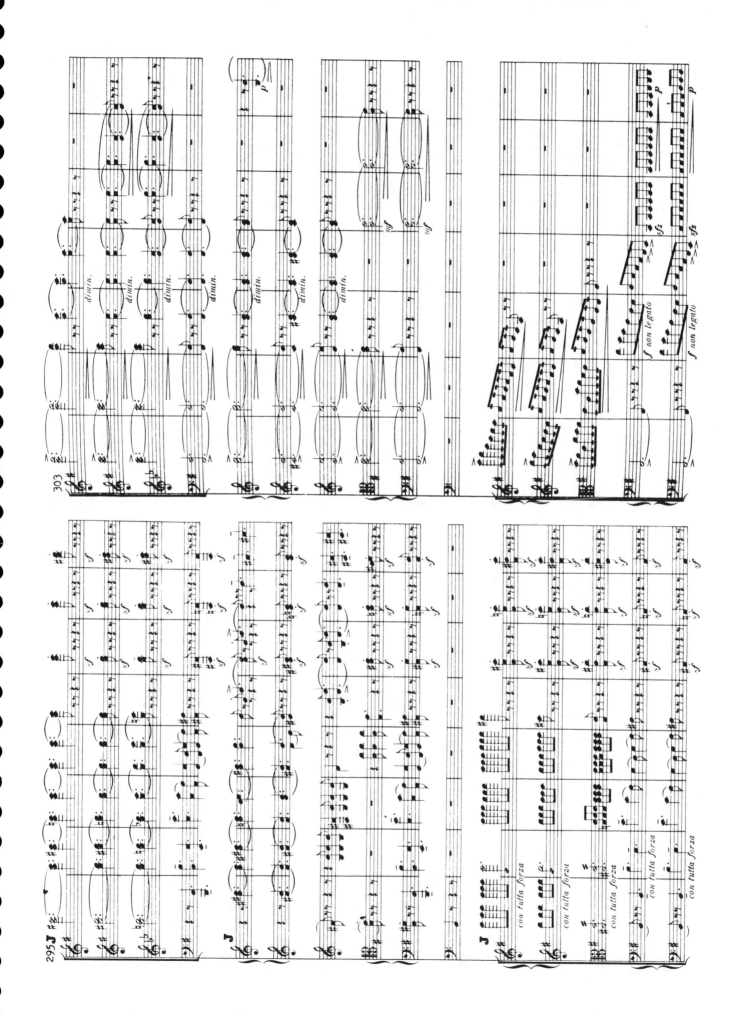

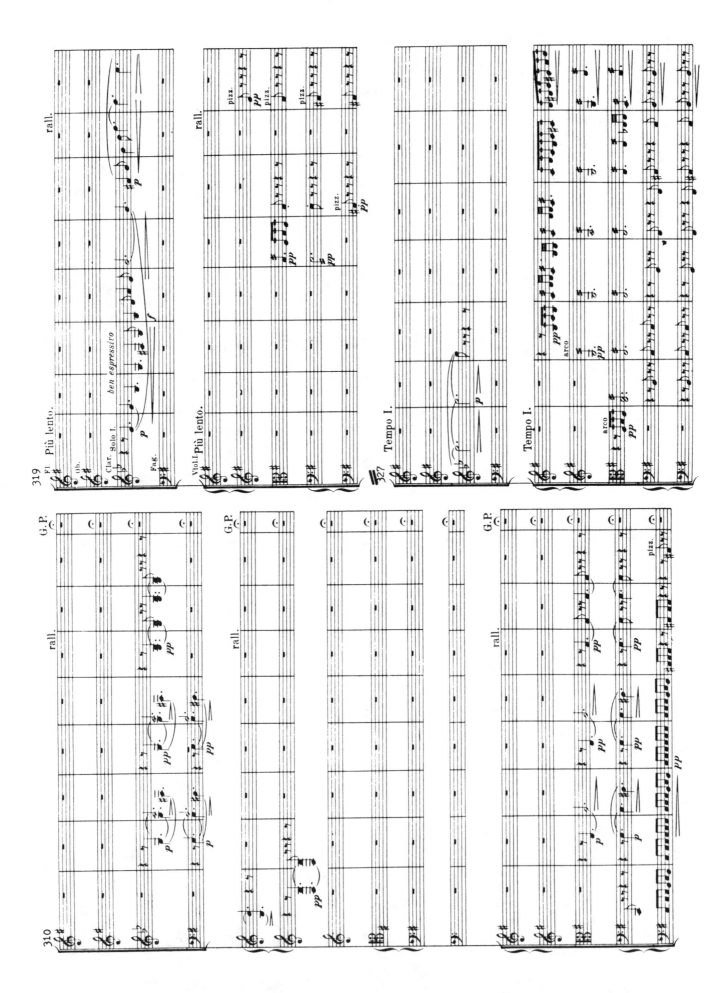

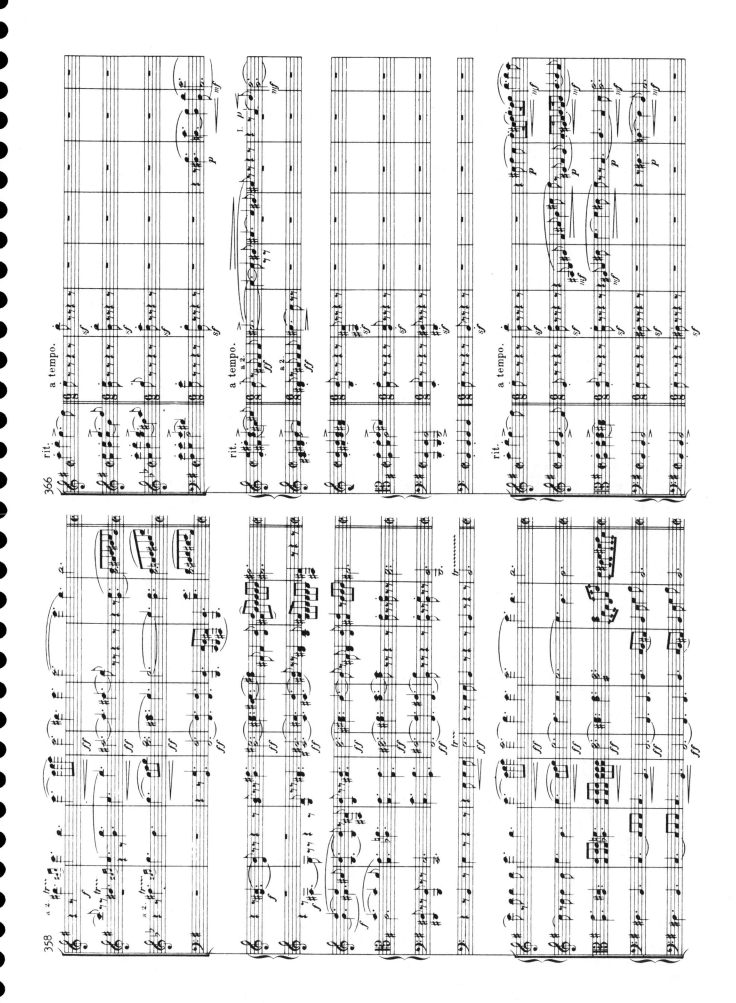

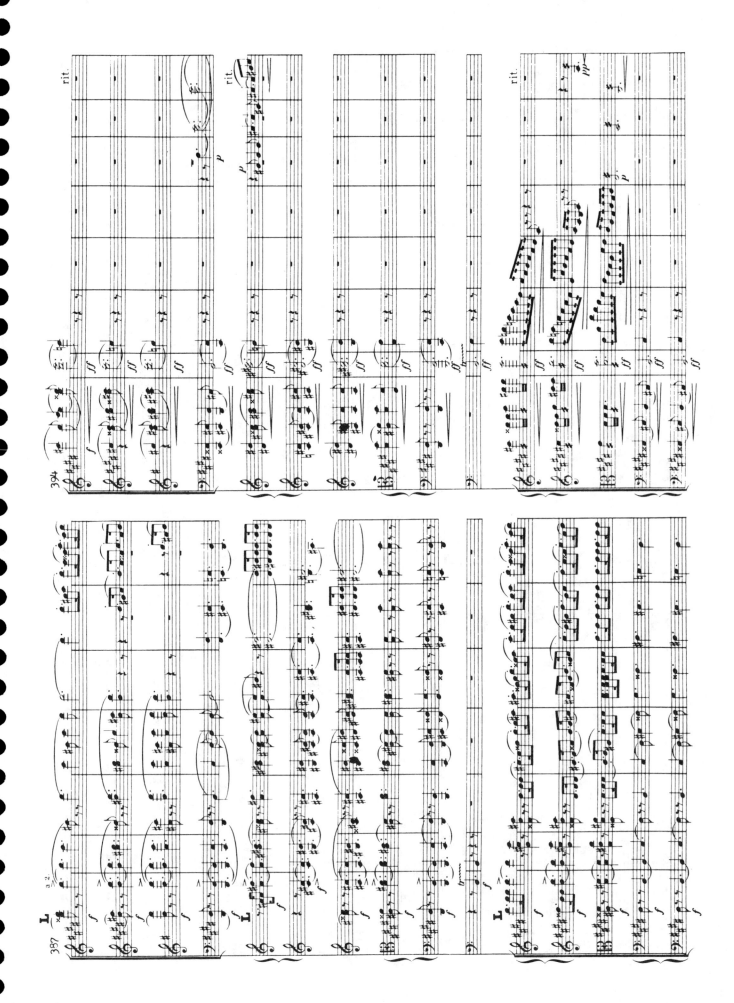

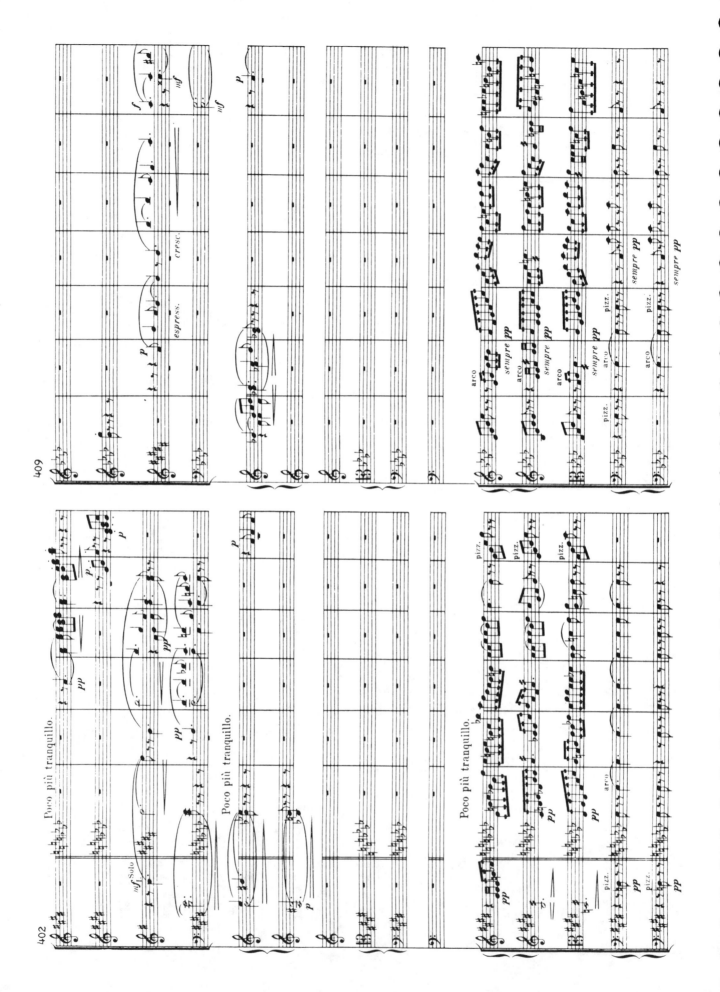

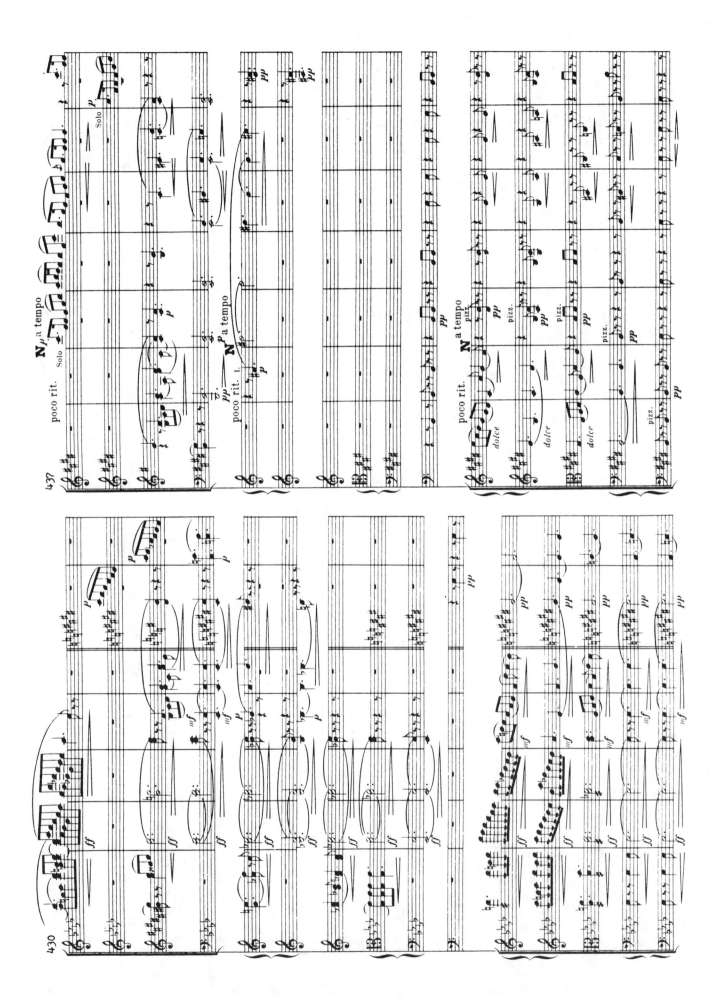

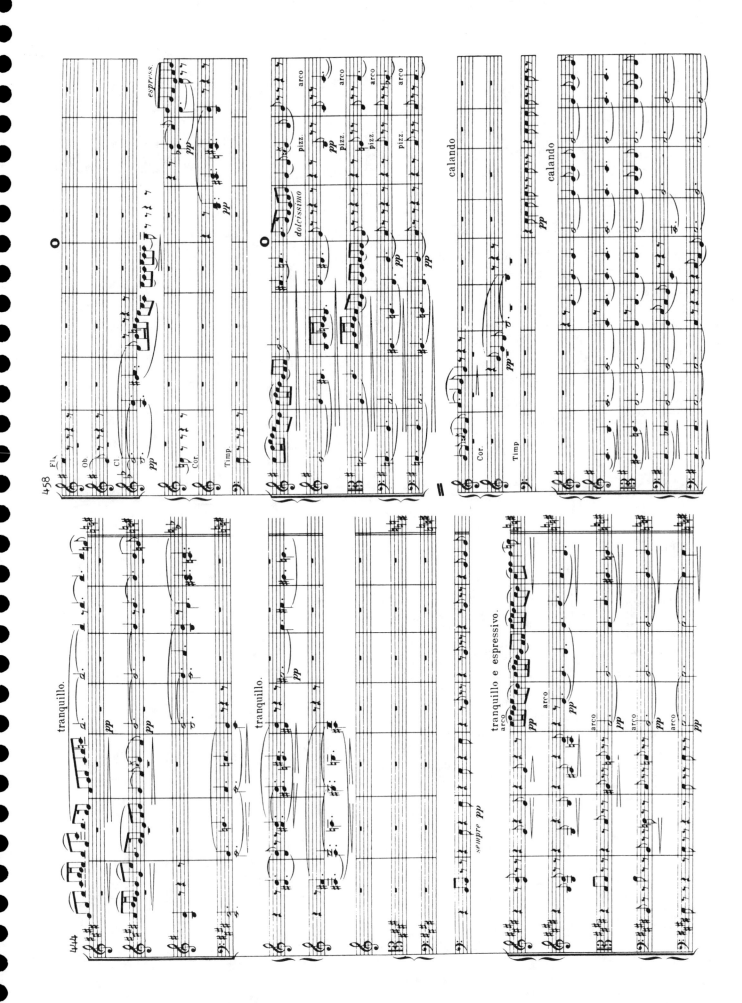

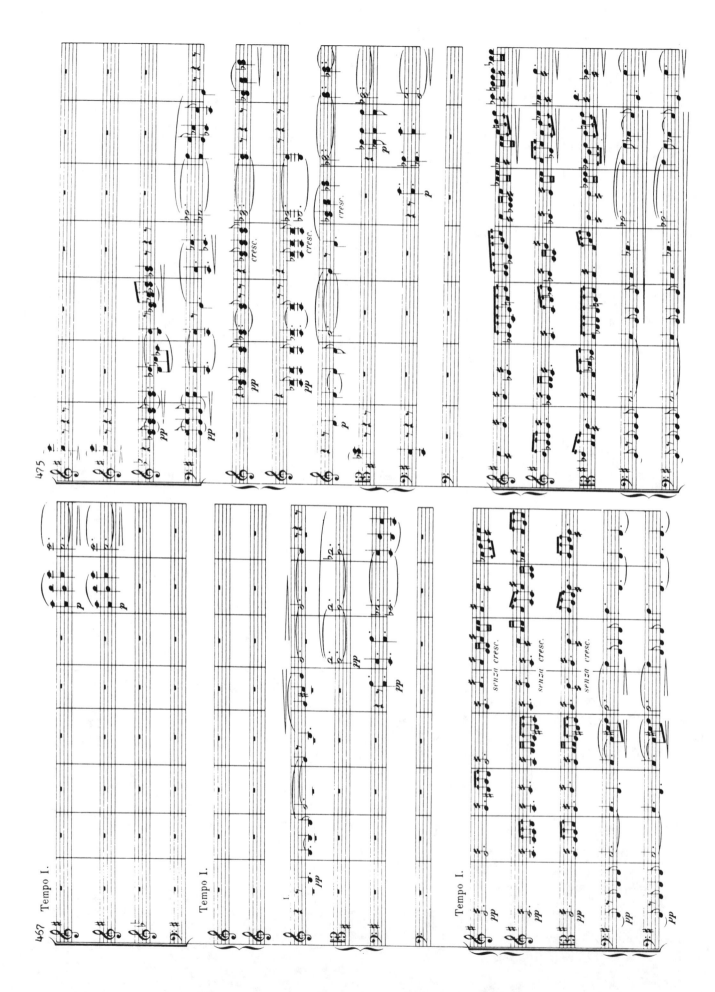

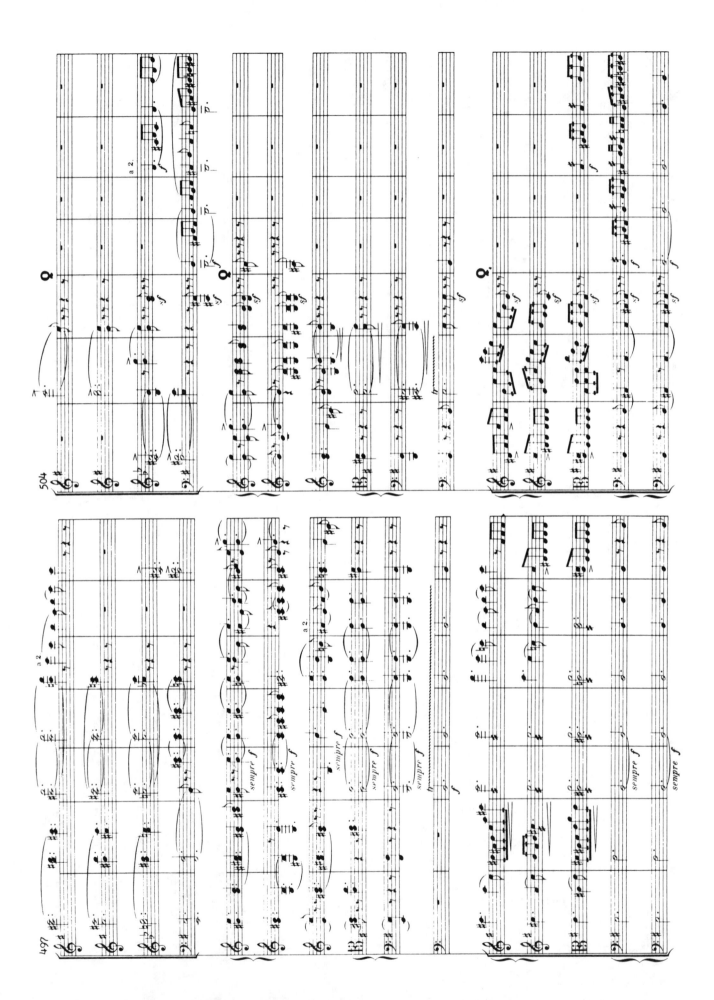

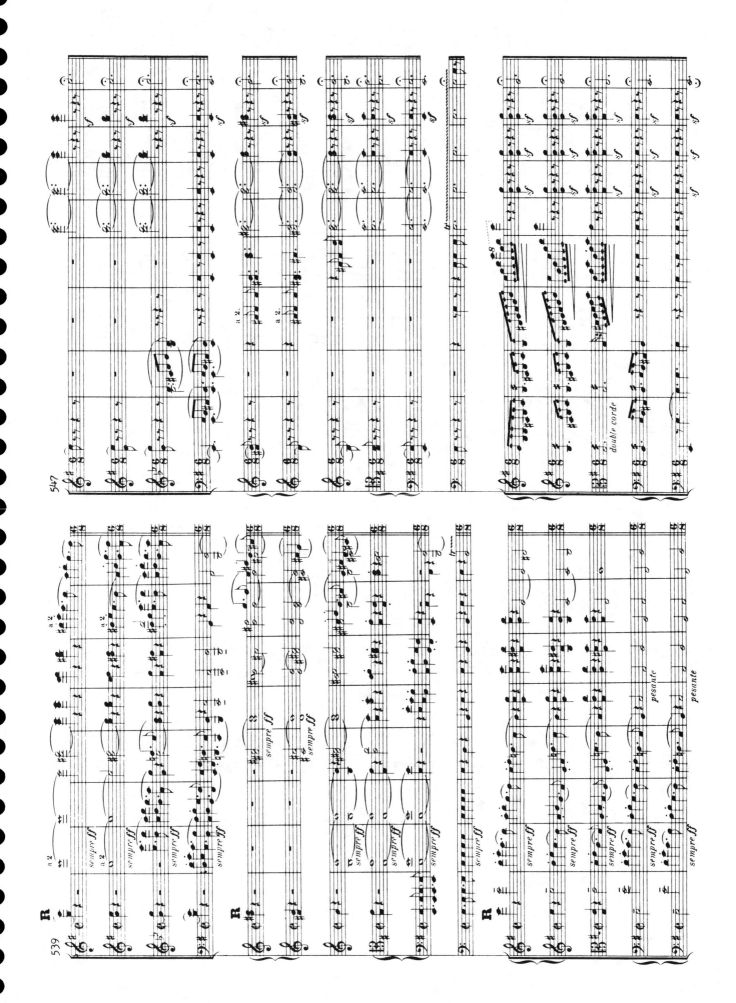

A Hermit Thrush at Morn

Mrs. H. H. A. Beach

* *These bird-calls are exact notations of hermit thrush songs, in the original keys but an octave lower, obtained at Mac Dowell Colony, Peterborough, N.H.*

Reprinted by permission of the MacDowell Colony, copyright holder.

Cécile Chaminade (1857–1944)

JAMES R. BRISCOE

Cécile Louise Stephanie Chaminade was born in Paris. From earliest childhood she exhibited a composer's imagination. Writing in the music magazine *Etude* in 1908, she explained that her games involved musical composition: "I was perpetually under the influence of music, so that my dolls danced to my pavans and I made up slumber-songs for my dogs." By age eight she had composed sacred works; and on hearing her perform, Georges Bizet advised her parents to provide her with a sound musical education. She studied piano with Le Couppey; counterpoint, harmony, and fugue with Savard; and composition with Benjamin Godard, whose taste seems to have marked her own decisively. A practical jokester, Chaminade at one lesson determined to repay Savard for his dry pedantry and patronizing approach to her aspirations as a composer. She recopied an obscure fugue by J. S. Bach and presented it as her own work. Proclaimed Savard, "But it's all full of blunders! You will not listen! Why do you not remember what I tell you?" To which Chaminade replied, "Oh, I beg your pardon, *maître,* but I have made a mistake. The fugue is not mine—it is one of Bach's." Savard followed with a long silence and then carefully continued his criticisms, skillfully turning them little by little into praise of the excellent counterpoint.

Cécile Chaminade made her debut as a pianist at eighteen, and in 1875 she toured France and England, frequently performing her own works. In 1892 the French government appointed her an Officer of Public Instruction and later named her Chevalière de la Légion d'Honneur. She died in 1944 in Monte Carlo.

Chaminade's compositions became the vogue in the elegant salons of the Belle Epoque. This very popularity among amateurs has led to the conclusion, perhaps unjustified, that her music lacks depth. Her own remarks in the 1908 *Etude* article apply to her current appreciation as well as to that of many women composers: "How limited is the number of those whose criticisms are unaffected by what others say. The great majority of people . . . are prevented by inertia and often by ignorance from revising opinions which are incomplete or hastily formed."

A renewed assessment is needed of Chaminade's *oeuvre,* which consists of more than 350 works in virtually all major genres. Among the most popular today is her Concertino for Flute and Orchestra (1905). In 1908 Chaminade made her American debut with the Philadelphia Orchestra, performing her *Concerstück* of 1896. She also wrote a large choral symphony, *Les Amazones* (1890); a symphonic ballet with full orchestra, *Callirhoe* (1888); and a comic opera, *La Sevillane* (1882). She composed more than 100 *mélodies*, to texts by Silvestre, Sully Prudhomme, Hugo, and Grandmougin, poets also favored by Fauré and Massenet.

Chaminade's piano compositions number over 200, of which her Sonata in C minor, Opus 21, is perhaps the finest example. Reprinted here is the second movement, Andante, which shows at once her quintessential lyric idiom, her capacity for deep inspiration, and her excellent compositional skills. The movement is cast in an ABA' form, with the sections beginning in mm. 1, 40, and 84. The opening motive of four notes unifies the entire compositon skillfully: Chaminade treats it to successive variations of register, intervallic set, texture, and dynamics in the A section, then recalls it subtly in mm. 52 and 75 of the strongly contrasted B section. She employs the overall key relationship of A-flat major to B major to A-flat major, an enharmonic lowered mediant relationship of the sort preferred throughout the nineteenth century and cultivated widely by her late-century contemporaries in France and Germany. The key of the B section is implied by related progressions, and the effect of tonality is rarified by reserving the tonic chord until the section closes. Paralleling a practice heard frequently in her contemporaries Brahms and Fauré, Chaminade obscures the recapitulation of the first section by blending the transition out of section B, which relies on the A section motive, with the outright return of the main theme. The sense of formal blurring is enhanced by the delay of the tonic A flat until m.85. Originally published in 1895, Chaminade's Sonata in C minor is an eloquent example of late-Romantic piano music, and it relates more closely to Brahms's Opus 117 and Opus 118 piano works than to post-Romantic French contemporaries. One ought to judge the merits of the Sonata in C minor solely on the basis of its inherent accomplishments in realizing the idiom Chaminade adopts. Dare we fault Brahms's Opus 118—a close parallel in time and style—for lacking the tonal explorations of the young Schoenberg?

Recording

Sonata in C minor for Piano. Pines, piano. Genesis 1024.

Sonata in C Minor, Second Movement

Cécile Chaminade

Reprinted from *Cécile Chaminade, Three Piano Works.* Women Composers Series, Da Capo Press, 1979. By permission. Original edition by Enoch et Cie., Paris, 1895.

218

Dame Ethel Smyth
(1858–1944)

JANE A. BERNSTEIN

One of the most original figures of the Victorian-Edwardian period, Ethel Smyth achieved international acclaim as a composer of opera. She was hailed by her contemporaries as the only woman to make "a name for herself in the field of opera." Critics praised her works as "virile, masterly in construction and workmanship." Yet despite their early success, most of her works remain unknown today.

Ethel Mary Smyth was the daughter of a major-general in the British army. With the begrudging consent of her family, she attended the Leipzig Conservatory, then considered the best European music school. After one year, she decided to study privately with the Austrian composer Heinrich von Herzogenberg, who was a close friend of Johannes Brahms. This connection enabled Smyth to make the acquaintance of both Brahms and Clara Schumann. Smyth's works dating from her apprenticeship consist mainly of chamber music.

On her return to England, Smyth composed two orchestral works, a four-movement *Serenade* (1889) and the Overture to *Antony and Cleopatra* (1890), both premiered by August Manns at the Crystal Palace. Smyth's most important work of this period was her Mass in D, which demonstrated her masterly control of a large musical structure. The turning point for the composer came when she showed her Mass to the great German conductor Hermann Levi. Impressed by her dramatic abilities, he urged her to write opera. From that time on, she devoted herself almost exclusively to musicodramatic composition.

In all, Smyth composed six operas and one symphonic work for voices and orchestra. In her first two operas, *Fantasio* (1898) and *Der Wald* (1902), she was clearly influenced by nineteenth-century German opera, particularly Wagner's works. Smyth's third and most important opera, *The Wreckers (1904)*, reveals her British background, with its dramatic plot and evocation of the sea. The notable conductor Sir Thomas Beecham championed the work as "one of the three or four English operas of real musical merit and vitality." Smyth collaborated with her close friend Henry Brewster on the libretto. The work was written in French (*Les Naufrageurs* was its original title), but ironically it never received a performance in that language. The first two productions took place in Germany, as *Strandrecht*. Smyth translated the work into English, and its British premiere, on May 28, 1908, under the direction of Artur Nikisch, was a concert version of the first two acts. Beecham conducted a complete stage production the following year, and in 1910 he included it in his debut season at Covent Garden.

The Wreckers is set in an eighteenth-century Cornish sea town at the time of the Wesleyan Revival. The economic survival of the town depends on shipwrecks deliberately caused by the townspeople by means of false beacons. Thirza, the young wife of the preacher, and Mark, a fisherman, are lovers who contrive to thwart the savage community. Caught by the Wreckers' committee, they are condemned by a secret court to die in a sea cave. The scene presented here occurs at the beginning of the opera, following a hymn sung by the church congregation. A storm is up and the frenzied chorus sings of its plans to wreck a ship.

The music of this scene epitomizes Smyth's style, with its colorful orchestration, dense contrapuntal writing, powerful theme, and impressive use of the chorus. The principal motive, found four measures after 33, appears at crucial moments in the opera. It pervades the overture as well as the climactic love duet and is reminiscent of the main *leitmotiv* of another opera of the sea, Wagner's *Der fliegende Holländer*.

On the whole, *The Wreckers* must be viewed as an important predecessor to later twentieth-century British operas. Its portrayal of the sea, the integration of the chorus into the action, and its characterization of an isolated sea town demonstrate a common bond with one particular work—Benjamin Britten's *Peter Grimes*.

Dame Ethel Smyth stands out as a crucial figure in the history of women in music. Besides her musical endeavors, she was a talented author who wrote candidly about herself and the many famous people she knew. She played an active role in the violent suffragist movement, and she later campaigned for the rights of women musicians. For her work as a composer and writer, Smyth was made Dame Commander of the Order of the British Empire in 1922. She received honorary doctoral degrees in music from the University of Durham in 1910 and from Oxford University in 1926. Her pioneering efforts as an outspoken composer, writer, and feminist paved the way for a younger generation of women in the field of music.

Recordings

Music of the Four Countries, Scottish National Orchestra, Alexander Gibson, cond. Ethel Smyth, Overture: *The Wreckers*. EMI-Odeon ASD 2400, 1968.
The Wreckers (complete opera). Rare Record Editions. SRRE 193–4.

Further Reading

Bernstein, Jane A. " 'Shout, Shout, Up with Your Song!' Dame Ethel Smyth and the Changing Role of the British Woman Composer," in *Women Making Music. The Western Art Tradition, 1150–1950*, edited by Jane Bowers and Judith Tick. Urbana and Chicago: University of Illinois Press, 1986, pp. 304–24.

The Wreckers, Scene from Act I

Ethel Smyth

Completed 1904. Printed by Universal Edition, Vienna, n.d., under the composer's copyright.

225

226

227

228

229

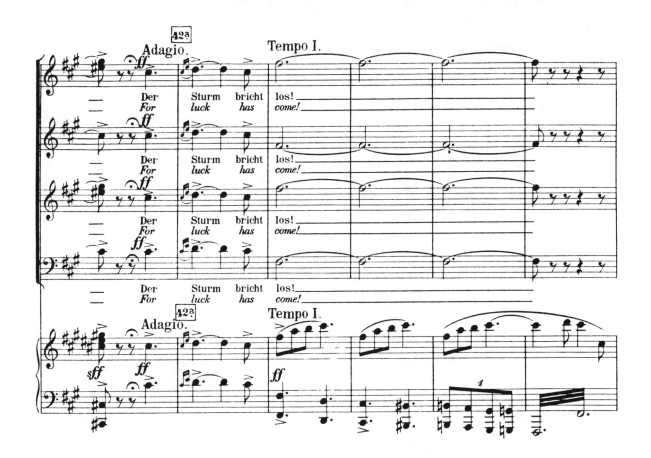

Lili Boulanger
(1893–1918)

LÉONIE ROSENSTIEL

Born into a family of musicians active in France since the late eighteenth century, Lili Boulanger outshone all her relatives in creative ability. Her grandfather had been a cellist with the King's Chapel, her grandmother a popular singer at the Opéra-Comique. Her father, Ernest Boulanger, a professor of singing at the Conservatoire National de Musique in Paris and composer of comic operas, won the Prix de Rome in 1835. Late in life he married a Russian emigrée, the self-styled "Princess Mychetsky," who had been a student of his at the Conservatoire.

Although Lili's elder sister, Nadia (1887–1979), a pianist, organist, conductor, and sometime composer, was destined to become one of the twentieth century's most famous teachers of music and to break new paths in music for women, it was Lili who became the darling of the French music world while she was still in her teens. A semi-invalid from early childhood, Lili astonished her family and their friends, including Gabriel Fauré, with her ability to read music at sight. Her seemingly intuitive grasp of harmony, counterpoint, and composition enabled her to learn in months what took most other musicians years. As with most composers, Lili learned to play a number of instruments, among them violin, piano, organ, and harp.

Despite her delicate health, Lili managed to complete the rigorous courses at the Paris Conservatoire in only three years. She not only won a composition prize in the process but also decided to become a professional composer and win the Prix de Rome, which had not been awarded to Nadia. In 1913 she succeeded, much to the amazement of her compatriots. The controversy aroused by a teen-age girl winning a prize that often eluded men in their twenties, and in a competition that had been open to women for only a few years, brought the young composer much publicity. That, in turn, resulted in a publishing contract with the firm of Ricordi. World War I intervened in 1914, but Lili took time out from her vigorous activities on behalf of French war relief to compose, perform, and conduct, sometimes with Nadia.

The years 1913–18 were Lili's most productive period, during which she finished some 50 works. Her prize cantata, *Faust et Hélène*; *Vieille prière bouddhique* (Old Buddhist Prayer); and three Psalms for voice and orchestra are her major works in the larger forms. (An opera she began in 1916, to a text by Maurice Maeterlinck, was never finished.) In addition to short works for violin, piano, flute, and voice, Lili wrote a song cycle, *Clairières dans le ciel* (Rifts in the Sky), to poems by the Symbolist Francis Jammes. Often, the composer would rearrange her works for different combinations of instruments or voices. Her Psalms exist in various versions, as do some of her instrumental works and songs (with orchestra or piano, for example).

The song cycle, completed in 1914, shows Lili Boulanger at her deeply passionate and sensitive best. It is an ambitious, successful work, not only in its understanding and exploitation of the sonorities of both the voice and the piano, but also in its projection of the nuances of the text, in the French tradition. Knowing that she was already gravely ill with the ileitis and ulcerative colitis that would eventually kill her, the young composer identified with the heroine of the cycle, a girl who disappeared, seemingly evaporating into the mist.

In the songs "Je garde une médaille d'elle" (I keep a medal of hers) and "Demain fera un an" (Tomorrow it will be a year), Lili Boulanger shows us the range of her emotional power. They are the last two songs in a cycle of thirteen—a number that had mystical significance for the composer since it accorded with the number of letters in her name. Most of the finest art songs are based on minor poetry by great poets or on the better works of lesser ones, and these songs are no exception. The composer undoubtedly chose them for the freedom they afforded her to evoke moods, for the words themselves are deliberately vague, suggestive, and unabashedly emotional.

"Je garde une médaille d'elle" is a song of gentle melancholy, lasting less than a minute but poignant nonetheless:

> I keep a medal of hers on which are engraved a date, and the words: "pray, believe, hope." But, as for me, I see above all that the medal is dark; its silver has tarnished on her dovelike neck.

"Demain fera un an" is the longest and most ambitious song of the entire cycle. It is also the most complex, tying together the rest of the cycle and interweaving fragments of melody and accompaniment from earlier songs:

> Tomorrow it will be a year since, at Audaux, I gathered the flowers of which I have spoken on the wet prairie. Today is the most beautiful day of Eastertide.
> I am sunk deep in the blue of the plains, across woods, across meadows across fields.
>   How, O my heart, did you not die a year ago?
> My heart, I have again given you the Calvary of seeing once more this village where I have suffered so, these roses bleeding in front of the presbytery, these lilacs that kill me in their sad flowerbeds.
> I have remembered my old anguish and I do not know how it is that I have not collapsed on the ochre path, forehead in the dust.
>   Why is the day so beautiful and why was I born?
> I would have wished to place on your calm knees the weariness that rends my soul, that beds down like a beggarwoman in the ditch.
>   To sleep. To find repose. To sleep forever beneath the sudden blue showers, beneath the cool lightning.
> To feel no more. To know no longer of your existence.
> I seem to feel the lack, in my deepest soul, with a heavy silent sob, of someone who is not here. I write. And the countryside rings out with joy:
>   "She went down to the deepest prairie, and like the prairie she was all abloom."
> Nothing. I have nothing more, nothing more to sustain me.

Lili Boulanger's style in these songs is in the tradition of the French art song—Duparc, Fauré, and Debussy spring readily to mind as her role models—but she has made this musical language clearly and creatively her own.

Recordings

Clairières dans le Ciel. K. Ciesinski, soprano. Leonarda 118.
Clairières dans le Ciel. Paulina Stark, soprano; David Garvey, piano. Spectrum 126.
Faust et Hélène and *Pour les Funérailles d'un Soldat.* Varèse/Sarabande 81095.

Je garde une médaille d'elle

Lili Boulanger, revised by Nadia Boulanger

Durand & Cie. Reproduced by Permission of the Publisher, Theodore Presser Company, Sole Representative U.S.A. & Canada.

Demain fera un an

Lili Boulanger, revised by Nadia Boulanger

Durand & Cie. Reproduced by Permission of the Publisher, Theodore Presser Company, Sole Representative U.S.A. & Canada.

240

Dormir à tout ja_mais sous les a_ver_ses bleu_es, sous les tonner_res frais

Ne plus sen_tir. Ne plus sa_voir votre e_xis_

_ten_ce. Ne plus voir cet a_zur engloutir ces co_

_teaux dans ce verti_ge bleu qui mêle l'air à l'eau,

242

243

Alma Mahler
(1879–1964)

SUSAN M. FILLER

Alma Mahler was the daughter of the artist Emil Schindler. During her long life she became a confidante of important men from many different fields of creativity, and she married three of them. In 1902 she became the wife of Gustav Mahler, who was then the director of the Vienna Opera and was also building a reputation as a major composer. He died in 1911, and four years later, after an affair with the artist Oskar Kokoschka, Alma married the architect Walter Gropius. The pressure of separation from Gropius during his military service in World War I, combined with an affair with the young writer Franz Werfel, resulted in separation and eventual divorce from Gropius. Alma and Werfel were married in 1929.

Alma's involvement with various men has resulted in her popular reputation as a *femme fatale.* However, this image is unfair since it does not admit of her intellectual gifts. She was educated to be a composer, studying counterpoint with Robert Gound and the blind organist Josef Labor and, at the turn of the century, composition with Alexander von Zemlinsky. In her autobiography she wrote, "Alexander von Zemlinsky was one of the finest musicians and . . . the teacher par excellence. His technical brilliance was unique. He could take a little theme, . . . squeeze it, and form it into countless variations."

While still a comparatively uneducated teenager, Alma began to compose music in many forms, including instrumental works. However, all her surviving compositions are in the form of the lied, generally for medium voice and piano. Three books of songs were published: *Fünf Lieder* (Vienna: Universal Edition, 1910), *Vier Lieder* (Vienna: Universal Edition, 1915), and *Fünf Gesänge* (Vienna: Josef Weinberger, 1924). In addition to these fourteen published songs, two songs *Aus dem Zyklus "Mütter" von Rainer Maria Rilke* survive in manuscript. A manuscript of the four songs published in 1915 survives on film in the Toscanini Memorial Archive of the New York Public Library. No other sources for Alma Mahler's songs are known to exist; at the induction of the Third Reich in Austria, Alma and Franz Werfel left Vienna, leaving almost everything behind, including her manuscripts, which were destroyed when their house was bombed during World War II.

Alma and Werfel lived in France from 1938 to 1940; they were fortunate enough to escape when the Germans invaded France and to come to the United States. They lived in southern California near many of their friends, including Arnold Schoenberg, Thomas Mann, and Bruno Walter. Werfel died in 1945; eventually Alma settled in

New York, where she lived until her death in 1964, at the age of 85. Of her four children (three daughters and one son), only her second daughter, Anna Mahler, lived to marry and have children. Her elder daughter by Mahler, Maria, and her son by Werfel, Martin, died in childhood; her daughter by Gropius, Manon, died in 1935 at the age of eighteen.

In compositional style, Alma Mahler is something of a *Januskopf*. She has some affinity for the older piano style of Brahms and Liszt in her piano parts, which are demanding with wide ranges, full harmonies, and equal partnership with the vocal parts. In other ways, however, her style looks forward to the harmonic dissonance and tight forms of the Second Viennese School. Credence is lent to Alma's description of Zemlinsky as a teacher by comparison of her works with those of a fellow student of Zemlinsky, Arnold Schoenberg.

The surviving songs show a decidedly modern taste insofar as the selection of texts is concerned: poems by Rilke (in the case of the two unpublished songs) Richard Dehmel (a taste shared with Schoenberg, who was writing *Verklärte Nacht* when Alma was writing some of her early songs), Franz Werfel, and Otto Julius Bierbaum, among others. Rarely, it appears, did Alma choose poems written before her own time; most of her poets were her contemporaries.

Performances of Alma Mahler's songs have been rare; the most widely publicized in the United States was a performance of six songs by Lorna Myers, mezzo-soprano, accompanied by Thomas Fulton, piano, at the 1980 Ravinia Festival. Among the songs in that recital was "Der Erkennende," which is reproduced below. It has not been recorded to date, although it is one of the finest songs Alma wrote. The text is by her future husband, Franz Werfel. In her autobiography she wrote:

> An episode in the summer of 1915 was the first cause of an upheaval in my life. . . . I bought the latest issue of a monthly called *Die weissen blätter,* and when I opened it I saw a poem: "Man Aware" (*Der Erkennende*) by Franz Werfel. . . . The poem engulfed me. It has remained one of the loveliest in my experience. I was spellbound, a prey to the soul of Franz Werfel, whom I did not know. . . . I set the poem to music, arbitrarily concluding halfway through the second stanza.

The following is a translation of the full text of Werfel's poem, of which Alma set only the first three stanzas.

Human beings love us, and, unblessed,
They arise from table to lament us.
So we sit bowed over the cloth
And are indifferent and can deny them.

That which loves us, how we thrust it away!
And no sorrow will soften us callous ones.
That which we love snatches a place,
Becomes hard and no more reachable.

And the word that rules is: Alone!
When we impotently burn to each other.
One thing I know: Never and nothing is mine.
Mine alone to recognize that.*

*Alma's setting ends at this point.

See the friend who portions your food,
Behind brow and countenance gathering together.
Where your glance hastens to meet him too,
A rock abides to bar the entry.

When I float through the range of the lamps
And, evil wanderer, hear my steps,
Then I awaken and I am close by,
And I myself am one who sneers, and an Other.

Yes, who descends to this position,
Where the solitary one severs and cleaves himself asunder,
That one himself dissolves in his hand
And nothing exists to fold him up.

In no more slumber is he embodied,
He always feels, while we sustain ourselves.
And the night of life, which remains to him,
Is inescapably a forest of mourning.

Further Reading

Filler, Susan M. "A Composer's Wife as Composer: The Songs of Alma Mahler," *Journal of Musicological Research* 4 (1983):427–41.

Mahler-Werfel, Alma. *And the Bridge Is Love.* New York: Harcourt, Brace & Co., 1958. Autobiography.

Mahler, Alma. *Mein Leben.* Frankfurt am Main: S. Fischer, 1960.

Schollum, Robert. "Die Lieder von Alma Maria Schindler-Mahler," *Oesterreichische Musikzeitschrift* 34 (1979):544–51.

Werfel, Franz. *Das lyrische Werk*, edited by Adolf D. Klarmann. Frankfurt: S. Fischer, 1967.

Der Erkennende

Alma Mahler

© 1924 by Josef Weinberger, Vienna/London. Reprinted by permission.

Rebecca Clarke
(1886–1979)

JANE A. BERNSTEIN

Rebecca Clarke is primarily remembered as a violist and a chamber music performer. She gained attention as a composer during the early decades of the twentieth century. Born in Harrow, England, Clarke began her musical studies as a violin student at the Royal Academy of Music. After her father removed her from the Academy in her third year, her interest turned to composition, and she was accepted as a student of Sir Charles Stanford at the Royal College of Music. Although several women had studied composition at the Academy (Maude Valerie White, for example, was the first woman to win the prestigious Mendelssohn Scholarship in 1879), Rebecca Clarke was the first female student of Stanford at the Royal College of Music.

When she left the Royal College, Clarke supported herself as a violist in several orchestras and ensembles in London. She played chamber music with many great artists, including Pablo Casals, Artur Schnabel, Jacques Thibaud, Jascha Heifetz, Myra Hess (who was a former classmate at the Royal Academy), Percy Grainger, and Arthur Rubinstein. In 1912, she became a member of the Queen's Hall Orchestra under the direction of Sir Henry Wood, who was the first conductor to admit women in his orchestra. Clarke made several tours of Europe and America as a soloist; she cofounded the English Ensemble, a piano quartet, and was a member of a string quartet with the sisters Adila Fachiri and Jelly d'Arányi, and Guilhermina Suggia.

Clarke gained recognition as a composer in 1919, when her Viola Sonata tied for first place with Ernst Bloch's Suite for Viola and Piano for a prize offered by Elizabeth Sprague Coolidge. Since there could be only one winner, the jury requested that Mrs. Coolidge cast the deciding vote. She chose the Bloch piece, but in view of the deadlock, the jury insisted that the name of the runner-up be divulged. The jury was surprised to discover that the piece was composed by a woman.

In 1944 Rebecca Clarke married the American pianist and composer James Friskin. She settled in New York, where she maintained an active schedule as teacher, lecturer, and writer. Clarke contributed essays on "Bloch" and the "Viola" for *Cobbett's Cyclopedic Survey of Chamber Music*. Her complete musical *oeuvre* includes 58 songs and part-songs and 24 instrumental works, mostly chamber music.

The Trio for Violin, Violoncello, and Piano won second prize at the Coolidge Festival in 1921. It has much in common with the French, so-called Impressionist style of Ravel in its predilection for harmonic opulence, instrumental color, clarity of melody and rhythm, and Classical structure. The first movement, presented here, adheres strictly to sonata form. Clarke based the entire movement on two chords set a tritone apart: E-flat minor and A minor. Used bitonally throughout the movement, these two chords not only serve as the pitch material for Clarke's powerful motto but also set up a conflict that is not resolved until the end of the entire work. This is demonstrated at the end of the first movement, where the violin sounds a low A against an E flat in the cello and piano. Clarke achieves some ravishing instrumental effects, such as the piano arpeggios against the pizzicato in the strings and the bariolage passages that occur in the violin and cello.

Recording

Piano Trios by Rebecca Clarke and Katherine Hoover, Suzanne Ornstein, violin; James Kreger, cello; Virginia Eskin, piano. Leonarda LP1–103, 1980.

Further Reading

Johnson, Christopher. Introduction to Rebecca Clarke, *Trio*. Women Composers Series. New York: Da Capo Press, 1980.

Trio

Rebecca Clarke

Reprinted from Rebecca Clarke, *Trio*. Women Composers Series, Da Capo Press, 1980. By permission.

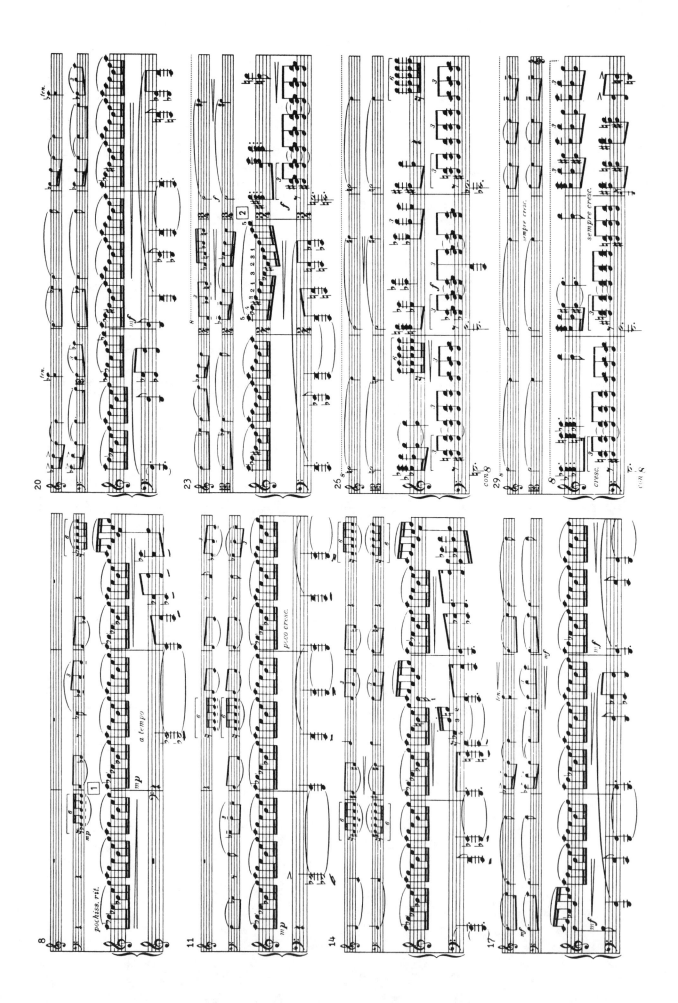

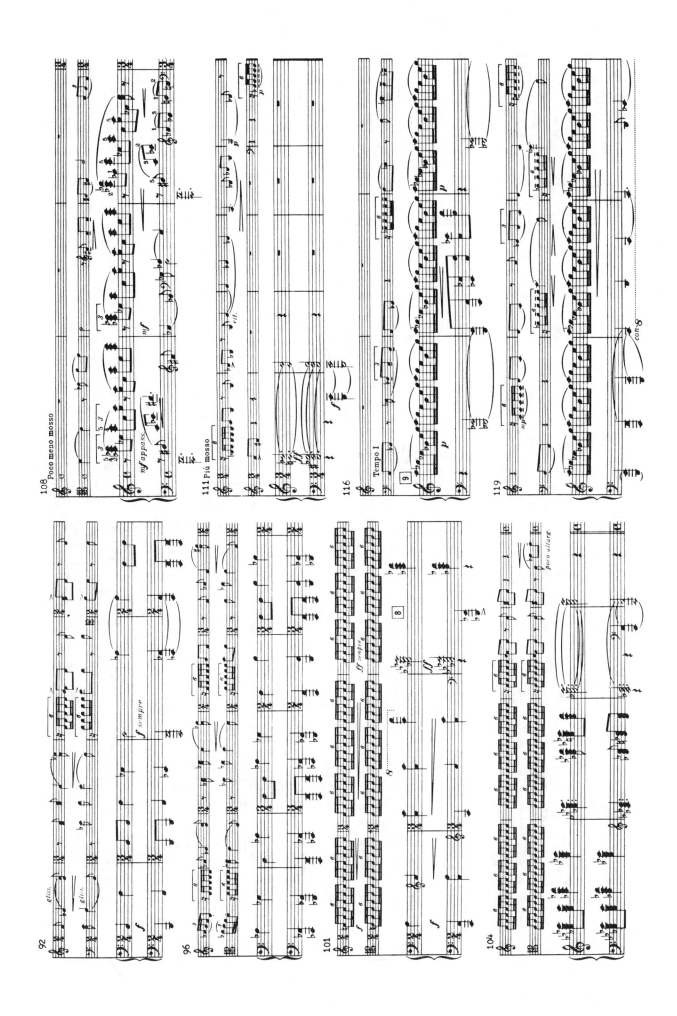

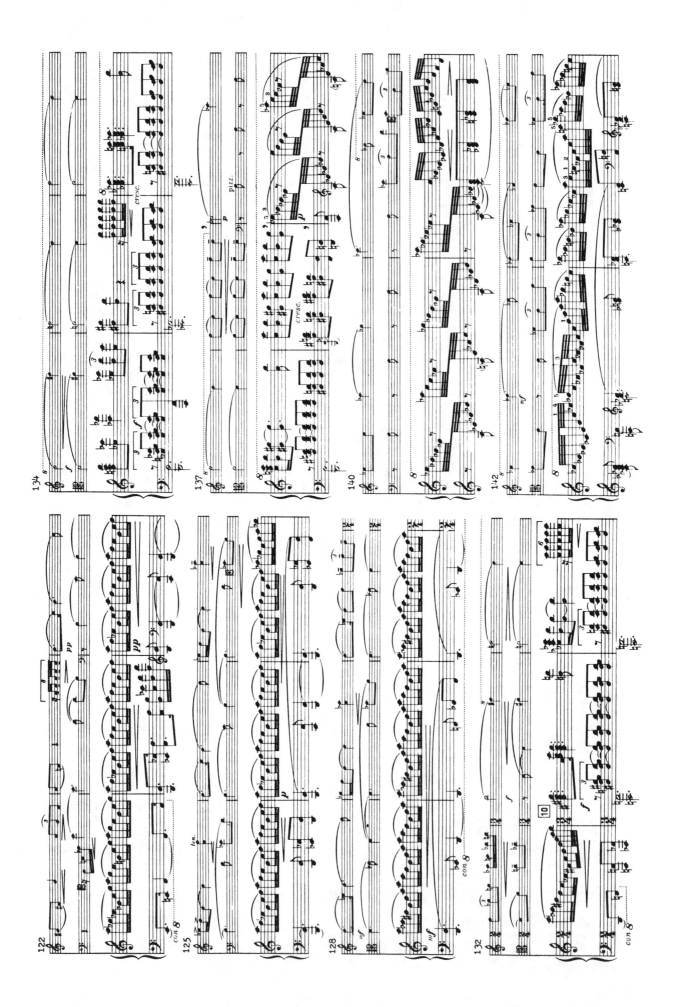

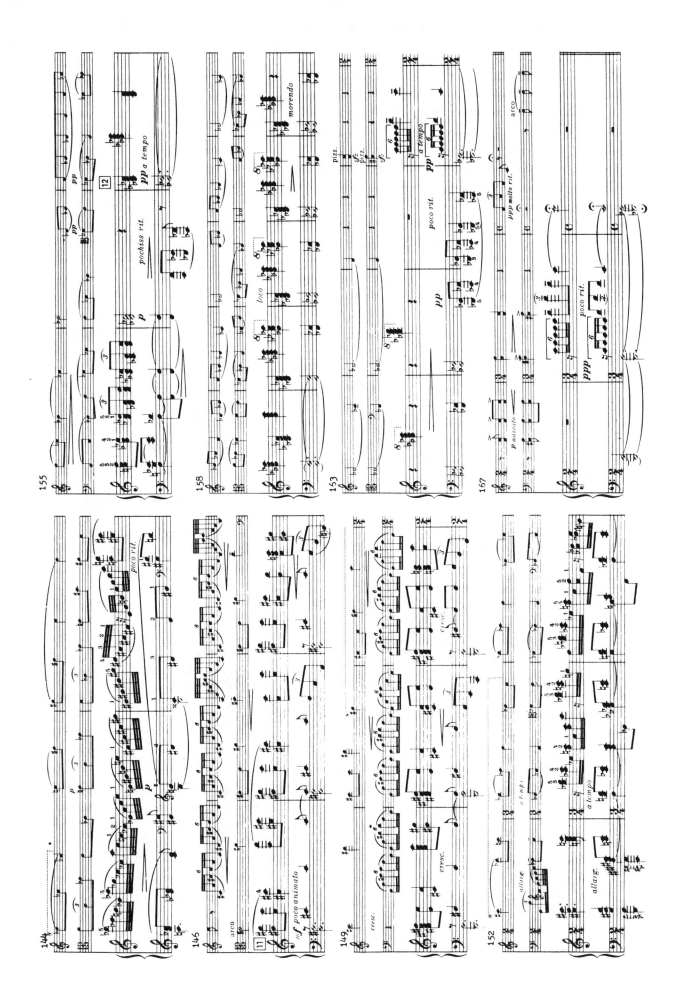

Germaine Tailleferre
(1892–1983)

LÉONIE ROSENSTIEL

Germaine Tailleferre showed her musical gifts at the age of four, when she picked out melodies by ear on the piano and even composed a short piano piece. Over her father's objections but with her mother's support and encouragement, she entered the Conservatoire in Paris in 1904. There, between 1906 and 1915, she walked off with first prizes in solfege, harmony, counterpoint, and keyboard harmony. She began her studies in orchestration with Charles Koechlin and completed them under Maurice Ravel.

Tailleferre and three fellow students at the Conservatoire—Darius Milhaud, Georges Auric, and Arthur Honegger—were later to create a sensation in musical circles. Along with Louis Durey and Francis Poulenc, and with the encouragement of Eric Satie, they formed a group, called at first the "Nouveaux Jeunes" (New Young Composers). In 1917 works by each of the six composers first appeared together, on a recital program by singer Jane Bathori. By 1918, Tailleferre's works had been introduced to an international audience by Erik Satie.

Satie's friend Jean Cocteau promoted the interests of the group and acted as its spokesperson. In his 1918 book *Le Coq et l'arlequin* (The Cock and the Harlequin), he spoke out against the German Romantic tradition, with its interest in pomp and complexity, and criticized such composers as Wagner, Strauss, and Schoenberg. Of the composers Cocteau mentioned, he praised only Satie—for his simplicity, wit, and lack of pretension—and he asked that composers take their inspiration from everyday life, to look to machines, the music hall, jazz, and the circus for their ideas.

Although the group was never completely cohesive artistically, in 1920 it received the name by which its members have been known ever since, "Les Six" (The Six). Tailleferre had the distinction of being known as "the only woman of Les Six," "The Smile of Les Six," and eventually "The Last Surviving Member of Les Six."

In June 1921, *Les Mariés de la tour Eiffel* (The Bride and Bridegroom of the Eiffel Tower), a ballet with two speaking voices, with text and choreography by Cocteau, had its premier in Paris. The speaking parts were supposed to represent phonographs describing a surrealistic wedding party; the music was a collective work of the group, with various pieces contributed by all the members except Durey. As a group their only other collective effort was an album of piano pieces. Only Poulenc retained his adherence to the group's initial, conscious simplicity. Satie and Honegger had a falling out; Durey became a Socialist; and Auric stayed on as Cocteau's collaborator on films in later years.

Tailleferre stood somewhat apart from these personal machinations, remaining on good terms with her former colleagues and collaborators. The music world gathered in her salon, and her fame grew not only for her music but also for her friendship with other musicians and artists, first between the world wars in Paris, then in the United States during and shortly after World War II. After the war she returned to Paris, where she spent her last years.

A prolific composer, Tailleferre worked in all genres, from film scores and music for radio to operas, concertos, chamber music, and songs. She was most active before the 1960s, feeling little sympathy for the newest serial and electronic musical developments. She summed up her artistic credo this way: "I create music because I enjoy doing it. It's not great music. I know that. It's cheerful, light music that sometimes gets me compared to the lesser 18th century masters, and I'm proud to be."

Her compositions are mainly in a spontaneous, fresh style, in the musical idiom of Fauré and Ravel, which invites immediate listener understanding without being pedantic. Not until 1958, in her Clarinet Sonata, did Tailleferre experiment with serialism and polytonality. But it was only an experiment, not a permanent part of her musical language, and for the rest of her life she remained opposed to formula music, by either live performers or electronic means. Tailleferre believed that if the listener could not identify a composer's style after three bars, the composition was lacking in artistry.

Sonate no. 1 for violin and piano, the first movement of which is presented here, shows Tailleferre at her most typical. It was completed in 1921, while Les Six were most active as a group, and published in 1923. It is dedicated to the great violinist Jacques Thibaud, a promoter of young composers in his day, who edited and fingered it for publication. The composer is clearly comfortable writing for the instrument, and the violin part is an encyclopedia of bowings, paying tribute to Thibaud's honorific title "master of the bow." In the interplay of complementary sonorities and the intertwined arabesques of the two instruments, the sonata is an exaltation of effortless technique. Tailleferre cheerfully avoids any pretensions to great musical depth, but her sonata, in its deceptive simplicity, combines enjoyable music with careful craft.

Recordings

Sonata for Violin and Piano, no. 1. Northeastern NR-222; cassette NR-222C/
Ballade for Piano and Orchestra. Turnabout 34754; CT-2276.
Concertino for Harp and Orchestra. Deutsche Grammophon 2543806.
Pastorale for Flute and Piano and *Six Chansons françaises.* Cambridge 2777.

Sonate

Germaine Tailleferre

I

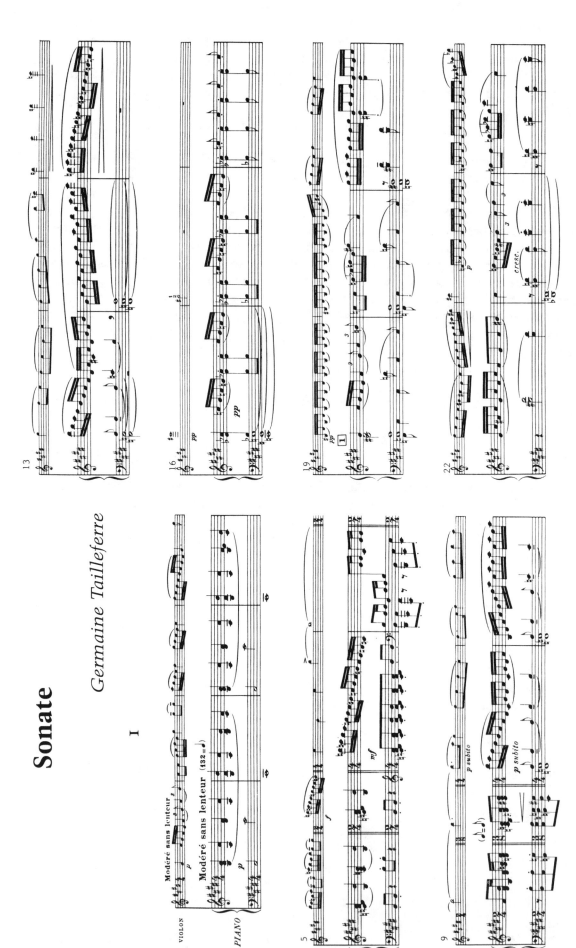

Durand & Cie. Reproduced by permission of the publisher, Theodore Presser Company, Sole Representative U.S.A. & Canada.

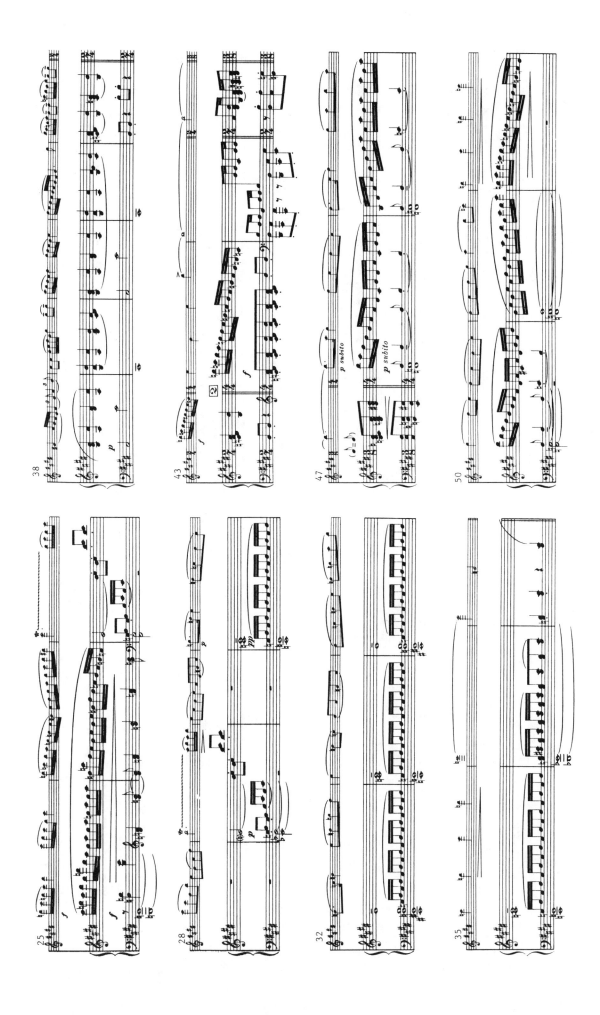

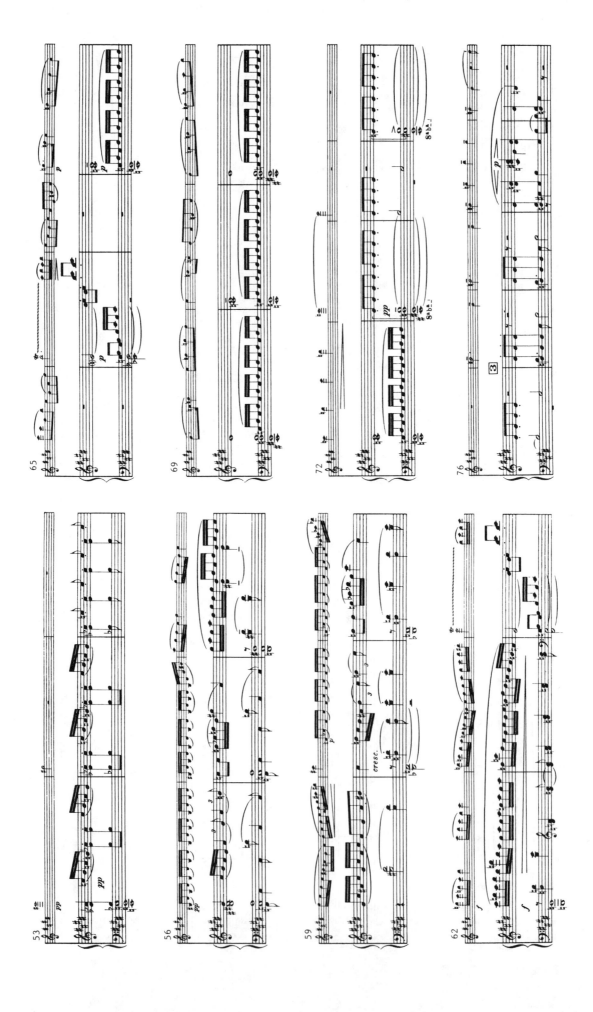

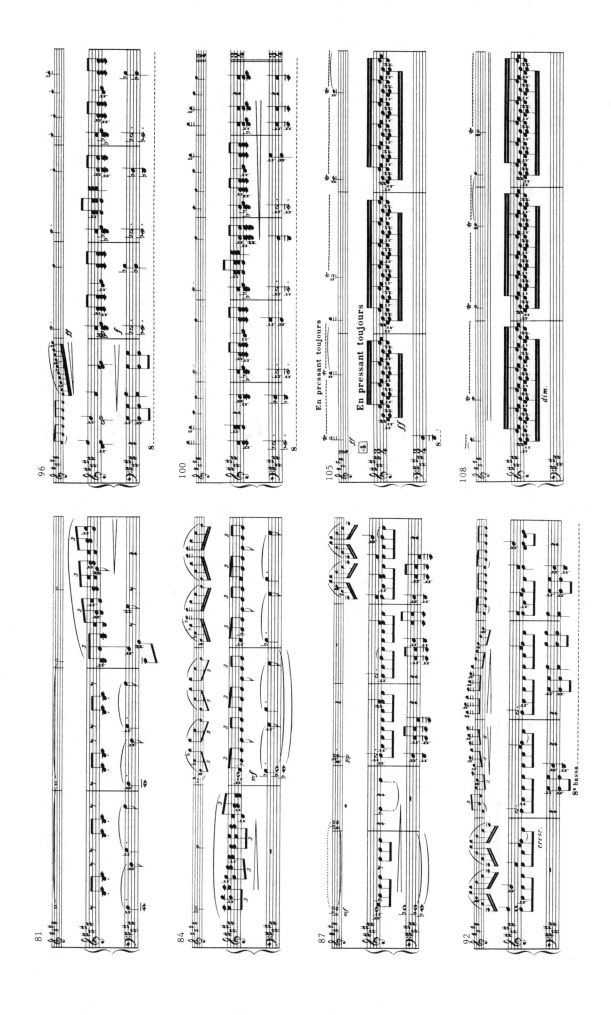

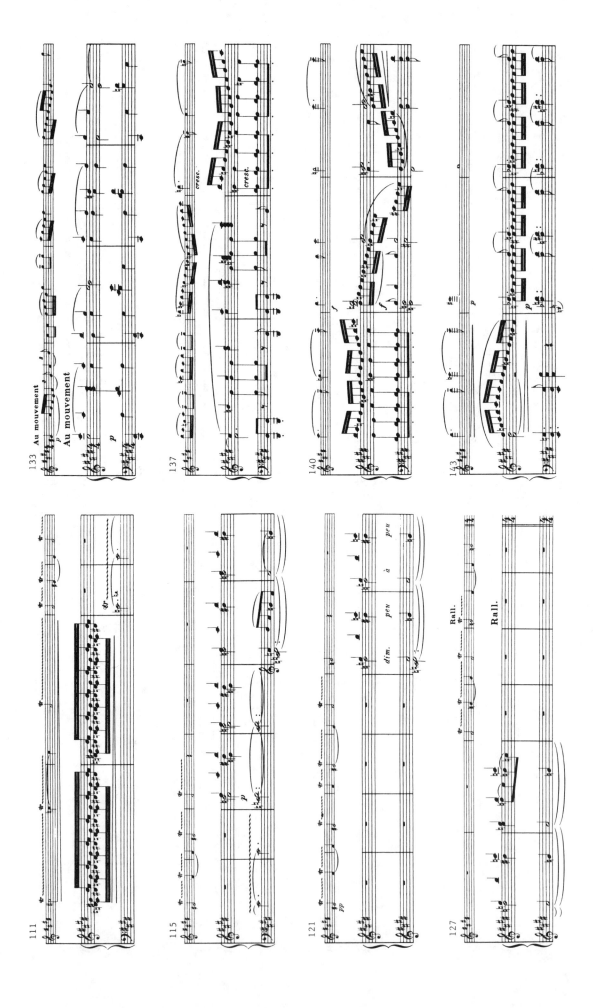

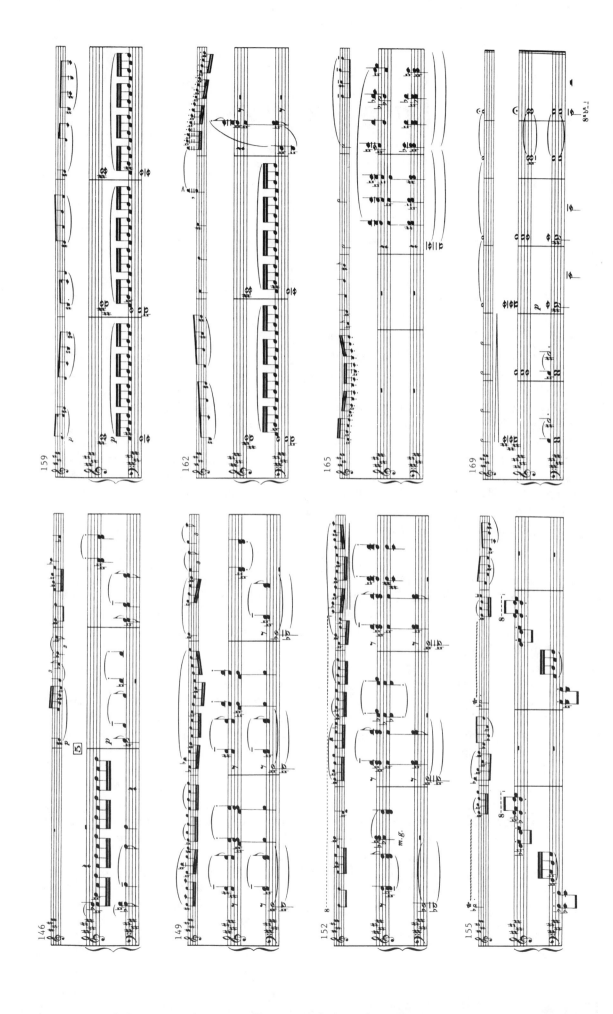

Ruth Crawford Seeger (1901–1953)

JUDITH TICK

As a composer in the 1920s and 30s, Ruth Crawford Seeger was a major artist in the American modernist movement; and as an editor, arranger, and music educator in the 1940s, she was a pioneering advocate of American traditional music.

Crawford Seeger was an "ultra-modern" composer, the 1920s label for the musical avant-garde, which included among its ranks Henry Cowell, Carl Ruggles, and Edgard Varèse. Her style has been called Expressionist and "constructivist," suggesting the combination of intensely emotional content within original schematic forms that is characteristic of her best work. Between 1924 and 1936 she composed most of her small corpus of about fifteen works, including nine preludes for piano; a violin sonata; a suite for small orchestra; a suite for piano and strings; *Piano Study in Mixed Accents*; *Three Songs for Contralto, Oboe, Piano, Percussion, and Orchestral Ostinati*; a string quartet; four *Diaphonic Suites* for instrumental solos or duos; and *Two Songs for Contralto and Piano*.

Crawford's compositions divide into two style periods, determined by the cities in which she lived and composed almost all her music: Chicago and New York. Crawford came to Chicago in 1921 from Jacksonville, Florida, where she had received her early training in piano. Her initial goal was to become a concert pianist, and she enrolled at the American Conservatory of Music for one year, with the plan of returning home a "finished" musician. She remained in Chicago for eight years, receiving a Master of Music degree in 1929. Composition became her primary interest partly because of her first classes in harmony in 1922, which enabled her creative gifts to surface, and partly as a consequence of muscular problems that thwarted her ambitions as a performer. Adolph Weidig, a fine violinist and Berlin-trained composer at the American Conservatory, was her major composition teacher, and some of her early works were performed at his annual student recitals.

In 1924 Crawford began to study piano with Djane Lavoie-Herz, a Canadian devoted to the philosophy and the music of the Russian composer Alexander Scriabin. Through Madame Herz, Crawford met Henry Cowell and Dane Rudhyar; her natural affinity for dissonance and chromaticism found a base on which to thrive, and she settled on a style to explore and refine for the next five years.

Prelude No. 2 (1924) was one of five preludes that Crawford wrote between the fall of 1924 and the spring of 1925. It was performed in New York in 1925 by Gitta Gradova, a brilliant young pupil of Herz, and was described by the critic for the *New*

York Sun as "sensational, pugnacious and curt." This work illustrates a number of the composer's style characteristics. Most important is her harmonic palette, which typically settles on a few chord-colors as the basis for the composition, exploring them through sequential repetition and extension through arpeggiation. The first chord, constructed of two perfect fifths separated by a minor second, is a revoicing of a seventh chord that emphasizes the parallel intervals rather than the triads. It becomes the basis of the arpeggiated figure in the middle section of the piece, starting at m.21. The melodic gesture of the tritone E flat–A, which introduces this chord, is equally developed. In m.8, the tritone skip up to F sharp is emphasized further by a chord built from fourths; and in mm.17–21, it directs the melodic motion. The influence of Scriabin is paramount in such choices. Another Crawford characteristic is the sense of movement achieved through rhythmic variety and extremities of range, particularly in the use of the upper and lower registers of the keyboard, which can be pitted against one another at climactic moments.

In 1927 Crawford confided to her diary that "Bach and Scriabin are to me the greatest spirits born to music." This statement foreshadows her affinity for the dissonant counterpoint she learned from Charles Seeger, who at that point in his eclectic career was a leading intellectual and theorist for American ultra-modern music. Crawford left Chicago on the advice of Cowell, who arranged for her to study with Seeger in New York in the fall of 1929. Her formal studies with him lasted about a year, but they were decisive in shaping her compositions from then on.

In March 1930 Crawford completed "Rat Riddles," which later became the first of a set of Three Songs for Contralto, Oboe, Piano, Percussion, and Orchestral Ostinati. It was premiered in New York in April 1930 and received a number of performances in the next few years. The most important were in Berlin, at a concert conducted by Nicholas Slonimsky in March 1932, and in Amsterdam, at the festival of the International Society of Contemporary Music in June 1933. "Rat Riddles" is a setting of a poem by Carl Sandburg, whom Crawford knew and admired; her careful attention to the formal aspects of the poem as well as to Sandburg's characteristic alliteration display her literary sensitivity.

Despite all the textural complexity of this work, its formal repetitions follow the verse structure: the opening two-line stanza, which in the poem is repeated with some variations four times, is set to virtually the same music, the instrumental *ritornello* that opens the work. Although there is little sense of triadic harmony, the oboe repetitions of D at key textual moments suggest extended tonality rather than avoidance of pitch centers. Crawford's vocal line is intended more as declamation than as lyrical melody. It interacts most with the oboe, which darts and scurries about in its witty depiction of Sandburg's wise hyperactive rats. Describing the frequent tritones and sevenths, particularly noticeable in the piano and oboe, Charles Seeger related "its vicious little stabs of dissonance" to the composer's earlier Chicago period. Of note also are the tone clusters in the piano part, associated with the pizzicato piano figure that first appears in m.5 and is indicated by square note shapes. The masterful handling of irregular rhythms, compounded by the homophonic ostinati that Crawford added to the work two years later, is characteristic of her mature style.

In 1930 Crawford won a Guggenheim Fellowship in composition. She was the first woman to receive that award and one of only five so honored until the 1970s. She spent most of her year in Berlin, composing, and the String Quartet was completed in Paris in the spring of 1931. The quartet is her most famous composition. It was premiered by the Pan American Association of Composers in New York in 1933. The slow movement was immediately singled out for special praise. In 1949 Virgil Thomson described it as "striking for intensity and elevation. Consisting entirely of notes juxtaposed in slowly changing chords of high dissonance content, the piece seemed

269

scarcely to move at all. And yet, it was . . . thoroughly absorbing." The composer herself pointed to its "heterophony of dynamics," in which "no high point in the crescendo in any one instrument coincides with the high point in any other instrument."

The fourth movement is based on a ten-tone row, which is presented ten times, on successive tones of the row. At m.21 the row is transposed a whole step higher; at m.60 the material retrogrades. The texture is two-voice counterpoint, with each voice systematically gaining or losing a pitch at each successive entry. Given that Crawford was in Berlin when Arnold Schoenberg was teaching there, it is easy to conclude that these serial techniques show his influence. But in fact, Crawford, who knew his classic twelve-tone method, never met him, did not consider herself a follower, and evolved her own methods, partly from Seeger's teachings, to handle idiosyncratic concepts.

Crawford returned from Europe in the fall of 1931, and she and Charles Seeger were married the following year. In 1935 the Seegers left New York for Washington, D.C., a move that had decisive consequences, for Crawford Seeger as a composer never again matched the period of her late youth in either brilliance or productivity. Instead, she and her husband were caught up in the folk-music renaissance that was a by-product of many New Deal programs. Traditional music routed composition from its status as her primary artistic medium. Captivated by the beauty and candor of field recordings, she dedicated the rest of her life to the dissemination of folk music through transcription and arrangement.

There were many reasons for her defection from composition. There was a pervasive disillusionment with the avant-garde in the wake of the disasters of the Great Depression; there were the pressures of family life—the Seegers had four children within ten years. But had she been so inclined, Crawford Seeger might have used traditional music as a new medium for composition, as did so many other American composers in the 1930s. Her Woodwind Quintet (1952), which marked her return to composition, certainly showed some absorption of traditional melody. However, her own evolution as a composer demonstrated the idiosyncratic and individualistic nature of her creative gift. She did not naturally lean toward reconstructed tonality or neo-classicism. Crawford Seeger's achievement as a composer was to find her individual voice within a very young avant-garde movement in American music and do battle on the fronts of musical modernism.

Recordings

Music by Women Composers, vol. II. "Prelude no. 2." Rosemary Platt, piano. Coronet LPS # 3121, 1982.
String Quartet. Composers Quartet. Nonesuch H-71280, 1973.
String Quartet. Fine Arts Quartet. Gasparo 205. "Rat Riddles." Beverly Morgan, voice, Speculum Musicae. New World Records, NW-285, 1978.

Further Reading

Carter, Elliott. "Expressionism in American Music," in *Perspectives on American Composers*, edited by Benjamin Boretz and Edward T. Cone. New York, W. W. Norton, 1972.
Gaume, Matilda. "Ruth Crawford Seeger," in *Women Making Music*, edited by Jane Bowers and Judith Tick. Urbana and Chicago: University of Illinois Press, 1986.
Seeger, Charles. "Ruth Crawford," in *American Composers on American Music*, edited by Henry Cowell. New York: Frederick Ungar Publishing Co., 1962, pp. 110–18.

Prelude No. 2

Ruth Crawford Seeger

Reprinted by permission of the family of Ruth Crawford Seeger, Mike Seeger, representative.

274

Autumn, 1924

Rat Riddles

Ruth Crawford Seeger

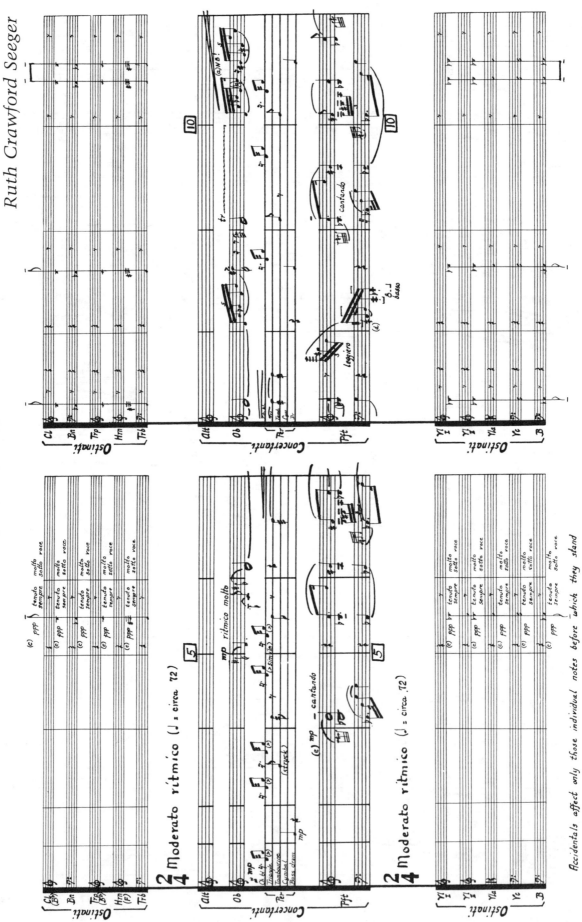

Copyright © 1933 by New Music Edition. Reproduced by permission of the publisher, Theodore Presser Company.

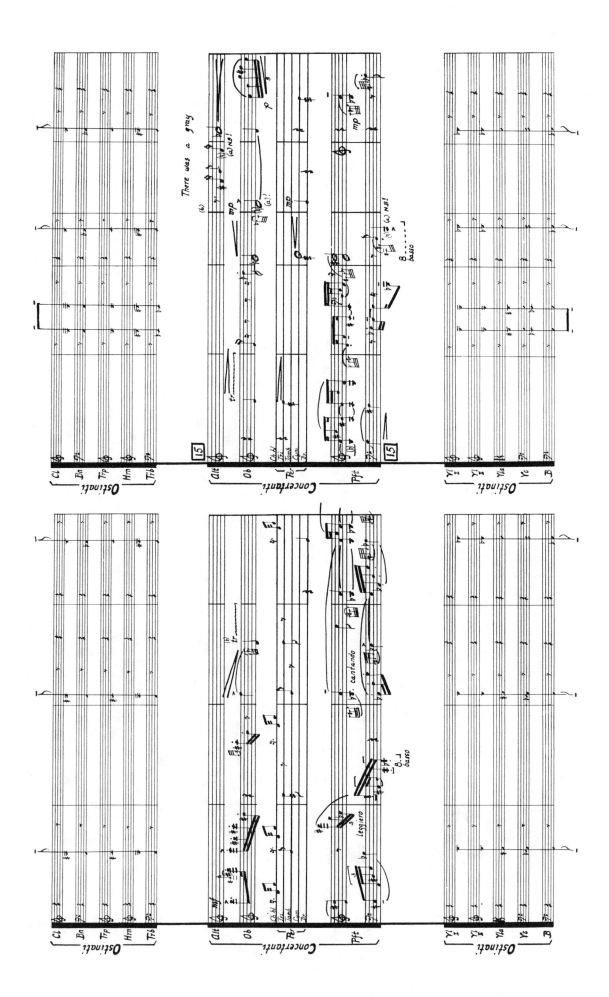

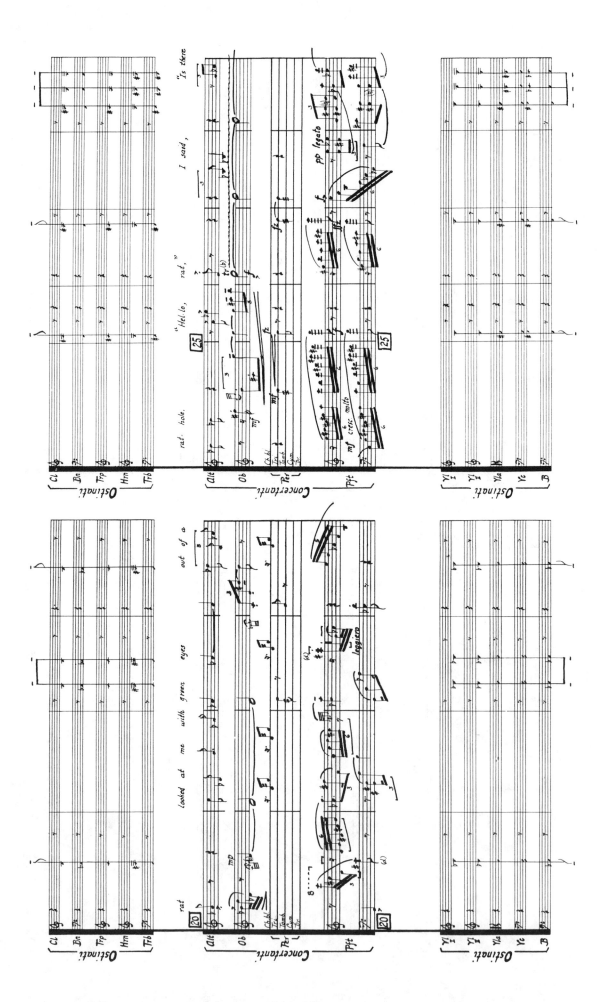

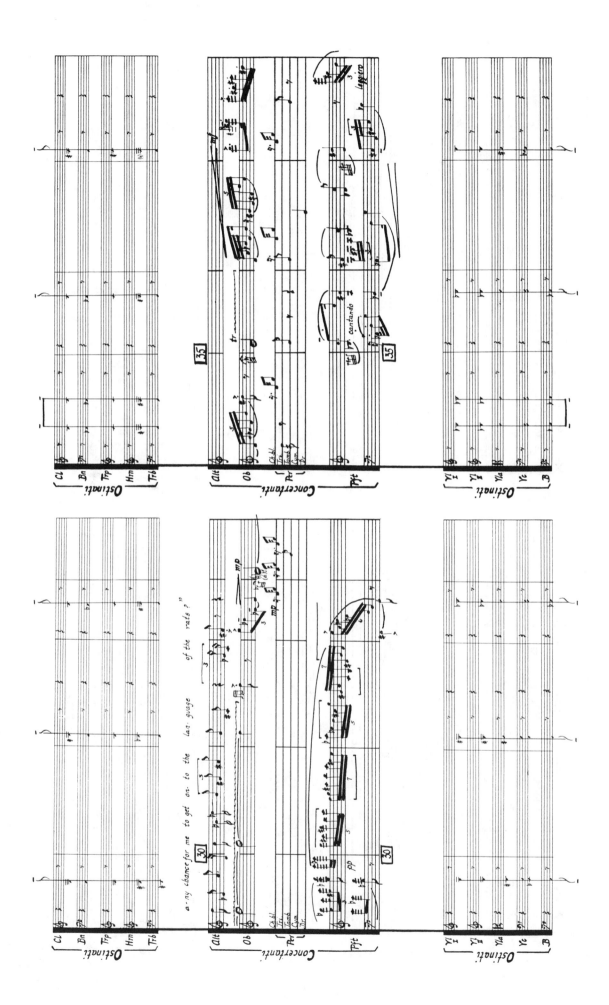

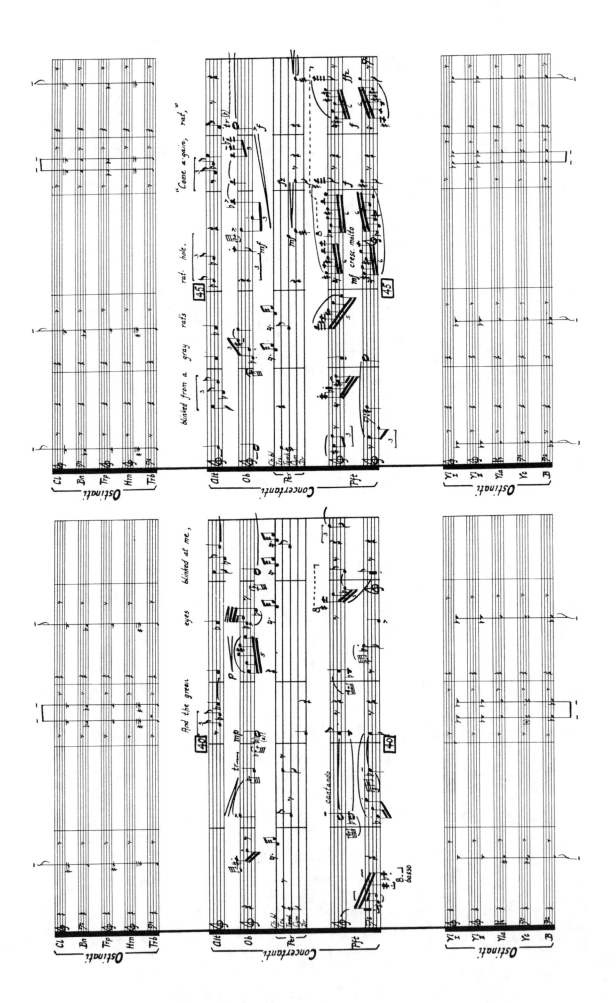

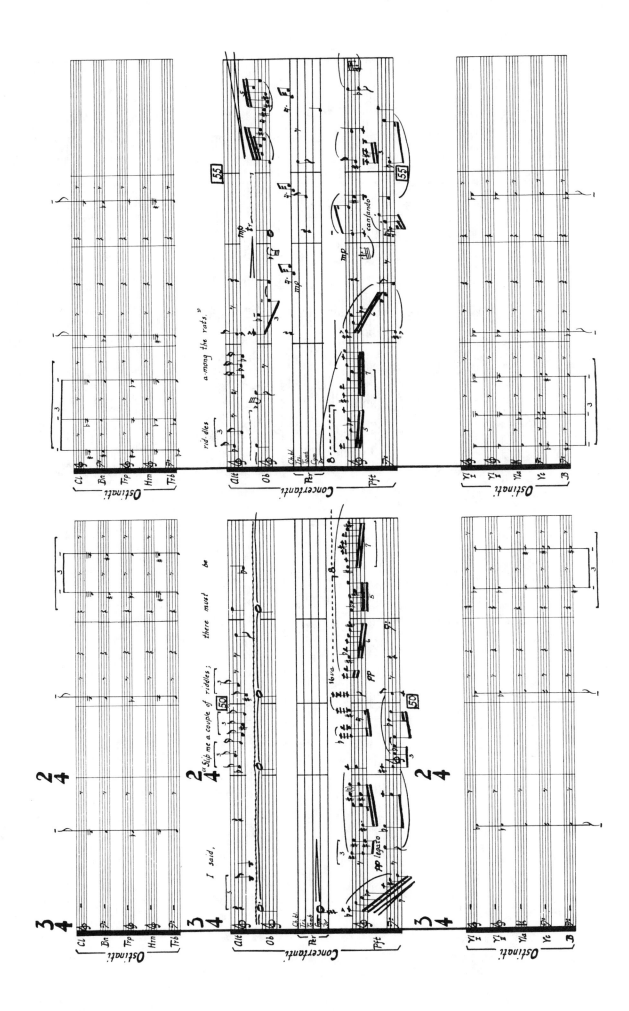

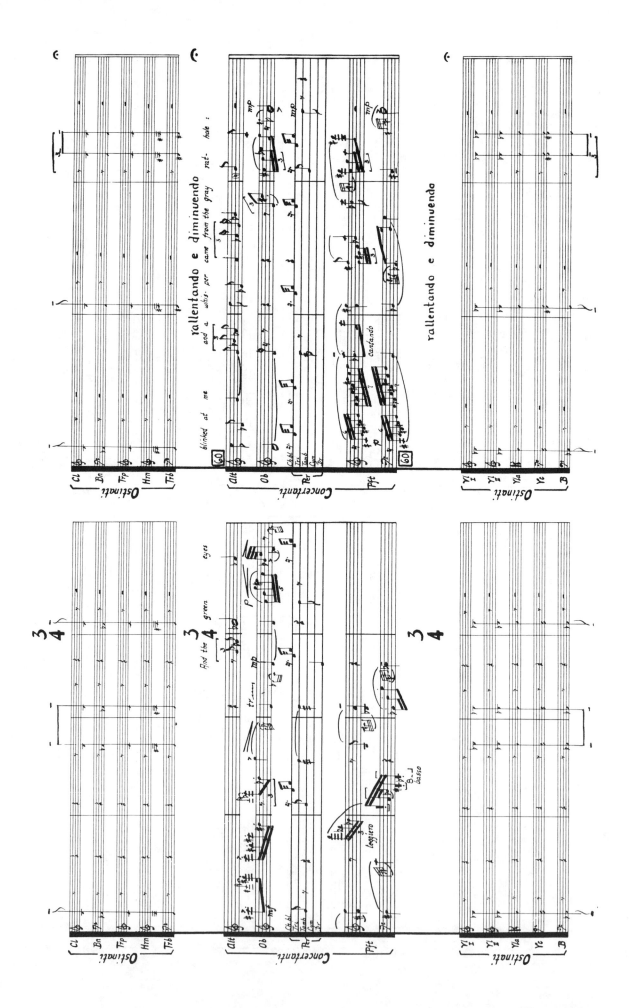

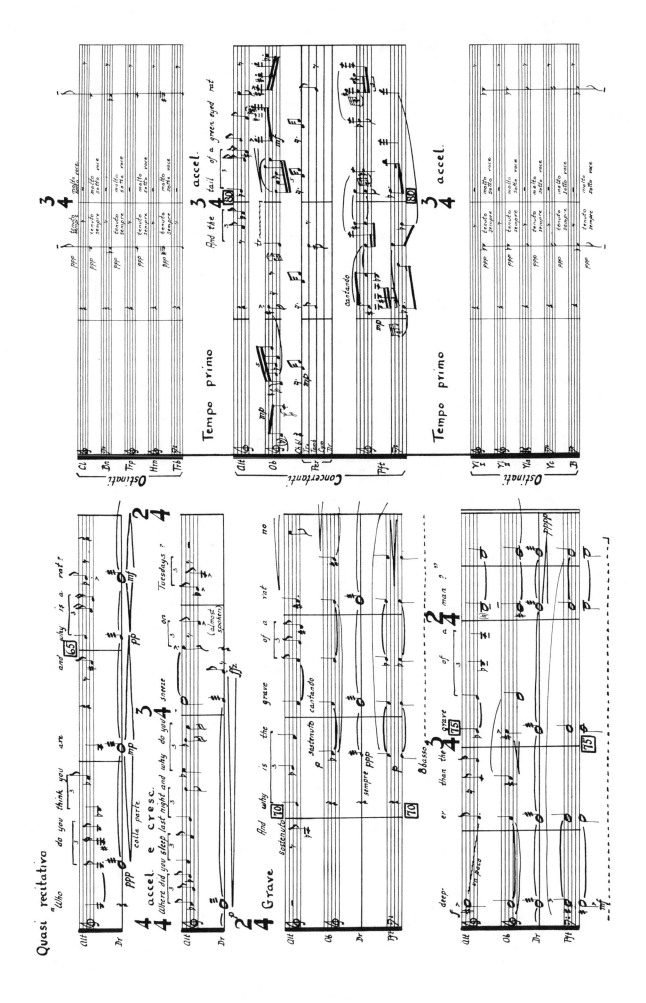

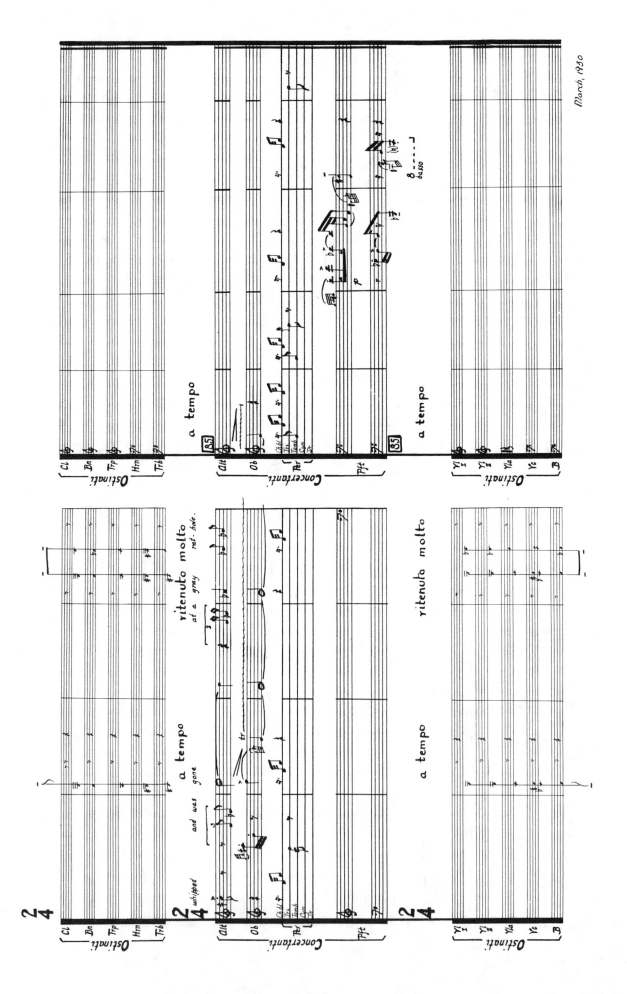

March, 1930

String Quartet

III

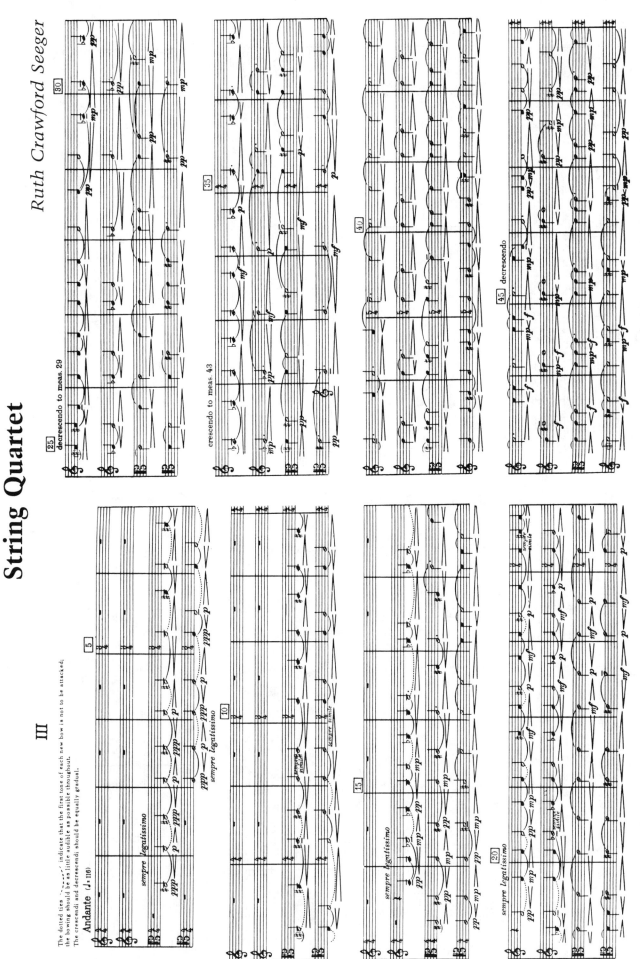

*The dotted ties '⌣‿‿⌣' indicate that the first tone of each new bow is not to be attacked;
the bowing should be as little audible as possible throughout.
The crescendi and decrescendi should be equally gradual.*

Copyright © 1941 by Merion Music Inc. Reproduced by permission of the publisher, Theodore Presser Company.

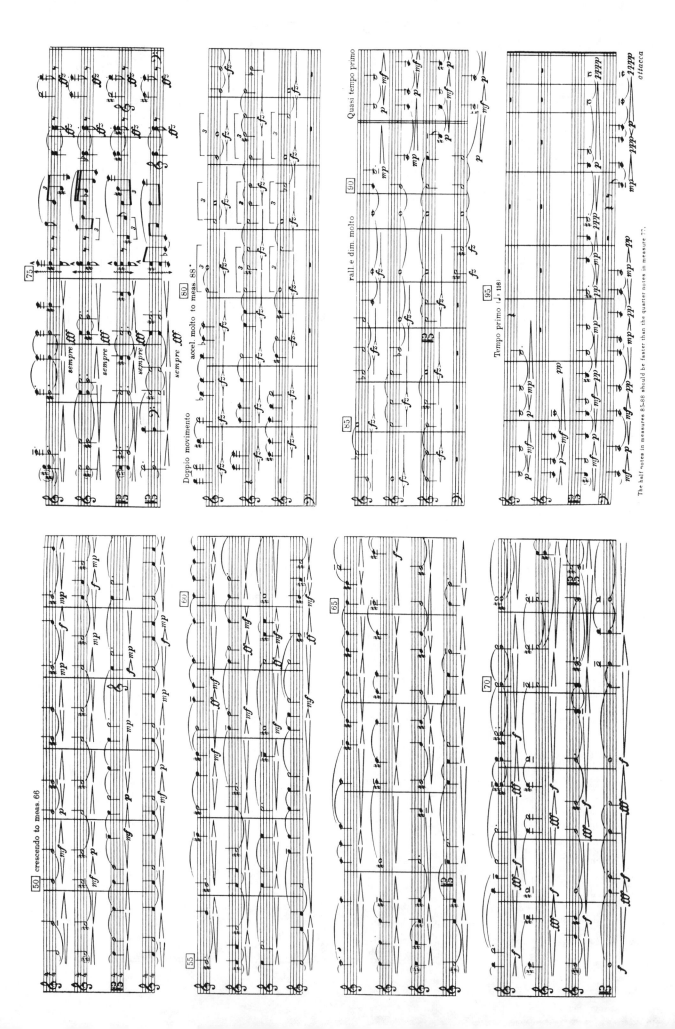

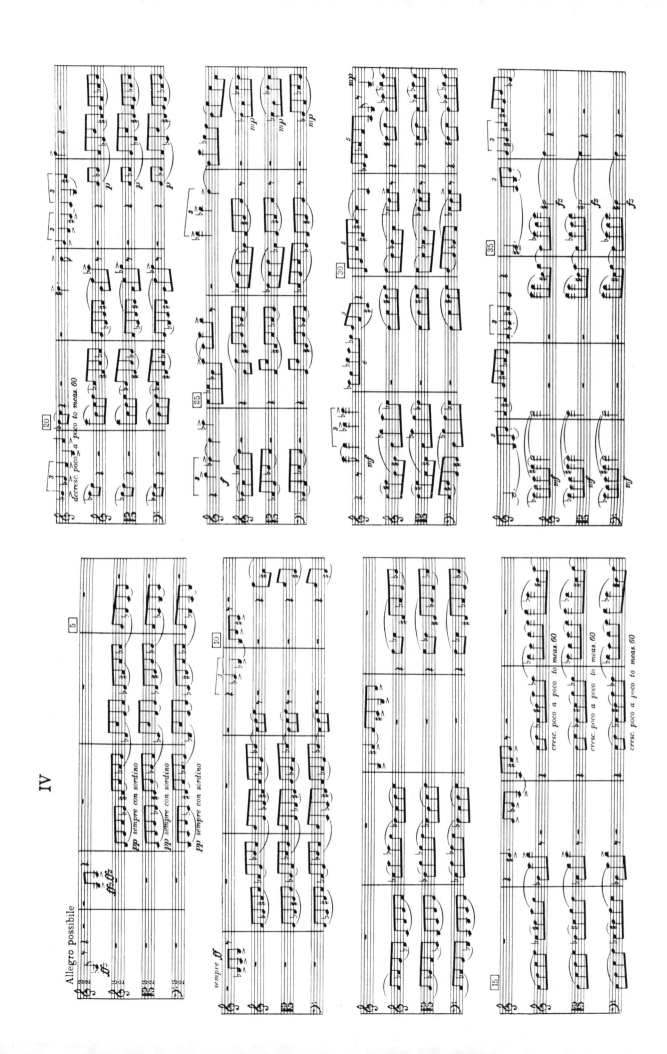

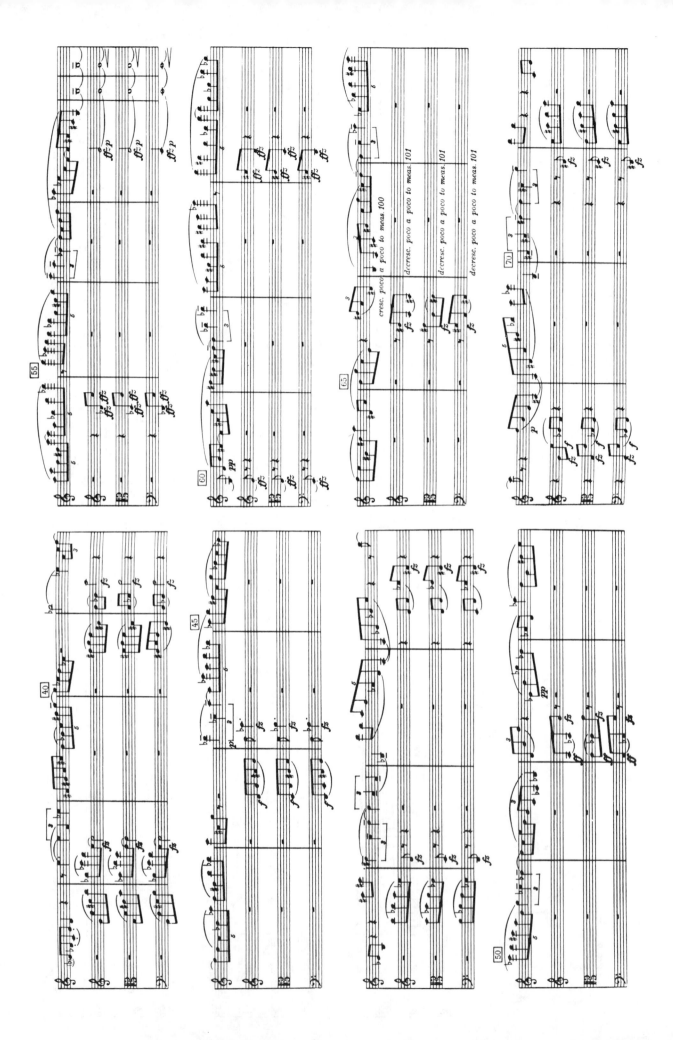

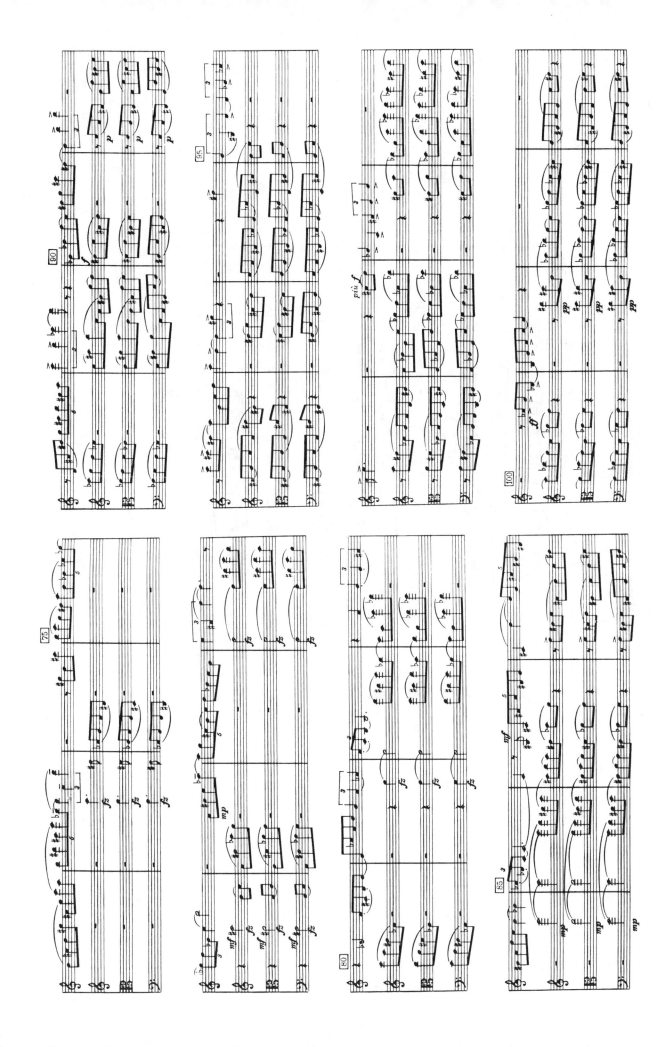

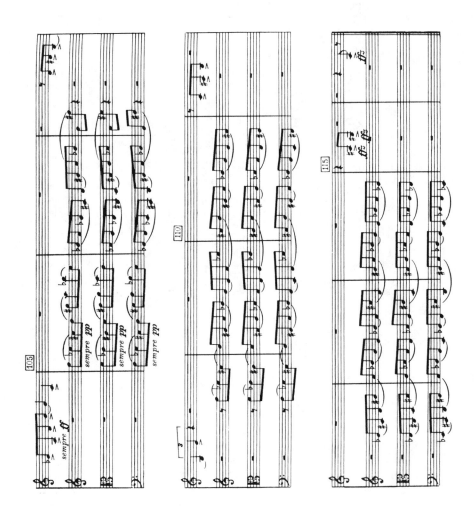

Miriam Gideon
(born 1906)

BARBARA A. PETERSEN

Without a doubt Miriam Gideon ranks as one of America's foremost women composers of today. Still active (at this writing) as a composer and teacher as she approaches her 80th birthday, Gideon has created over 60 compositions in a career spanning six decades. She was born in Greeley, Colorado, but her family moved eastward, and she studied piano and music theory in both New York and Boston. Her academic degrees include a B.A. in French from Boston University (1926), an M.A. in musicology from Columbia University (1946), and a D.S.M. in composition from Jewish Theological Seminary of America (1970). Gideon considers the late Roger Sessions, with whom she studied from 1935 to 1943, her major composition teacher and strongest influence. She herself has taught at Brooklyn College and City College of the City University of New York; she continues to teach at the Manhattan School of Music and the Jewish Theological Seminary as well as in her private studio. Among her many honors are election to the American Academy and Institute of Arts and Letters (1975), as the second woman composer to be named to the Institute (Louise Talma was the first), and honorary doctorates from Jewish Theological Seminary and Brooklyn College (1981, 1983).

Gideon's concentration as a composer has been on chamber music, especially works for voice and mixed ensembles. From the early conservative style of her German Songs, Opus 1 (1930–37), which evoke the musical and poetic worlds of Mendelssohn and Schumann, Gideon moved toward a more Expressionistic style with strong elements of chromaticism and dissonance. Most of her works are on a small scale, with clear designs, in a freely atonal idiom, and with a harmonious balance of lyrical and dramatic elements. Without following any rigid compositional doctrine, she has created a remarkably consistent body of works that fuse abstract ideas, poetic images, and subjective emotional experience. Her concerns have always been with "illuminating her inner feelings" and with combining words and music into a meaningful whole. As she has said on many occasions, she writes not as a *woman* composer or a *Jewish* composer but as a *composer*, period. Of utmost importance is her declaration, "What I write has to *mean* something to me."

Gideon's interests extend to many languages, cultures, and periods. She has set texts in several languages, sometimes within the same work: *The Condemned Playground* (1963) uses poems in Latin, English, Japanese, and French. In some works she sets the poems in the original language as well as in translation (*Songs of Youth and*

Madness, 1977), and in others she uses English translations of ancient originals (from the Japanese in *The Seasons of Time*, 1969, and from the Greek in *Voices from Elysium*, 1979). The text of *The Hound of Heaven* is drawn from an extended poem by Francis Thompson (1859–1907), an English poet and essayist known for his devout Catholicism. Whereas the poet was recording his reactions to specific disappointments in life (rejection for both the priesthood and the practice of medicine), Gideon selected verses that evoke the purification through suffering that underlies the Jewish experience. In crossing cultural boundaries she has created a poignant musical setting that emphasizes the suffering common to all humankind. *The Hound of Heaven* was commissioned by Lazare Saminsky, one of Gideon's early composition teachers, to celebrate the centenary of the founding of Congregation Emanu-El in New York City; it was first performed there on March 23, 1945.

Although it is the first in a series of fifteen works for voices and small ensemble, *The Hound of Heaven* displays the most important stylistic features of Gideon's writing. As in most of her works in the genre, the vocal line may be taken by either a male or a female (medium) voice. The "mixed consort" of instruments, here oboe and string trio, is also a common characteristic. Lasting approximately seven minutes, *The Hound of Heaven* is atypical only in its being in a single movement; here the text is drawn from a single poem, whereas in most of Gideon's other chamber works there are separate movements for individual poems. Interludes such as the one in mm.62–86—or complete, if short, instrumental movements—occur in many of her chamber works and offset the surrounding texted passages. The sinuous vocal line, mainly syllabic text setting, fluctuating meters, and close interweaving of voice and instruments found here are hallmarks of her later works as well.

Recording

The Hound of Heaven. CRI (Composers Recordings, Inc.). SD 286.

Further Reading

LePage, Jane Weiner. *Women Composers, Conductors and Musicians of the Twentieth Century: Selected Biographies*, vol.2. Metuchen, NJ: Scarecrow Press, 1983, pp. 118–41.
Petersen, Barbara A. "Music by Miriam Gideon for Voice and Chamber Ensemble," in *The Musical Woman: An International Perspective*, vol.2, edited by J. L. Zaimont. Westport, CT: Greenwood Press, forthcoming.

The Hound of Heaven

Text by Francis Thompson

Miriam Gideon

Copyright © 1975 by Columbia University Music Press. Used by permission of Galaxy Music Corporation, New York, sole U.S. agent. This work is fully protected by copyright law and may not be reproduced without permission of the publisher. No performance materials may be reproduced from this edition. Performance materials are available for sale from Galaxy Music Corporation, New York.

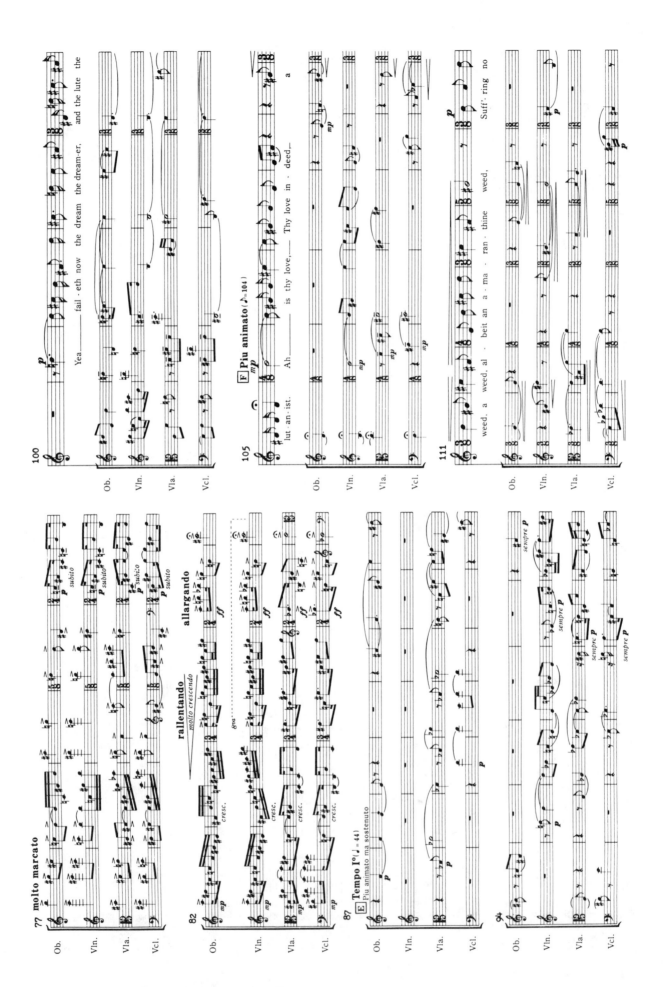

Grażyna Bacewicz (1909–1969)

ADRIAN T. THOMAS

Grażyna Bacewicz was one of the most-accomplished women composers of her generation, and, within her native Poland, she was highly regarded by her peers. Along with many of her generation, she studied not only at the Warsaw Conservatory but also in Paris, with Nadia Boulanger (1932–33). Being abroad also enabled her to further her violin studies—with André Touret and, in 1934, with Carl Flesch. Bacewicz spent the war years in Poland and withstood the successive pressures imposed on Polish culture by Nazi and by Stalinist ideology with fortitude and poise. She performed as a concert violinist until the early 1950s.

To describe her style as neoclassical is to utter a half-truth. Certainly, Bacewicz seems to have found the interwar Parisian blend of neobaroque and neoclassical gestures much to her taste. She admired clarity and directness, but equally she was no lover of formulae; her ability to surprise the listener by deft twists and turns was entirely her own. Her heyday was during the 1940s and 1950s, when she wrote such works as the Third String Quartet (1947) and the Concerto for String Orchestra (1948). Bacewicz went on to embrace a greater degree of experimentation than might have been expected, as seen in the *Music for Strings, Trumpets and Percussion* (1958). Her music of the 1960s was unfortunately fraught with inconsistencies, as she struggled to accommodate the avant-garde trends sweeping through contemporary Polish music. The absence of clearly defined thematic hierarchies and an over-reliance within an atonal context of the very gestures that had so suited her tonally oriented music of the postwar decade suggest that it is her earlier music, rather than more-recent compositions, that will survive on the concert platform.

The Second Piano Sonata (1953) justly maintains its position in the repertoire. It is a rich blend of neoclassical style and a folk-derived idiom, and, like a number of Bacewicz's works of the period, it refers to the music of Karol Szymanowski (cf. his Twelve Studies for piano, Opus 33, 1916, and the finale of his *Symphonie Concertante* for piano and orchestra, Opus 60, 1932).

The vigorous opening movement, Maestoso—Agitato, is typical of her style and methods. Bacewicz worked essentially as a rhapsodist, constantly reshaping her materials through the developmental association of motivic ideas. The simple and initially unimposing second theme of this movement (poco meno, m.44) gradually comes to dominate, leaving the distinct impression of the composer's giving good ideas their head rather than forcing them into too strait a sonata jacket. This folklike theme is

298

followed in the second movement, Largo, by an even more direct acknowledgment of the ever-present "socio-realist" requirement for musical relevance. Here, an unmistakeably folk-derived theme in the Dorian mode now soothes, now hectors; its preeminence is threatened only briefly by the unexpected artifice of a fugato toward the end of the movement.

Bacewicz was no mean pianist (she gave the premiere of the Sonata), and the final Toccata is a brilliant piece of keyboard writing. It is cast in the mold of an oberek (a fast-moving cousin of the mazurka). As in the first movement, Bacewicz makes recourse to fourths (perfect and Lydian), modal folk themes, and swirling chromaticism to create this muscular folk dance, which is arguably her most successful finale.

Recordings (of Sonata No. 2)

Regina Smendzianka. Muza SXL 0977.
Nancy Fierro. Avant AV 1012.
Krystian Zimerman. Muza SX 1510 (live recording).

Further Reading

Rosen, Judith. *Grażyna Bacewicz: Her Life and Works.* Polish Music History Series, 2. Los Angeles: University of Southern California, 1984.
Thomas, Adrian. *Grażyna Bacewicz: Chamber and Orchestral Music.* Polish Music History Series, 3. Los Angeles: University of Southern California, 1985.

Sonata II

Grażyna Bacewicz

Published by Polskie Wydawnictwo Muzyczne, Krakow, n.d. [1953]. Reprinted by permission.

302

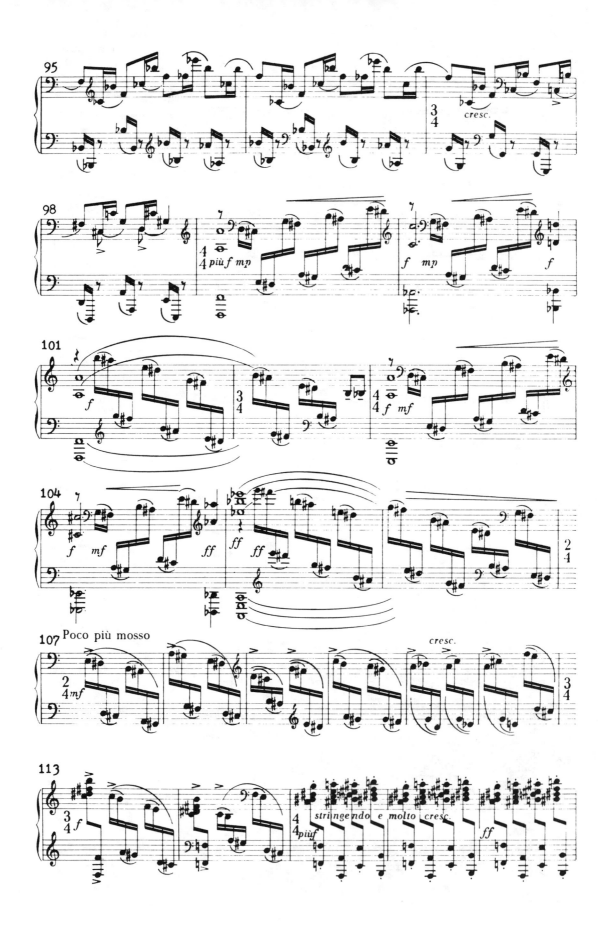

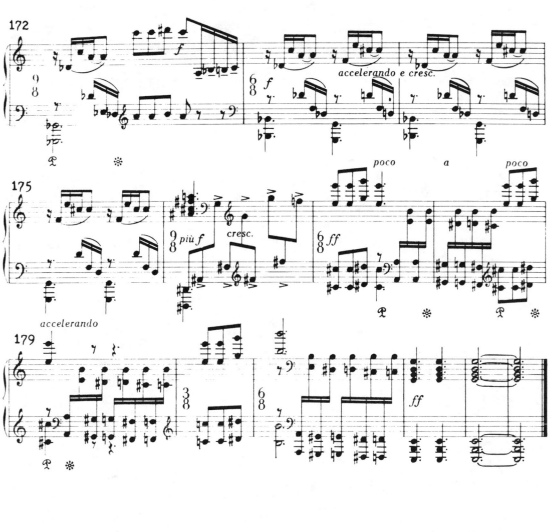

Toccata

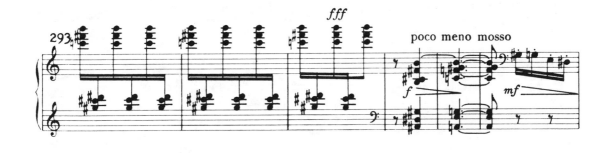

316

317

Louise Talma
(born 1906)

JAMES R. BRISCOE

Louise Talma was born in Arcachon, France, and came to the United States in her teens. At the Institute of Musical Art in New York, she studied counterpoint and composition with Percy Goetschius and Howard Brockway. She earned a bachelor's degree in music from New York University in 1931 and a Master of Arts degree from Columbia University in 1933. She attended the Fontainebleau School in France each summer from 1926 through 1939, serving in later years as the first American on the faculty. There she studied piano with Isidor Philipp and composition with Nadia Boulanger. She had a distinguished career on the faculty of Hunter College in New York, from 1928 to 1979.

A pioneer among American women composers, Louise Talma has compiled a record of many "firsts": she was the first woman to receive the Sibelius Medal for Composition, in 1963; she was the first woman to receive two Guggenheim awards in composition, in 1946 and 1947; she was the first woman composer to be elected to the National Institute of Arts and Letters, in 1974; and she was the first American woman whose work was produced by a major European opera company—*The Alcestiad*, in Frankfurt-am-Main in 1962. Her other, numerous awards include the Prix d'Excellence de Composition from the French government, a Senior Fulbright Research Grant for the composition of *The Alcestiad*, major grants from the National Endowment for the Arts, and honorary doctoral degrees from Hunter and Bard colleges. Since 1943 Talma has worked regularly at the MacDowell Colony for composers in New Hampshire, which has played a major role in her creativity. Beyond her recognition as the dean of contemporary American women composers, she is renowned, as she deserves to be, as a foremost American composer—without the qualification "female."

Louise Talma has composed in all genres. Her three-act opera *The Alcestiad*, based on a text by Thornton Wilder, was composed in 1958. Among large choral works, Talma's oratorio *The Divine Flame* (1948), her triptych *The Tolling Bell* (nominated for a Pulitzer Prize in 1970), and her *Mass in English* (1984) have received important acclaim. Her *Toccata for Orchestra, Alleluia in Form of Toccata for Piano, Piano Sonata Number 1*, and *Piano Sonata Number 2* have been recorded and frequently performed. Louise Talma is represented primarily by the publisher Carl Fischer.

Louise Talma is an outstanding representative of main tendencies in twentieth-century composition in the United States. In general, she is a neoclassicist, although

319

with her Six Etudes for piano (1954), she began to use a serial approach. With *The Alcestiad* she began to combine serial and tonal elements. In regard to broad stylistic predilections and adaptations, she therefore parallels Stravinsky and Copland.

On the genesis of *La Corona (Seven Sonnets by John Donne)*, Talma says:

> The work came to be written by way of a suggestion made to me in 1954 by Donald Aird, who was then connected with the Illinois Wesleyan University Collegiate Choir. He asked if I had ever thought of setting this sonnet sequence, at the time unknown to me. I looked into it and was immediately struck by the interesting form the repeated lines could give to the music. The set is literally a "corona," in that the last line of each sonnet becomes the first line of the next one, and the last line of the last one is the first line of the first one. This is, of course, carried out in the music. I was commissioned to write the work by the Illinois Wesleyan Choir. Its first New York performance [and perhaps its premiere—ed.] was given on November 19, 1964, by the Dorian Chorale, Harold Aks, conductor.

Recordings

La Corona—Holy Sonnets by John Donne. The Dorian Chorale, Harold Aks, conductor. Composers Recordings Inc., 187.

La Corona—Holy Sonnets by John Donne. The Gregg Smith Singers. GSS Recordings, forthcoming.

Further Reading

Cohn, A. "Louise Talma," *The New Grove Dictionary of American Music.*

Holcomb, D. "Louise Talma," *The New Grove Dictionary of Music and Musicians.*

Teicher, Susan. "The Solo Works for Piano of Louise Talma," D.M.A. diss., Peabody Conservatory, 1982. Ann Arbor: University Microfilms.

Holy Sonnets
LA CORONA

Louise Talma

Texts by John Donne

Reprinted from the original manuscript, by permission of the composer.

ANNUNCIATION

16
chuse But die, Loe, faith-full Vir-gin, yeelds him-self to lye In pri-son
yet can-not chuse but die, Loe, faith-full Vir-gin, yeelds him-self
poco marcato
yet can-not chuse But die, Loe, faith-full Vir-gin, yeelds him-self in thy
21
dim. pp
in thy wombe; and though he there can take no sinne, nor thou give, yet
cresc.
he Can take no sinne, yet
dim. pp cresc.
wombe; and though he there can take no sinne, nor thou give, yet he will weare
cresc.
nor thou give,
26
molto marcato
he will weare Ta-ken from thence, flesh which deaths force may trie.
molto marcato
he will weare flesh will weare flesh which deaths force may trie.
molto marcato
Ta-ken from thence flesh which deaths force may trie.
molto marcato
yet he will weare Ta-ken from thence flesh which deaths force may trie
31
Ere by the spheares time Was cre-a-ted, thou Wast in his
Ere time was cre-a- - - ted, thou Wast in
Ere by the spheares time was cre-a- - ted, thou Wast in
Ere time Was cre- a- - - - ted, thou Wast in his minde, in
36
minde, who is thy Sonne and Brother, Whom thou con- ceiv'st, con-
his minde, Who is thy Sonne, and Bro-ther, Whom thou Whom thou con- ceiv'st, con- - -
his minde, Who is thy Sonne; con- - - -
his minde, Who is thy Sonne, and Bro-ther, Whom thou con- ceiv'st;
41
poco cresc. dim.
ceiv'd; yea thou art now Thy Makers maker, and thy
ceiv'd; and
ceiv'd; yea thou art now Thy Ma- kers ma-ker
poco cresc. dim.
yea thou art now Thy Ma- - - - Kers ma-

NATIVITIE

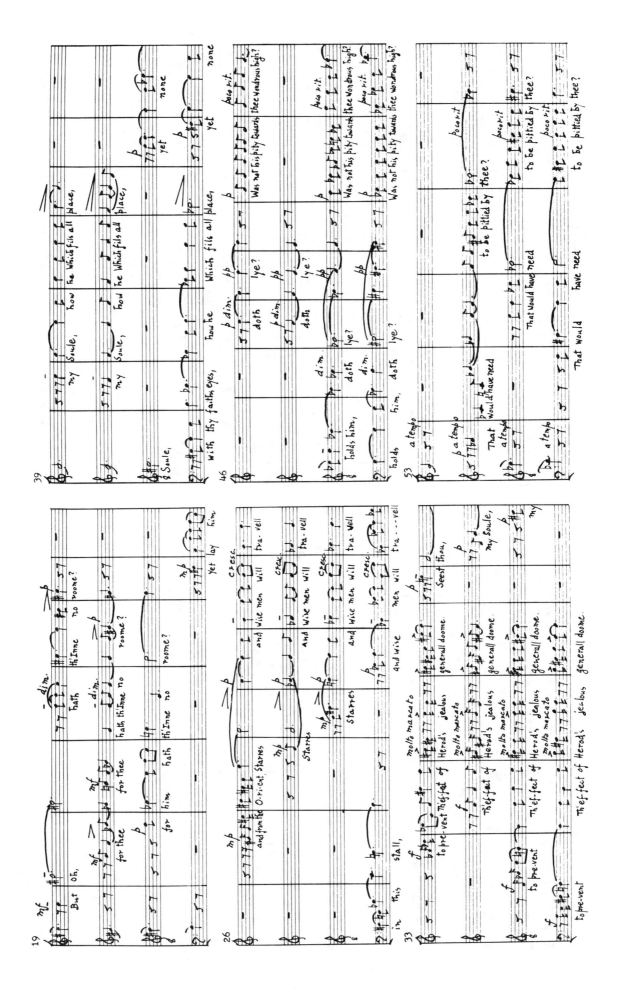

TEMPLE

August 12-31, 1954,
Peterborough, N.H. 2'40"

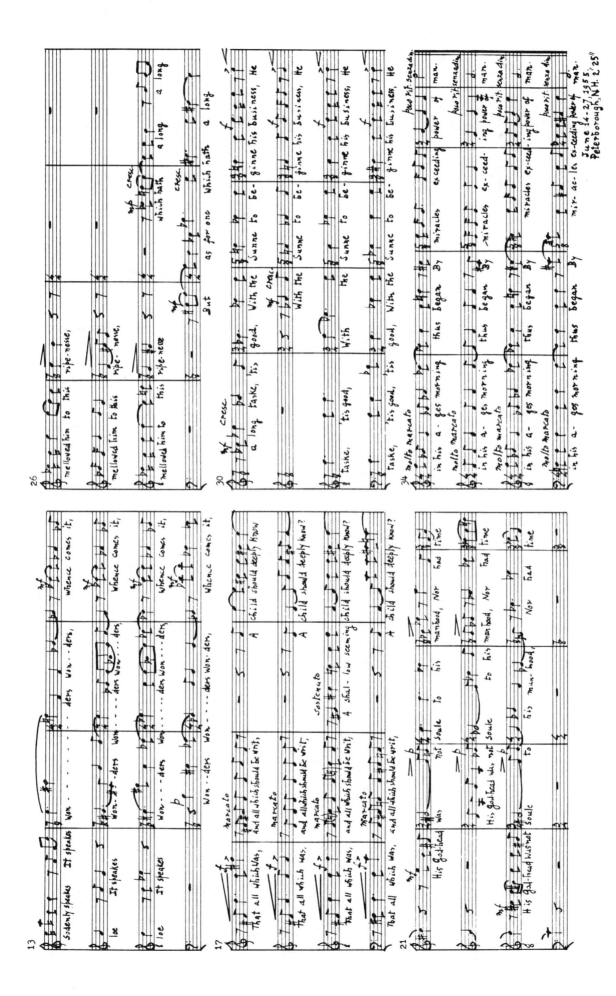

CRUCIFYING

Allegro ♩=120
By miracles exceeding power of man, Hee faith in some, envie in some begat,
For what weake spirits ad-mire, ambitious hate;
In both affections many to him ran, But Oh! the worst are most,
18
they will and can, A-las, and do unto the im-maculate, Whose creature Fate is, now pre-
24
scribe a Fate, Measuring selfe-life's in-fin-i-ty to a span, Nay to an
30
inch. Loe, where condemned hee Beares his owne crosse, with paine,
with

RESURRECTION

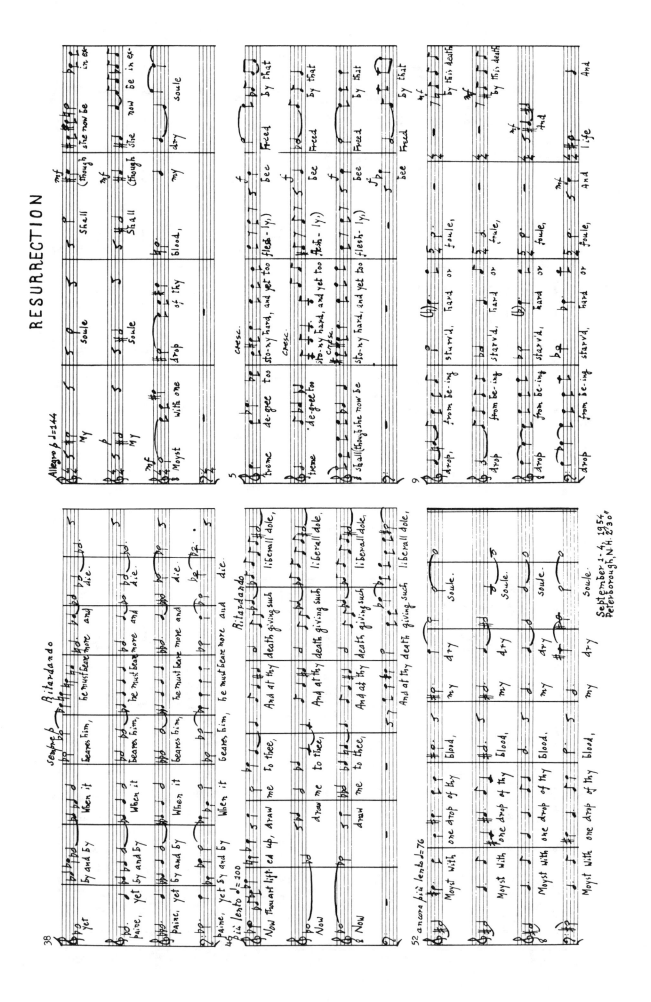

September 1-4, 1954
Peterborough, N.H. 2730

41
meanes be glo-ri-fied. May then sinnes sleep and
senza dim.
46
deaths soone from me passe, That wak't from both, I a-
mf cresc.
51
gain risen may salute the last and ev-er-last-ing day.
gain risen may Sal-ute may Salute the last and ev-er-last-ing day.
marcato
senza dim.
June 29 - July 6, 1955
Peterborough, N.H. 1' 35"

ASCENTION

Allegro ♩=126
Sa-lute the last and ev-er-last-ing day,
Sa-lute Sa-lute the last and ev-er-last-ing day,
Salute Sa-lute the last and ev-er-last-ing day,
Sa-lute the last and ev-er-last-ing day,
6
Joy at the up-ris-ing of this Sunne, and Sonne, Yee whose just teares, or trib-u-
12
la-tion Have pure-ly washt, or burnt your drossie clay;
Be-
Be-hold the High-est
Be-hold the High-est
Be-hold Be-hold the

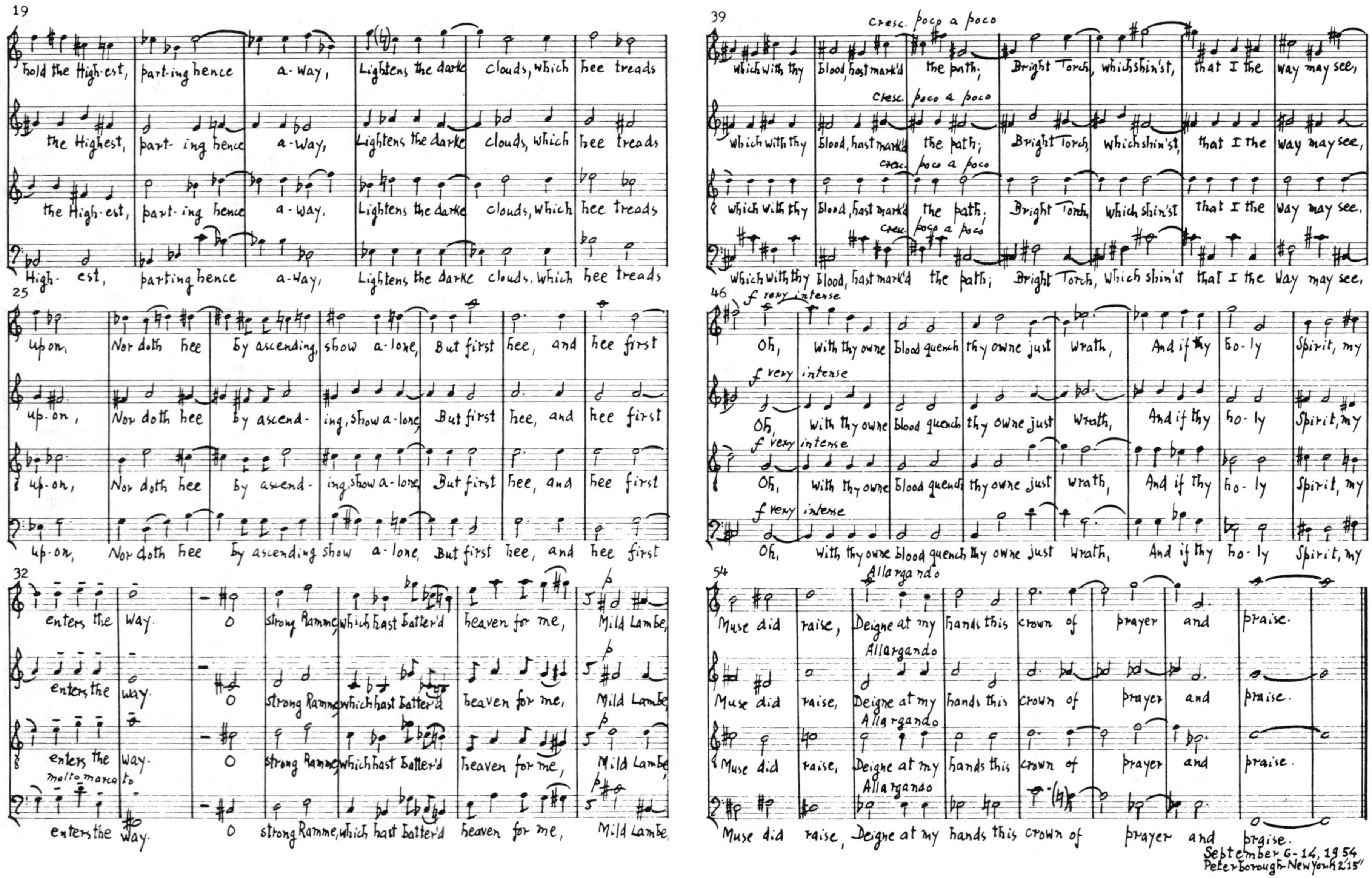
September 6-14, 1954
Peterborough-New York 2'15"

Julia Perry
(1924–1979)

MILDRED DENBY GREEN

The musical style of Julia Perry includes various compositional techniques. Although some of her music reflects her Black heritage, many of her major works, especially the later ones, make liberal use of dissonance and unconventional harmonies. Perry's compositions include symphonies, operas, chamber works, choral anthems, art songs, and arrangements of spirituals.

Julia Perry was a native of Lexington, Kentucky, but grew up in Akron, Ohio, where she received her first musical training. Her musical sensitivity was strongly shaped by the influence of a local voice teacher. Perry subsequently studied at the Juilliard School of Music in New York. Although composition was the area in which she showed the greatest talent, she also studied piano, violin, voice, and conducting. She found conducting a rewarding means of expressing her artistic ideas. She also earned a bachelor's and a master's degree at Westminster Choir College.

Two Guggenheim fellowships afforded Perry the opportunity to study in Europe. The first was awarded in 1952, allowing her to study with Luigi Dallapiccola in Florence (she had studied with him at Tanglewood during the summer of 1951) and with Nadia Boulanger in Paris, during which time she received the Boulanger Grand Prix at Fontainebleau for a viola sonata. The second fellowship, awarded in 1955, permitted additional study with Dallapiccola in Italy. In 1957 Perry organized a concert tour of European cities under the sponsorship of the United States Information Agency. The concerts were acclaimed by a number of European critics.

When Perry returned to the United States she continued to compose and teach. She held positions at Florida A. & M. University in Tallahassee and the Atlanta University Center. Among her prizes are a 1964 American Academy and National Institute of Arts and Letters Award, and a 1969 Honorable Mention in the ASCAP Awards to women composers for symphonic and concert music. An illness necessitated Perry's early retirement, and her last years were spent in seclusion in Akron.

Perry's unconventional style is revealed in *Homunculus C.F.*, a chamber work for percussion, harp, and piano in which she fittingly used a logical structure to contain the unorthodox. The work was composed during the summer of 1960 in Perry's apartment, which was located on the top floor of an office building belonging to her father, a medical doctor. According to Perry's record jacket notes for this piece, the clinical surroundings reminded her of "the medieval laboratory" in which Wagner, Faust's young apprentice in alchemy, fashioned and brought to life "a creature he called *homunculus* (Latin for 'little man')."

Perry used percussion instruments for her musical imitation of a test-tube creation. She maneuvered and distilled them "by means of the chord of the fifteenth (C.F.)" and brought her musical test-tube being to life. The structural chord is built on E and consists of a major third, a perfect fifth, a major seventh (with a minor seventh appearing frequently in one section), a major ninth, an augmented eleventh, a major thirteenth, and an augmented fifteenth. Perry described her work as a "pantonal" composition. *Homunculus C.F.* has four sections: one rhythmic (mm.1–40), one primarily melodic (mm.61–94), one primarily harmonic (mm.95–105), and one that combines these three elements (mm.106–80).

The first half of the first section serves as an introductory passage (mm.1–20). The main feature of this section is a rhythmic canon. Melodic material is introduced by the timpani in a transitional passage beginning at m.41. The third, seventh, and ninth of the structural chord of the fifteenth are also introduced in this transition leading to the second section. The root of the C.F.—the chord of the fifteenth—is presented in the second section. The three tones presented in the transition are continued here, and the fifth is added. A brief chord by the harp (mm.76–80) anticipates the harmonic section.

The third section is based on the E_7 and E_9 chords. The fundamental idea of the work is further demonstrated here as the chord of the fifteenth continues to build. The final section combines the three elements (rhythm, melody, harmony) and continues the presentation of the tones of the C.F. until the entire chord appears in m.177. Great energy and strength are suggested with the ascending pitches, increasing volume, and rapid tempo leading to a sudden climactic ending, which can be equated with birth and the successful completion of the "experiment."

Other works of particular note by Perry include *Stabat Mater* for contralto and string orchestra or string quartet (1951); *Ye Who Seek the Truth,* an anthem for tenor solo, mixed chorus, and organ with text by the composer (1952); *Song of Our Saviour,* an anthem for unaccompanied mixed chorus with text by the composer (1953); *The Cask of Amontillado,* a one-act opera performed at Columbia University in 1954; Symphony No. 1 (1959); *Pastoral,* for flute and string quartet (1962); *The Selfish Giant,* a three-act opera and ballet (1964); and Symphony No. 8 (1968).

Perry's works reflect the variety of sources that formed her musical vocabulary. Her eclectic style makes use of the Black idiom, traditional European techniques, and twentieth-century methods.

Recording

Homunculus C.F. Manhattan Percussion Ensemble, conducted by Paul Price. Composers Recordings, Inc. CRI S-252.

Further Reading

Abdul, Raoul. *Blacks in Classical Music.* New York: Dodd, Mead & Co., 1977.
Green, Mildred Denby. *Black Women Composers: A Genesis.* Boston: Twayne Publishers (a division of G. K. Hall & Co.), 1983. (This essay was adapted from pp. 71–77.)
Southern, Eileen. *Biographical Dictionary of Afro-American and African Musicians.* Westport, CT: Greenwood Press, 1982.
———. *The Music of Black Americans: A History.* New York: W. W. Norton & Co., 1983.

Homunculus C. F.

Julia Perry

*) Xylophone is not transposed

Copyright © 1966 by Southern Music Publishing Co., Inc. All rights reserved. Reprinted by permission.

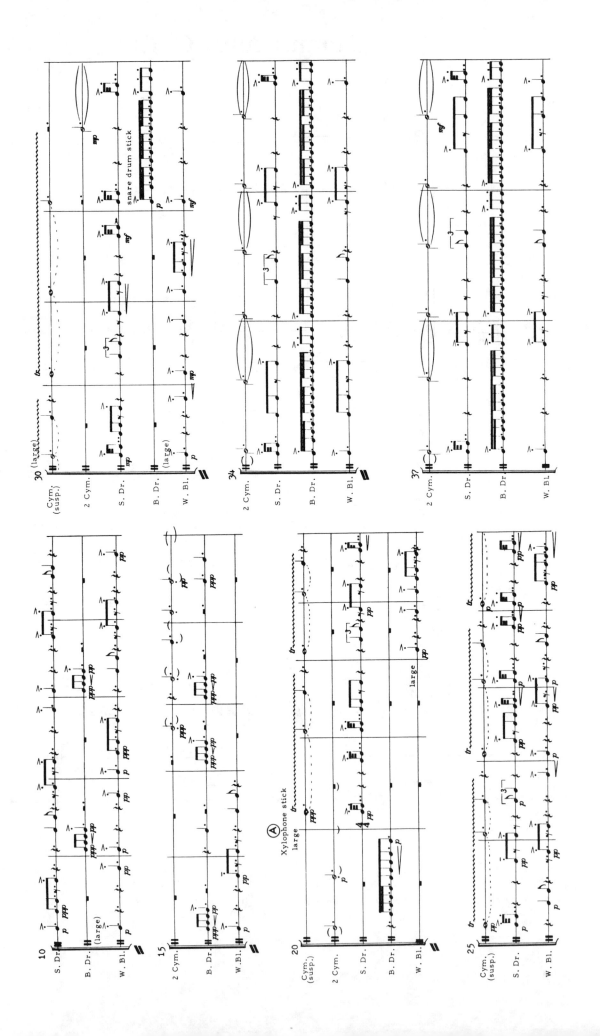

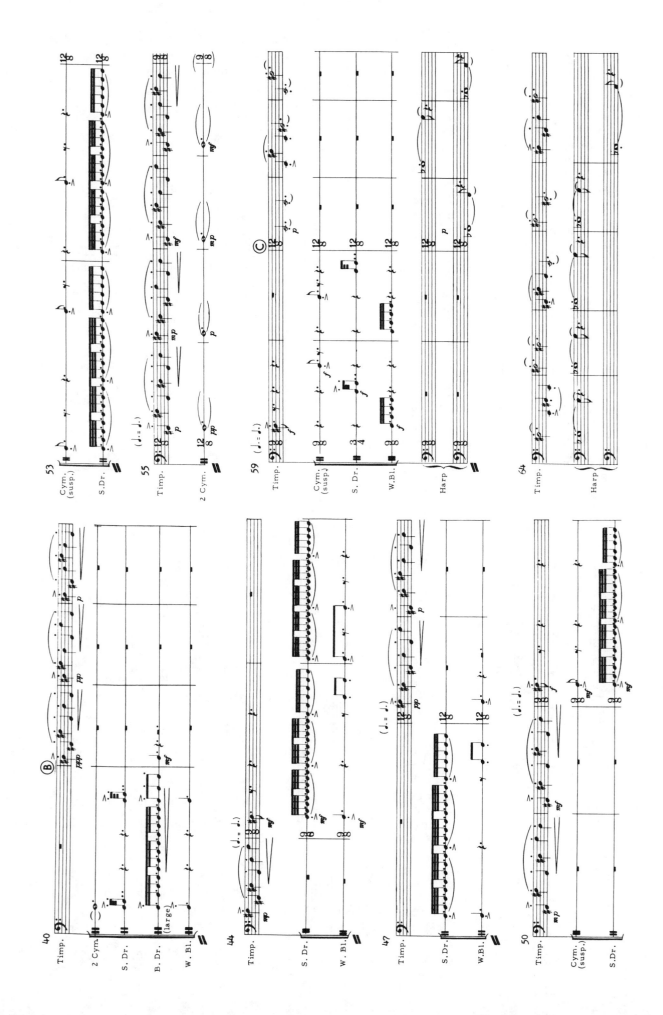

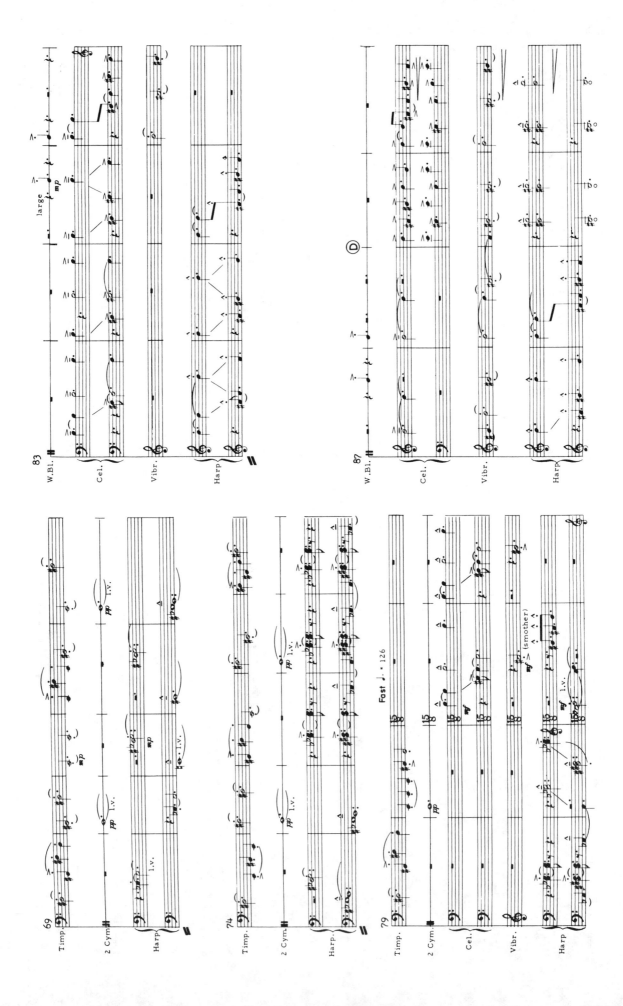

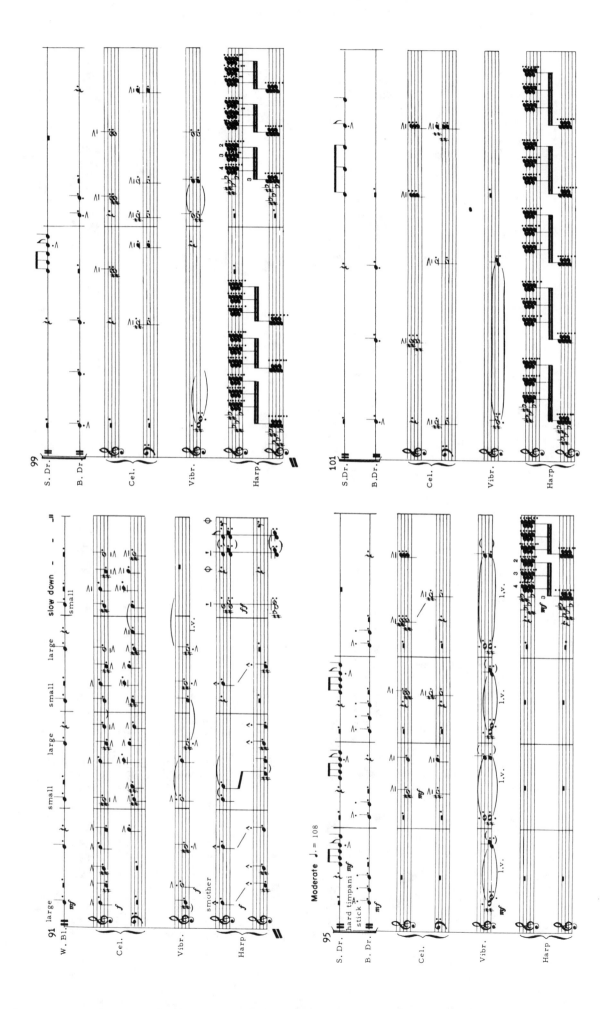

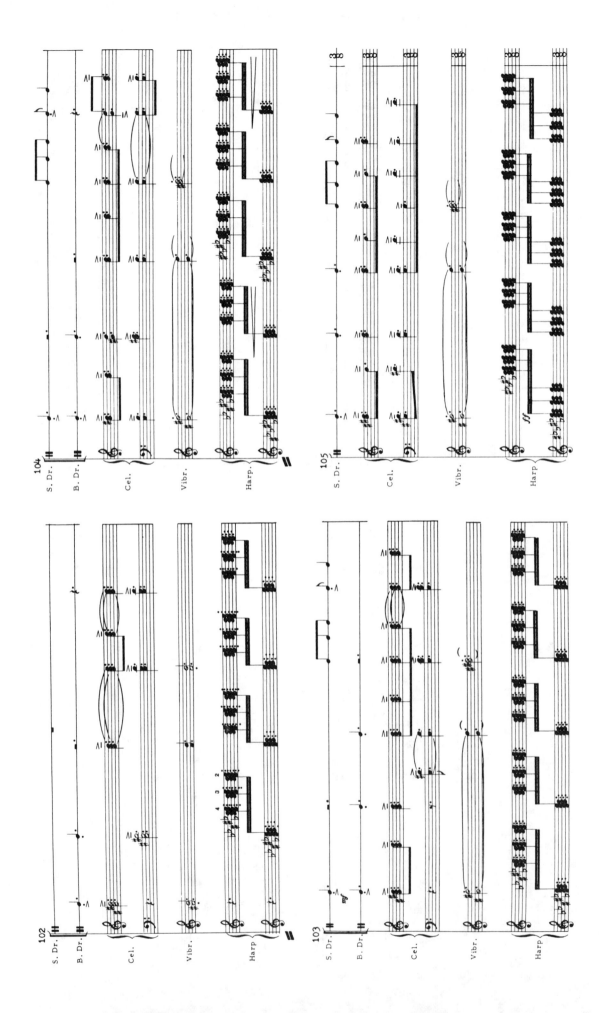

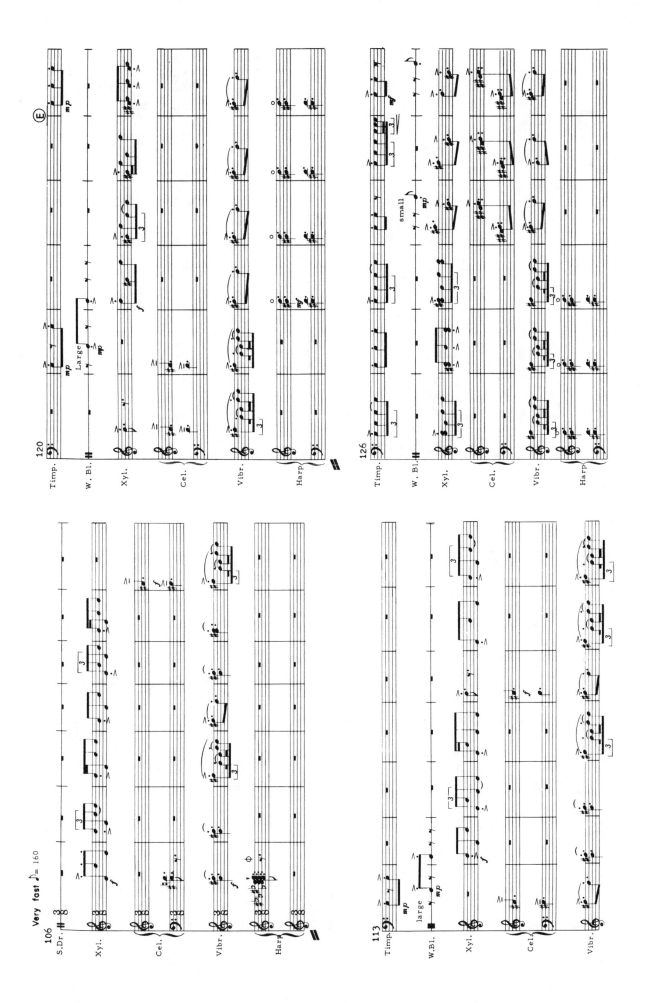

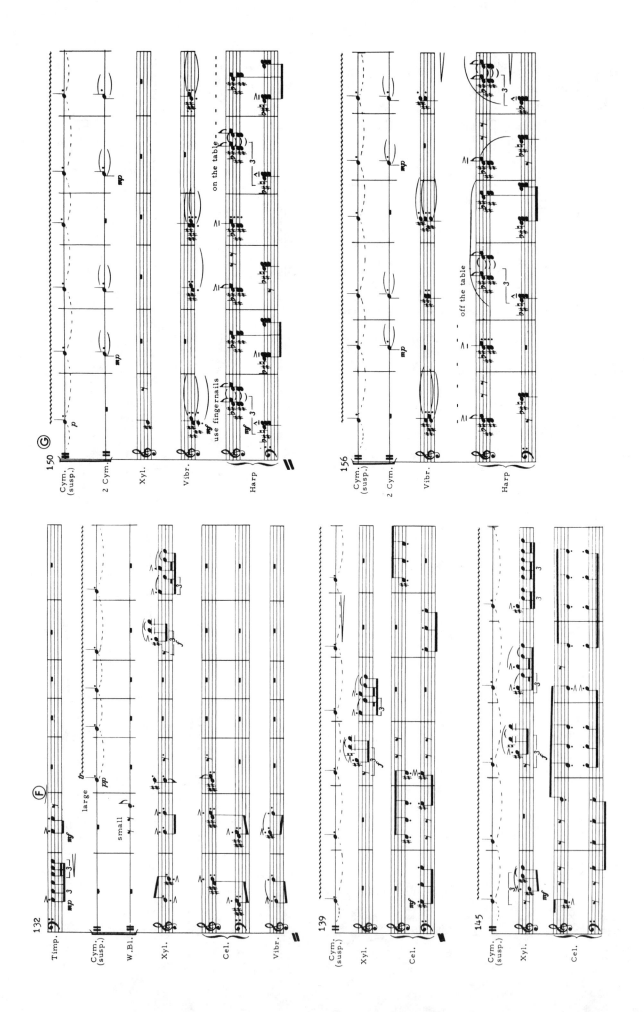

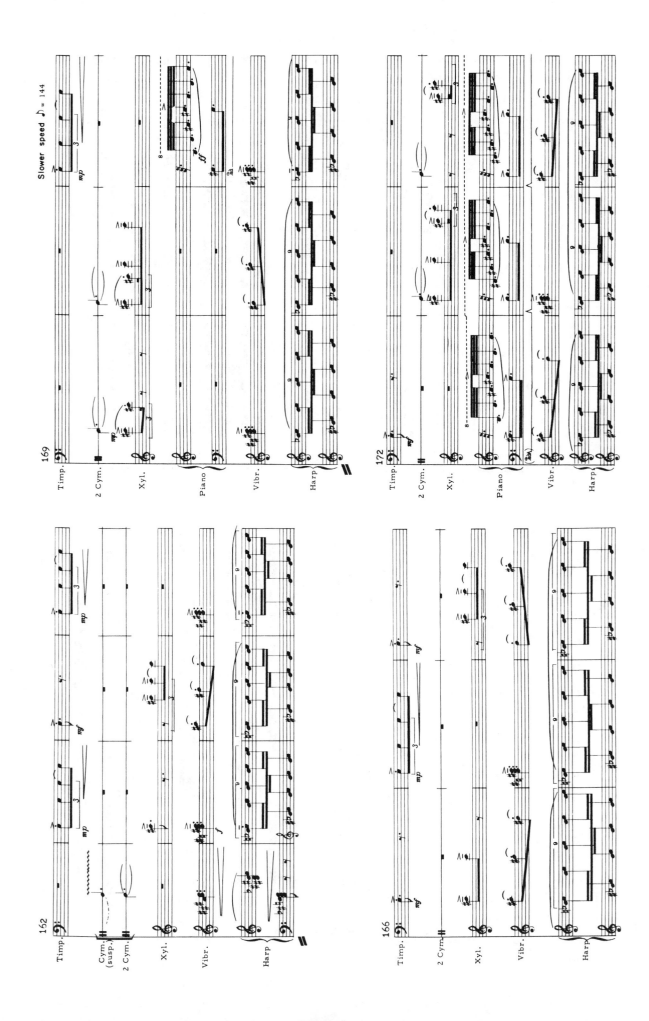

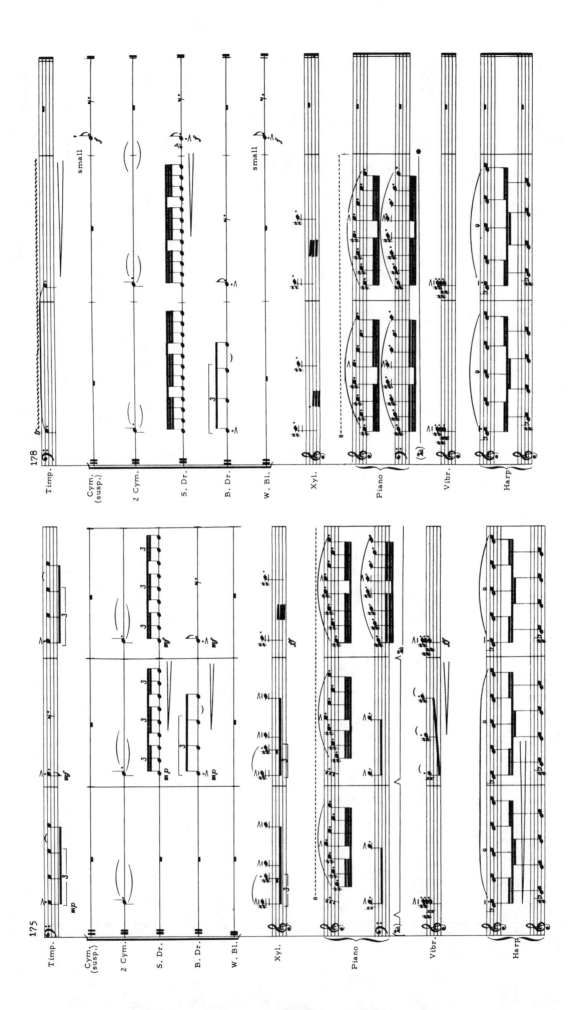

Vivian Fine
(born 1913)

VIVIAN FINE

Vivian Fine was born in Chicago, Illinois, and began to study the piano at the age of five with her mother. In later years her principal piano teachers were Djane Lavoie-Herz and Abby Whiteside. At age twelve Fine began studies of theory and harmony with Ruth Crawford Seeger, and she began to compose at thirteen. Upon moving to New York in 1931, she studied composition with Roger Sessions and orchestration with George Szell. Henry Cowell arranged for her debut as a composer when Fine was sixteen, presenting *Solo for Oboe,* and he saw through her first publication, *Four Songs,* in the New Music Edition in 1933.

Fine was one of the founders of the American Composers Alliance and was its vice-president from 1961 to 1965. She has served as composer and piano accompanist for modern dance groups led by Doris Humphrey, Charles Weidman, and Hanya Holm and has held teaching posts at New York University, the Juilliard School of Music, and the New York State University at Potsdam. Since 1964 she has been a member of the faculty of Bennington College. She was musical director of the Rothschild Foundation from 1953 to 1960, and she received the Dollard Award in 1966 and a Ford Foundation Award in 1970. In 1980 Vivian Fine received a Guggenheim Fellowship and was elected to the American Academy and Institute of Arts and Letters.

Particularly representative of Fine's works are her 1937 composition for the stage, *The Race for Life;* the ballet *Alcestis,* of 1960; and the instrumental works Concertante, for piano and orchestra (1944); Concertino, for piano and percussion (1972); and *Romantic Ode,* for string trio and string orchestra (1976). Her vocal works include *The Great Wall of China* (1947), on a text by Franz Kafka; *Valedictions* (1959), on a text by John Donne; *Morning* (1962), on a text of Henry David Thoreau; and *Paean* (1969), for narrator, female chorus, and brass. Prominent among her more recent vocal works are Missa brevis (1972), for taped voices and four violoncellos; *3 Sonnets* (1976), on poems of John Keats; and *Meeting for Equal Rights 1866* (1976), for soloists, narrator, chorus, and orchestra.

Recent compositions written on commission include *Drama for Orchestra,* by the San Francisco Symphony and premiered in 1983; *Ode to Purcell,* by the Elizabeth Sprague Coolidge Foundation and performed at the Library of Congress in 1985; *Poetic Fires,* by the Koussevitsky Music Foundation and performed in 1985 by the American Composers Orchestra, with the composer as piano soloist and Gunther Schuller as conductor; and *A Song for Saint Cecelia's Day,* by Trinity College and performed in 1985.

345

"Dance of Triumph: The Rescue of Alcestis" is the fourth and final section of the ballet suite *Alcestis*. It was commissioned by Martha Graham and performed by her and her dance company in 1960. The Alcestis myth concerns the sacrifice of Alcestis's life for her husband, Admetus, so that he may thereby attain immortality. As the household of Admetus mourns for Alcestis, Hercules arrives. The news of Alcestis's death is kept from him, and he feasts and drinks in heroic fashion. When he learns from a servant of her death, he seeks out Thanatos (Death) and battles with him for her life. Victorious, Hercules rescues Alcestis and returns her to Admetus.

The movement is marked alla breve, allegro energico, and is scored for woodwinds, brass, timpani, xylophone, piano, harp, and strings. The "Dance of Triumph" involves a rush of energy that subsides only momentarily. It ends with an emphatic punctuation by timpani and piano. The writing is primarily contrapuntal, and the piece attains its expressive purpose largely through the choice of intervals in the separate parts and by the gestural tension between the top and bass lines.

Recording

Alcestis. Composers' Recordings CRI 145.

Further Reading

Riegger, Wallingford, "The Music of Vivian Fine," *American Composers Alliance Bulletin* 8, no. 1 (1958).
"Vivian Fine," *The New Grove Dictionary of Music and Musicians*, VI:564.

Dance of Triumph: The Rescue of Alcestis

Vivian Fine

© 1960 by Vivian Fine. Reprinted with the composer's permission. Published by Catamount Facsimile Edition, Box 245, Shaftsbury, VT 05262.

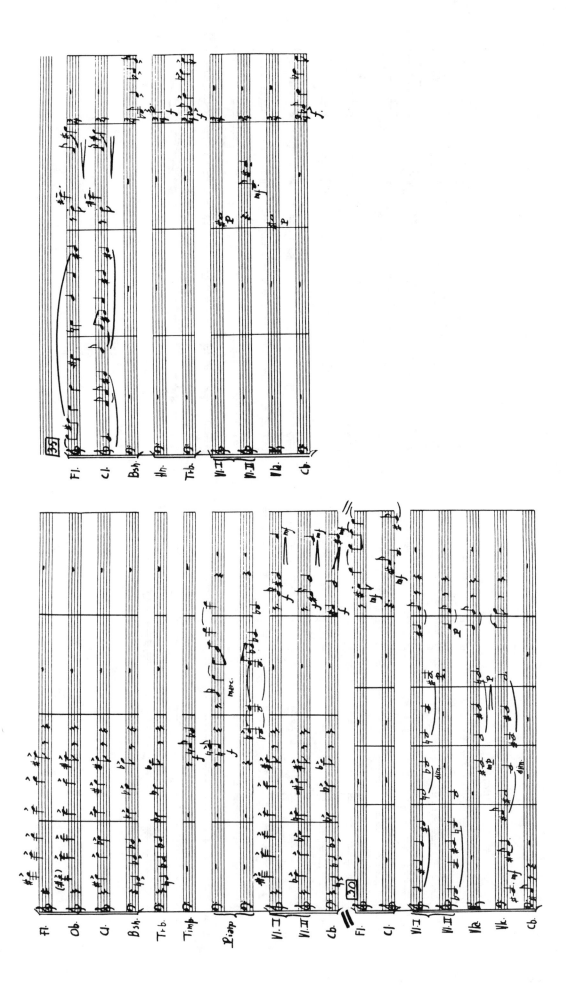

352

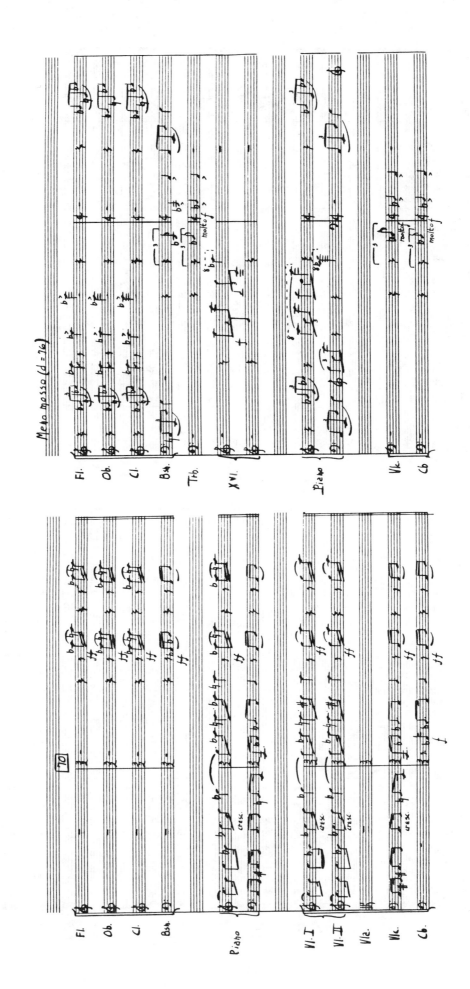

353

354

Violet Archer
(born 1913)

ROBERT WEBER

Violet Archer is both a widely performed composer and a dedicated, influential educator. Admirers of her music point to its melodic vigor and seamless craftsmanship, while her former students credit her with nurturing in them both a formidable technique and an inquiring musical mind. This, together with her tireless promotion of Canadian music, has long made her a prominent participant in Canada's musical life.

Violet Archer was born in Montreal. Her own musical life began early, for she was composing seriously for the piano before she was out of her teens. In 1930 she entered the Conservatory of Music at McGill University, where her teachers included Claude Champagne and Douglas Clarke. To pay her way through school, she took jobs as a chamber musician, accompanist, church organist, and music teacher. Working prevented her from receiving her Bachelor of Music degree and Teacher's Licenciate in piano until 1936, but it gave her varied and valuable experience of practical music making. After graduation, she added composition to her other professional musical activities.

Eventually desiring further study, Violet Archer spent the summer of 1942 in New York as a pupil of Béla Bartók. Bartók's lessons brought a new discipline and economy to her writing, as well as a more sympathetic approach to folk materials. In 1947, she studied with Paul Hindemith at Yale University. Along with his usual emphasis on the practical aspects of composing and music making, Hindemith honed her technique and taught her how to organize her music better. Both Bartók and Hindemith had profound impacts on Violet Archer, and she considers them "the greatest musical minds of this century."

After Yale granted Archer a Master of Music degree in 1949, her academic career began. For the next thirteen years she taught in several American universities. She returned to Canada in 1962, to the fledgling music department of the University of Alberta in Edmonton. Through the efforts of Violet Archer and her colleagues, the department was soon flourishing. Today, many of her former students are successful and active composers both in Canada and abroad. Even though she retired from the university in 1978, her interest in teaching has never flagged, and she remains active in music education.

Violet Archer's creative output is both prodigious and diverse. In 1985 her catalogue numbered over 220 works for many media—from solo flute to full orchestra and chorus. Solo song and choral cycles form an important part of her *oeuvre*, and she has also written two operas, *Sganarelle* (1973) and *The Meal* (1983). From her own powerful style, as influenced by Hindemith and Bartók, she has forged a musical language marked by forceful counterpoint, soaring melodic lines, and traditional forms, which has lately been modified by Expressionist techniques.

Archer's music has been performed worldwide, and among her many awards are an Honorary Doctorate from McGill University (1971), an Honorary Fellowship in the Royal Canadian College of Organists (1985), the Order of Canada (1984), and an Honorary Membership in Sigma Alpha Iota.

The sonata for Alto Saxophone and Piano is one of Archer's most popular chamber works. It was commissioned in 1971, through the Canadian Broadcasting Company, by Paul Brodie, who also recorded the work. The Sonata was premiered in 1972 by Eugene Rousseau at the World Saxophone Congress in Toronto. The saxophone and the piano are equal partners in this piece, which exploits the lyrical quality and wide range of the saxophone. The movements are entitled Preamble (reproduced here), Interlude, Valsette, and Rondo.

The Preamble is cast in sonata form. The first theme appears immediately. Two notes in the first measure of the saxophone part—D–D sharp—reappear at the start of each of the following movements and form a unifying element. The brief second theme contrasts with the first through its slower rhythmic movement. The following development section is drawn largely from the first theme. A dialogue between the saxophone and piano forms the recapitulation, and a short coda completes the movement.

The Interlude is in ternary form and projects a blues feeling through its "swinging" dotted eighth notes and the Gershwinesque parallel chords in the piano. The middle section begins with three notes taken from the climax of the opening theme.

The opening phrase of the Valsette expands the D–D sharp motif from a semitone to an augmented octave. This charming movement is formally quite strict, based solidly on the eighteenth-century minuet.

The opening figure of the Rondo borrows both the D–D sharp motif and the rhythmic figure from the Preamble. Following the opening statement, the Rondo goes through two digressions, the first animated and the second lyrical. Both are derived from the main theme, as are the transitional materials between the sections. A register shift in the last return of the theme heightens the tension moving into the final cadence and serves as a coda.

Recording

Sonata for Alto Saxophone and Piano. Paul Brodie, saxophone; George Brough, piano. Radio Canada International. RCI 412.

Sonata for Alto Saxophone and Piano

Violet Archer

Reprinted by permission of the publishers, Berandol Music, Ltd., Toronto.

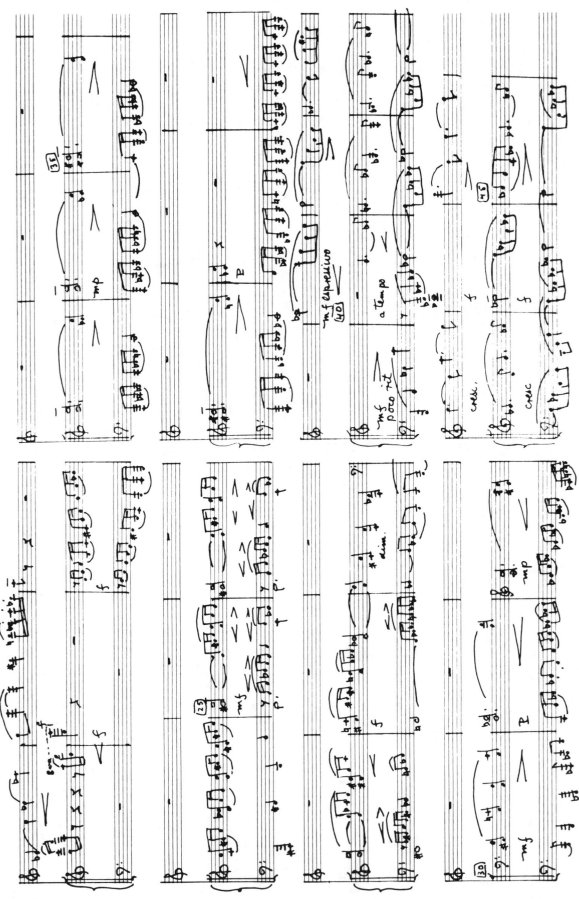

358

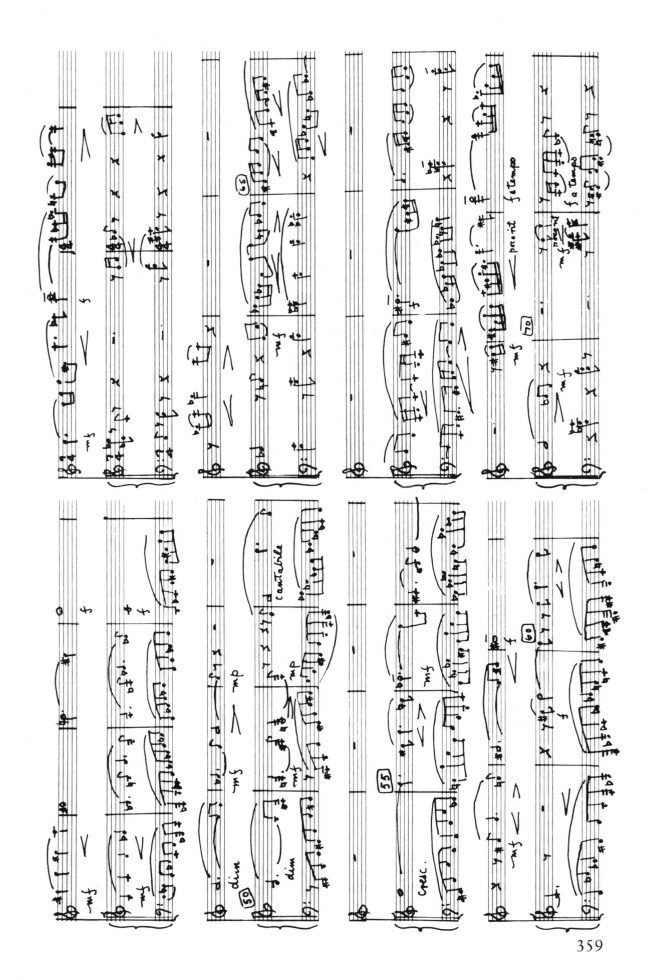

359

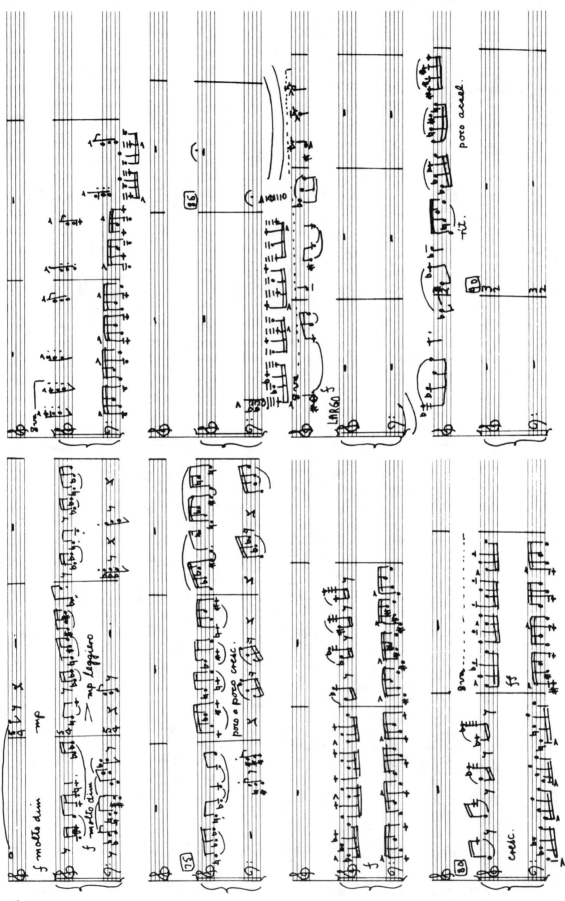

360

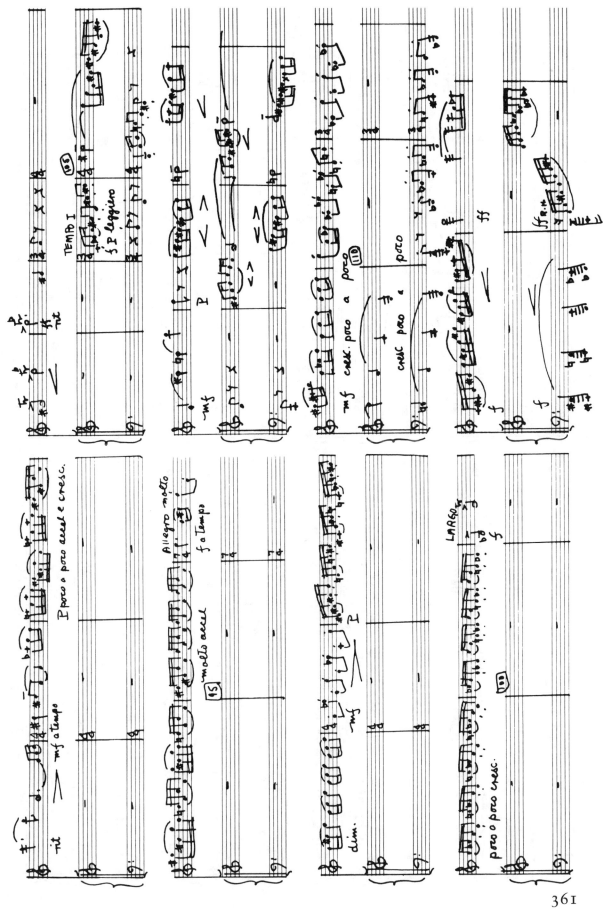

361

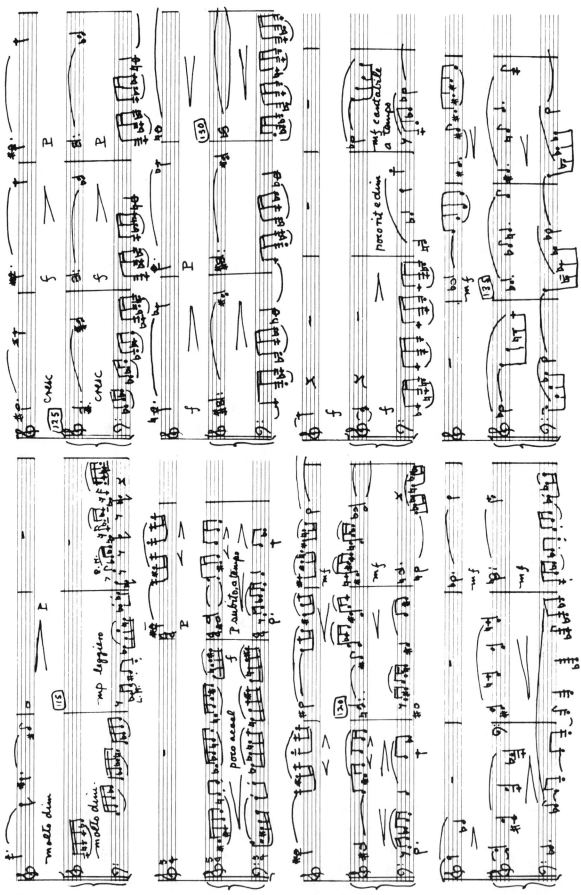

362

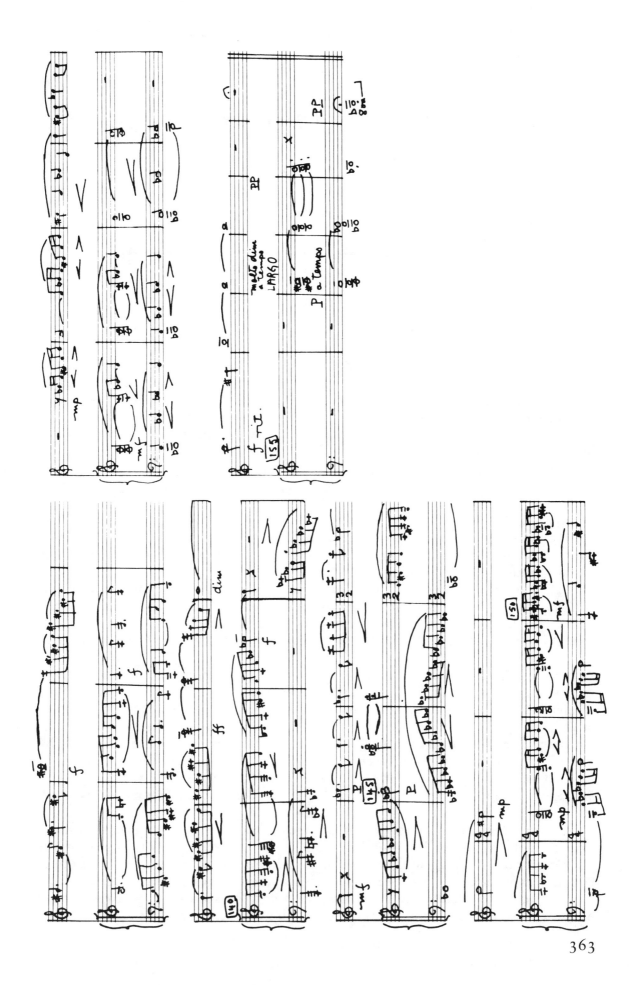

363

Pauline Oliveros
(born 1932)

HEIDI VON GUNDEN

Pauline Oliveros is a contemporary American composer who has written experimental compositions in the areas of improvisation, electronic music, theater music, ceremonial music, and sonic meditations. She is best known for her *Sonic Meditations*, and the three selected for this anthology are among the easier ones; anyone can perform and understand them regardless of previous experience with meditative techniques.

At an early age Oliveros knew that she wanted to be a composer. Since both her mother and her grandmother made their living by teaching piano, it did not seem unusual that she should pursue a musical career. At age nineteen she left her home in Houston, Texas, and moved to San Francisco in search of a composition teacher. During the early 1950s Oliveros decided that she would try to be always aware of what she heard. This dedication to listening is evident in all her compositions, especially in the *Sonic Meditations.*

The numerous articles Oliveros has written about her music are collected in *Software for People.* Of special interest in this volume are her articles "And Don't Call Them 'Lady' Composers," which was first published in *The New York Times* on September 13, 1970, and "On Sonic Meditation," which discusses "Teach Yourself to Fly."

Oliveros's credentials are impressive. In 1962 her composition *Sound Patterns* (1961) for *a cappella* mixed chorus won the Gaudeamus prize in Holland for the Best Foreign Work. From 1967 to 1980 Oliveros was a faculty member at the University of California, San Diego. At the time of her resignation she was a full professor, an amazing accomplishment in academe, as Oliveros has only a bachelor's degree. She has received awards from the Guggenheim Foundation and the city of Bonn, Germany; has had her music performed at several world's fairs; and has been guest composer at many festivals and universities. Currently she lives at Mount Tremper, New York, and is a free-lance composer.

The 24 *Sonic Meditations* reflect Oliveros's interest in consciousness studies, karate (she holds a black belt), world religions, and world music. Oliveros considers the *Meditations* to be physically beneficial because they can produce a calming effect and heightened states of awareness. Most of the *Meditations* are for voice, although several can be translated into instrumental sound. The scores are in prose and are explained in short, clear statements. Each score must be carefully studied and constantly checked to ensure that the correct interpretation is being followed, because performers often try to substitute something different, an idea of their own that the *Meditations* might have suggested to them.

In "Teach Yourself to Fly", *Sonic Meditation I*, the performers' attention is focused on breathing. The result of this tuning is that involuntary sounds begin to be made; the performers do not consciously try to make sounds. This meditation resembles waves of sound and should last at least fifteen minutes, so that all the performers have an opportunity to experience the effects of observing the breath:

> Any number of persons sit in a circle facing the center. Illuminate the space with dim blue light. [It would be possible to perform this meditation without the dim blue light.] Begin by simply observing your own breathing. Always be an observer. Gradually allow your breathing to become audible. Then gradually introduce your voice. Allow your vocal cords to vibrate in any mode which occurs naturally. Allow the intensity to increase very slowly. Continue as long as possible naturally, and until all others are quiet, always observing your own breath cycle.
> Variation: Translate voice to an instrument.

This meditation is simple to perform, although it helps to have an experienced leader who can begin the meditation. It will not take long before others join.

Each meditation is a prescribed tuning for hearing sound. During "Zina's Circle" one actively makes sound. Some of the other meditations require imagining sound, listening to present sound, or remembering past sound. Each one uses either active or passive listening and sound making, and some can be complex. "Tumbling Song" and "Zina's Circle" specify active listening.

"Tumbling Song," *Meditation XIV*, should consist only of descending gestures. The score is as follows:

> Make any vocal sound, but always go downward in pitch from the initial attack. The initial attack may begin at any pitch level. Go downward in a glissando or in discrete steps continuously. Go any distance in range, at any speed, dynamic or quality, but the breath determines the maximum time length of any downward gesture.

The performers should observe the duration of their breath, which determines phrase lengths. Therefore, phrases will not be the same, and some will overlap because not everyone will begin at the same time. Also, as "Tumbling Song" progresses, the phrases will become longer, because observation causes the breath to become lower, slower, and deeper.

Depending on the number of performers, there will be a variety of descending gestures, which are like ribbons of sound. Ideally there should be no audience, because everyone can participate. During a performance of "Tumbling Song" people will discover new ways to use their voices, and all should be aware of the sounds of the moment. Deviations from these directions will produce an improvisation, a performance mode that Oliveros does not intend. In an improvisation performers imitate and are affected by each other, thus limiting the sonic vocabulary. Simply observing the breath will protect "Tumbling Song" and the other meditations from becoming improvisations.

"Zina's Circle," *Meditation XV*, demands intense concentration even though the actions are simple. Breaks in the sound, hesitation, and laughter are indications that

The scores for "Teach Yourself to Fly," "Tumbling Song," and "Zina's Circle" copyright © 1974 by Smith Publications. Used with permission.

the directions are not being followed, whereas an alert awareness of sound, a feeling of ensemble precision, and a renewal of energy are signs that the meditation is being properly performed:

> Stand together in a circle, with eyes closed facing the center. One person is designated the transmitter. After observing the breathing cycle, individually, gradually join hands. Then slowly move back so that all arms are stretched out and the size of the circle increased. Next stretch the arms towards center and move in slowly. Finally move back to the normal sized circle, with hands still joined, standing so that arms are relaxed at sides. Return attention to breathing. When the time seems right, the transmitter starts a pulse that travels around the circle, by using the right hand to squeeze the left hand of the person next to her. [The directions were originally written for a performance group called ♀, the Women's Ensemble.] The squeeze should be quickly and sharply made, to resemble a light jolt of electricity. The squeeze must be passed from left hand to right hand and so on to the next person as quickly as possible. The action should become so quick that it happens as a reflex, before the person has time to consciously direct the squeeze. Simultaneously with the squeeze, each person must shout *had*. This shout must come up from the center of the body (somewhere a little below the navel) before passing through the throat. There must be complete abdominal support for the voice. When the first cycle is complete, the transmitter waits for a long time to begin the next cycle. When the reaction time around the circle has become extremely short, the transmitter makes the cycles begin closer and closer together until a new transmission coincides with the end of the cycle, then continue trying to speed up the reaction time. If attention and awareness are maintained, the circle depending on its size, should be shouting almost simultaneously.
> Variations: 1. Reverse the direction of the pulse using the left hand to transmit and the right hand to receive. 2. Reverse the direction of each cycle. 3. Each person chooses which direction to send the pulse. The transmitter continues to control the beginning and ending of a cycle.

Further Reading

Oliveros, Pauline. *Software for People.* Baltimore: Smith Publications, 1981.

Turek, Ralph. *Analytical Anthology of Music.* New York: Knopf, 1984. Contains score of *Sound Patterns.*

Von Gunden, Heidi. *The Music of Pauline Oliveros.* Metuchen, NJ: Scarecrow Press, 1983.

Thea Musgrave
(born 1928)

JAMES R. BRISCOE

Scottish composer and conductor Thea Musgrave was born in Barnton, Midlothian. After graduation from Edinburgh University, she studied composition in Paris with Nadia Boulanger, from 1950 to 1954. Many of her early works were composed on commission and were of an expanded diatonic idiom. These include *Suite o'Bairnsangs*, written for the British Broadcasting Corporation, and the chamber opera *The Abbot of Drimock.*

After her return from Paris, Musgrave's style turned toward chromaticism and abstraction in form, as seen in her *Piano Sonata* and *String Quartet.* By the end of the 1950s, Musgrave had adopted serialism, and she had come to represent fully the mainstream of British composition in that regard and in her disavowal of the experimental avant-garde.

Her opera *The Decision* was staged by the New Opera Company in 1967. According to *The New Grove,* this work "forced an extroversion which her earlier works generally lacked, and the benefit is apparent in most of Musgrave's subsequent work." The 1960s saw a spate of commissions for major works, such as the Clarinet Concerto, for the Royal Philharmonic Society, and the Viola Concerto, for the BBC, first performed by her husband, Peter Mark. Musgrave has explained her concept of "dramatic-abstract" procedures in certain innovative instrumental compositions of the 1960s as "dramatic in presentation and abstract because of the absence of a program." One such work is *From One to Another,* which uses a prerecorded tape in conjunction with a solo viola.

Thea Musgrave is now a resident of the United States. Increasingly active as a conductor of her own works, she conducted her opera *Mary, Queen of Scots* at its premiere in August 1977 at the Edinburgh International Festival and again in 1979 with the Spring Opera Theater in San Francisco. *Mary, Queen of Scots* was first performed in the United States by the Virginia Opera Association, and it has had subsequent performances in New York, Chicago, London, and Stuttgart.

In his review for *The Spectator* concerning the Edinburgh premiere, Rodney Milnes stated:

> Against all odds it has a better chance of becoming established in the repertory than any new work seen here in the last ten years. . . . Musgrave's musical language, vaguely post-Britten, eschews the angular declamation that has been so depressing a characteristic of contemporary opera. . . . This is a twentieth-century *grand opera,* and it works.

367

Andrew Porter in *The New Yorker* added his accolades following the United States premiere:

> I found myself forgetting the careful planning, the parallels, the influences, and instead caring very much about Mary herself—move by move, event by event— and being at the same time rapt in the music, intent on the movement of the melodic lines, calmed or excited by the shifting patterns of harmonic tension, and stirred by the colors of the score. There is a visionary quality in *Mary.*

As with Wagner's operas, the remarkable dramatic force of *Mary, Queen of Scots* derives largely from a single authorship of both music and libretto. Musgrave based the latter on the play *Moray* by Emilia Elguera:

> Writing my own libretto has given me a heightened sensitivity to the perennial question of balance between musical and dramatic elements in opera: I wanted my opera to have vitality and depth; and I needed to find the right delicate balance between them. To achieve this I worked in the following way. After making the initial outline and sketching out a complete draft, I decided to leave detailed working out until I came to write the music. Thus the libretto could reflect the demands made by the music and vice versa. . . . In fact I was rewriting the libretto right up to the day the opera was finished.

Mary Stuart (1542–1587) was aptly called by her cousin Elizabeth I "the daughter of debate." The rightful heir to the throne of Scotland, Mary grew up in France and married the boy king François II. She returned to Scotland at age nineteen, already a widow. As a Roman Catholic she was unwelcome to many, Scotland having been led toward Protestantism by the forceful preacher John Knox. She first married the widely hated Lord Darnley and, following his murder, her cousin Henry Stuart. The Scottish nobles imprisoned Mary, but she escaped to England. There, however, Elizabeth feared her as second in line to the throne, placed her in confinement for eighteen years, and finally had her executed. In the composer's words,

> The whole work revolves around Mary, her personality expressed through the situations in which she finds herself. There is her marriage to Darnley, which goes wrong so soon; her stormy relationship with Bothwell; and all the confrontations with her brother James, each vying to gain . . . ultimate power and control. It is a struggle to the death. Mary is a tragic figure yet vitally alive.

The excerpt given here represents Mary at her most determined moment, when she vows to rely on her own inner resources and to reign without the aid of her presumed allies, who have deceived her at every turn.

Recording

Mary, Queen of Scots. Virginia Opera Association, Peter Mark, conductor. Moss Music Group, 1979.

Further Reading

Walsh, S. "Thea Musgrave," in *The New Grove Dictionary of Music and Musicians.*

Monologue of Mary, from Act III of *Mary, Queen of Scots*

Thea Musgrave

Reprinted from the vocal score by permission of Novello and Company Limited.

370

372

374

Ellen Taaffe Zwilich
(born 1939)

ELLEN TAAFFE ZWILICH
with BRUCE CREDITOR

Ellen Taaffe Zwilich was born in Miami, Florida. She studied at Florida State University and at the Juilliard School, where her major teachers were Roger Sessions and Elliott Carter. She received the 1983 Pulitzer Prize in music for her Symphony No. 1. Among her other principal works are *Symposium for Orchestra; Chamber Symphony; Sonata in Three Movements*, for violin and piano; the song cycle *Einsame Nacht; String Quartet 1974; Passages*, for soprano and instrumental ensemble (or chamber orchestra); *String Trio;* and *Divertimento*, for flute, clarinet, violin, and cello. Her *Celebration for Orchestra* was commissioned in 1984 by the Indianapolis Symphony Orchestra to inaugurate its new hall, Circle Theatre.

In addition to concert and radio performances in the United States and Europe, Zwilich's music has been heard at such major festivals as the International Society for Contemporary Music "World Music Days," the Edinburgh Festival, the Aspen Music Festival, the Festival of Contemporary Music at Tanglewood, and the Gulbenkian Festival in Portugal. Zwilich has received grants from, among others, the Guggenheim Foundation, the Martha Baird Rockefeller Fund for Music, the National Endowment for the Arts, and the Norlin Foundation. Her awards include the Gold Medal of the G. B. Viotti Annual International Competition in Vercelli, Italy; the Elizabeth Sprague Coolidge Chamber Music Prize; and the Ernst von Dohnanyi Citation.

Symphony No. 1 (Three Movements for Orchestra) was commissioned by the American Composers Orchestra and the National Endowment for the Arts. It also had the support of the Guggenheim Foundation. The symphony was premiered on May 5, 1982 by the American Composers Orchestra conducted by Gunther Schuller, in Alice Tully Hall, New York. About her work the composer has written:

> Symphony No. 1 grew out of several of my most central music concerns. First, I have long been interested in the elaboration of large-scale works from the initial material. This "organic" approach to musical form fascinates me both in the development of the material and in the fashioning of a musical idea that contains the "seeds" of the work to follow.

Adapted from the Foreword to Symphony No. 1.

Second, in my recent works I have been developing techniques that combine modern principles of continuous variation with older (but still immensely satisfying) principles, such as melodic and pitch recurrence and clearly defined areas of contrast.

Finally, Symphony No. 1 was written with great affection for the modern orchestra, not only for its indescribable richness and variety of color, but also for the virtuosity and artistry of its players.

The first movement begins in a contemplative mood, with a "motto": three statements of a rising minor third, marked accelerando. Each time the "motto" appears in the first movement, an accelerando occurs, prompting slight evolutions of character until an Allegro section is established. After the Allegro, the movement subsides in tempo and ends as quietly as it began.

Unlike the first movement, the second and third movements are cast in traditional molds: song form and rondo form, respectively. The material is, however, subject to continuous variation.

Throughout the entire Symphony, the melodic and harmonic implications of the first fifteen bars of the first movement are explored. My aim was to create a rich harmonic palette and a wide variety of melodic gestures, all emanating from a simple source.

Recording

Symphony No. 1, Prologue and Variations, and *Celebration for Orchestra.* Indianapolis Symphony Orchestra, John Nelson, conductor. New World Records.

Symphony No. 1
(Three Movements for Orchestra)

Ellen Taaffe Zwilich

Copyright © 1983 by Margun Music, Inc. Reprinted by permission of the publisher.

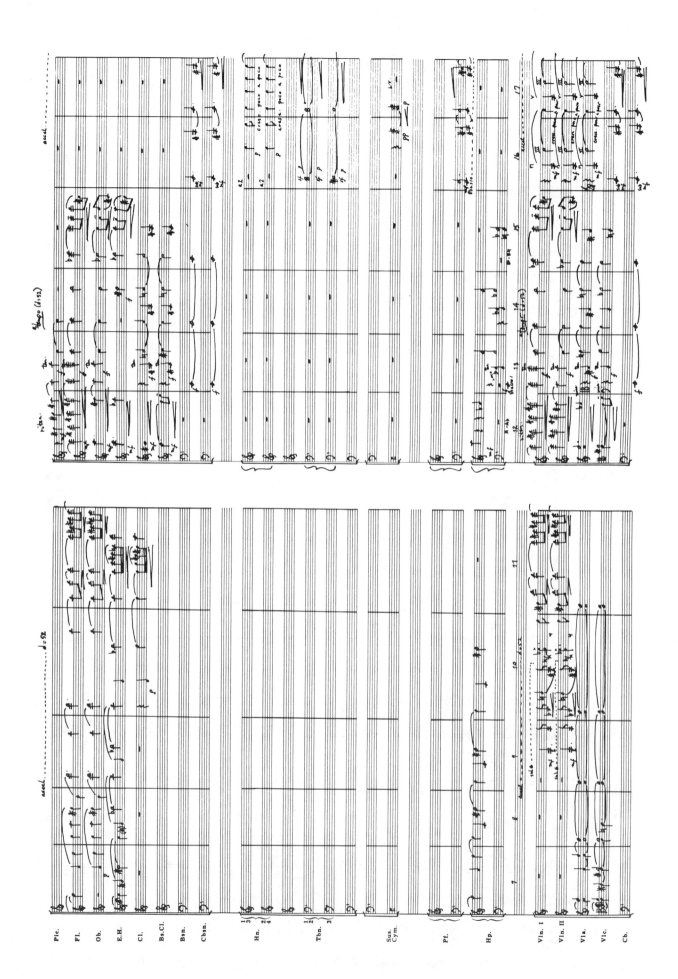

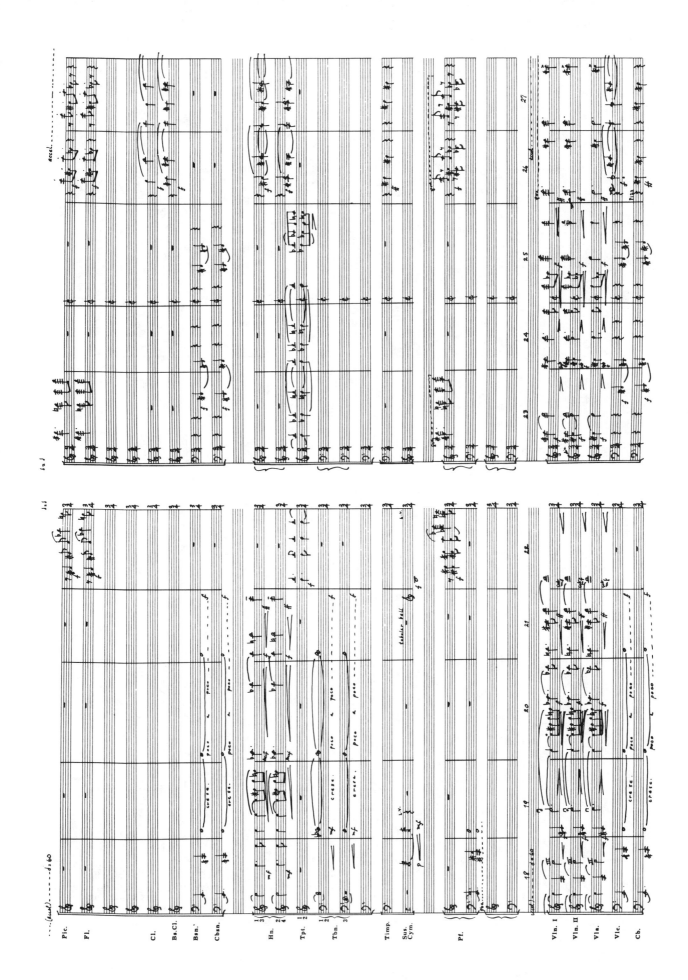

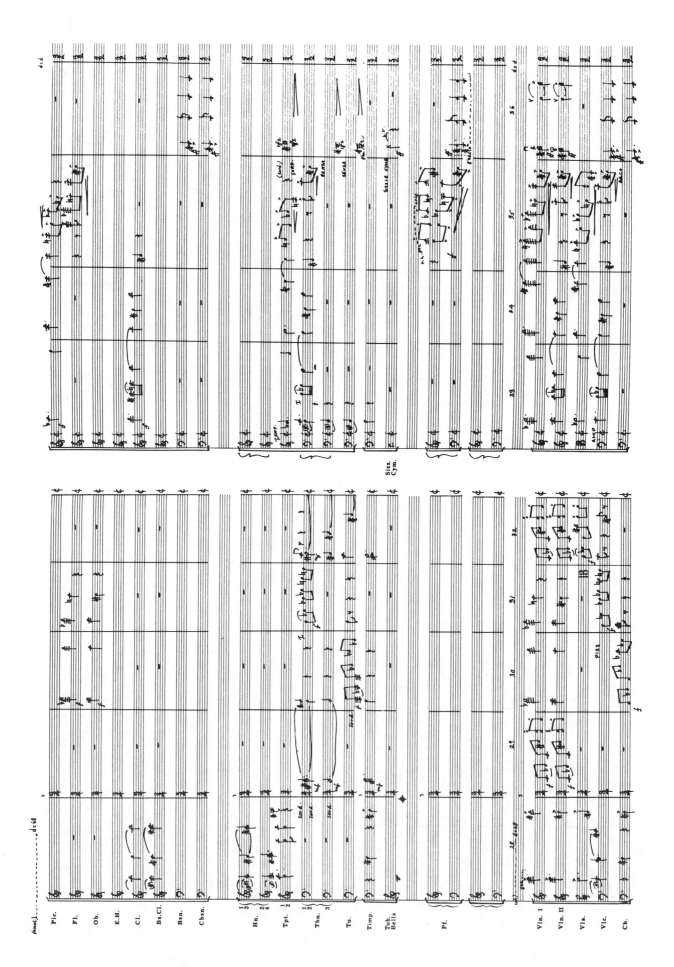

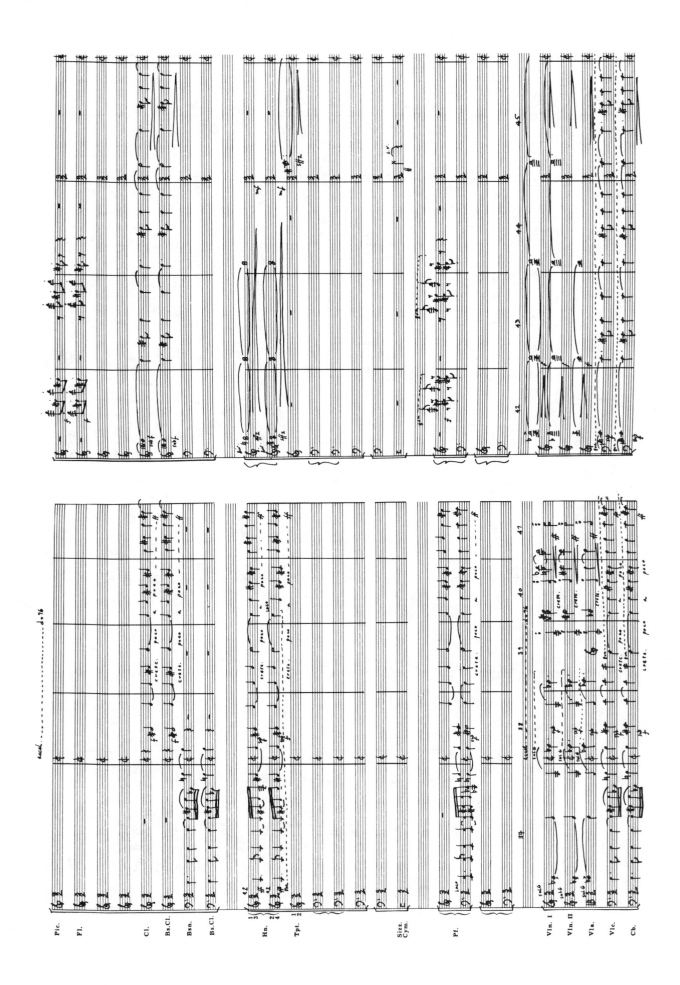

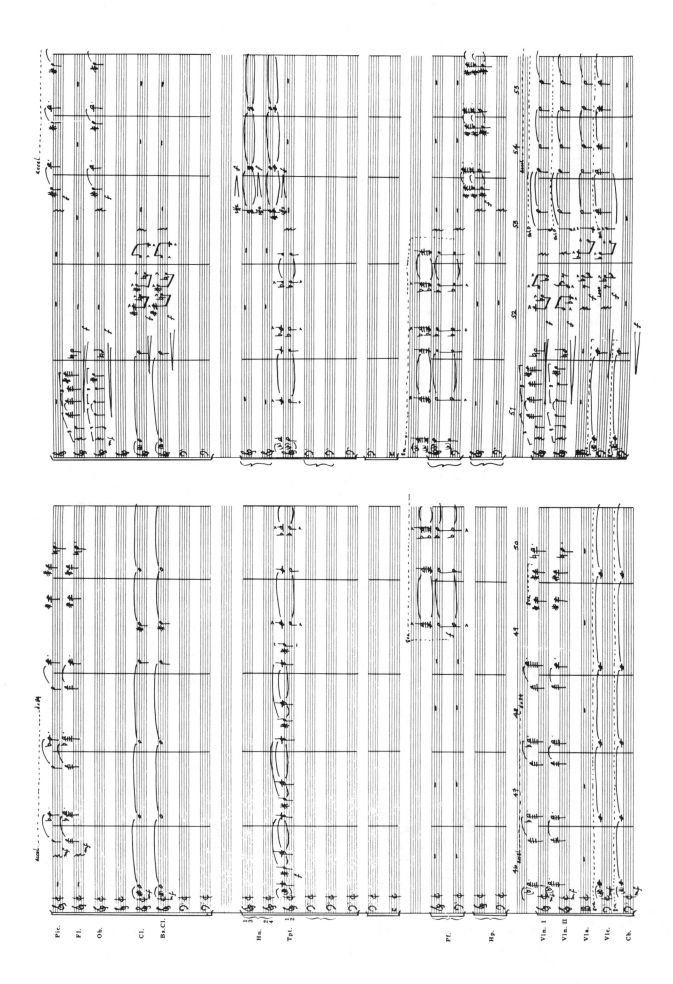

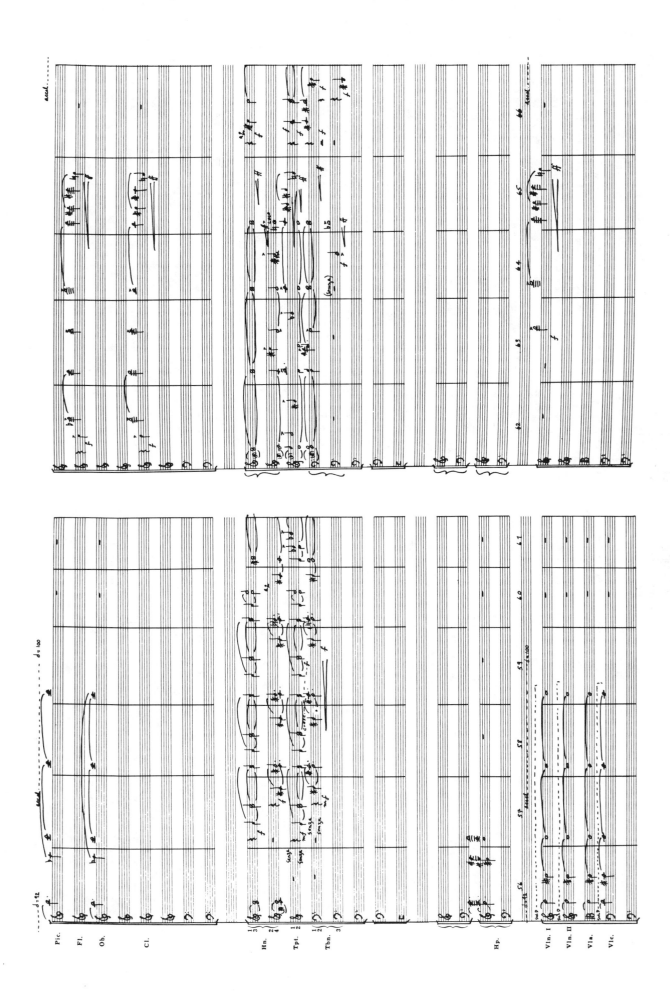

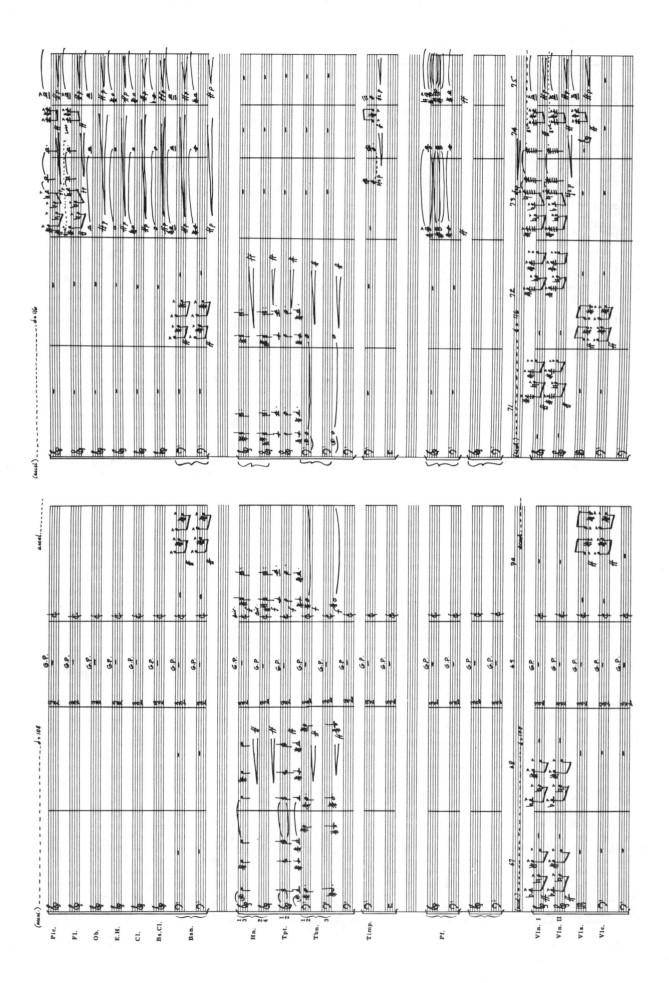

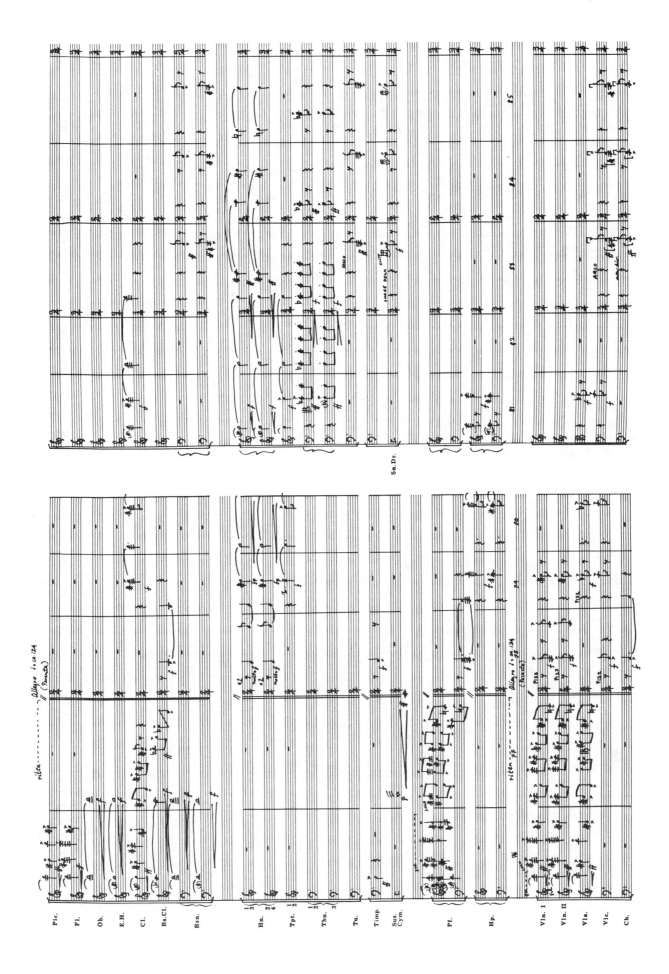

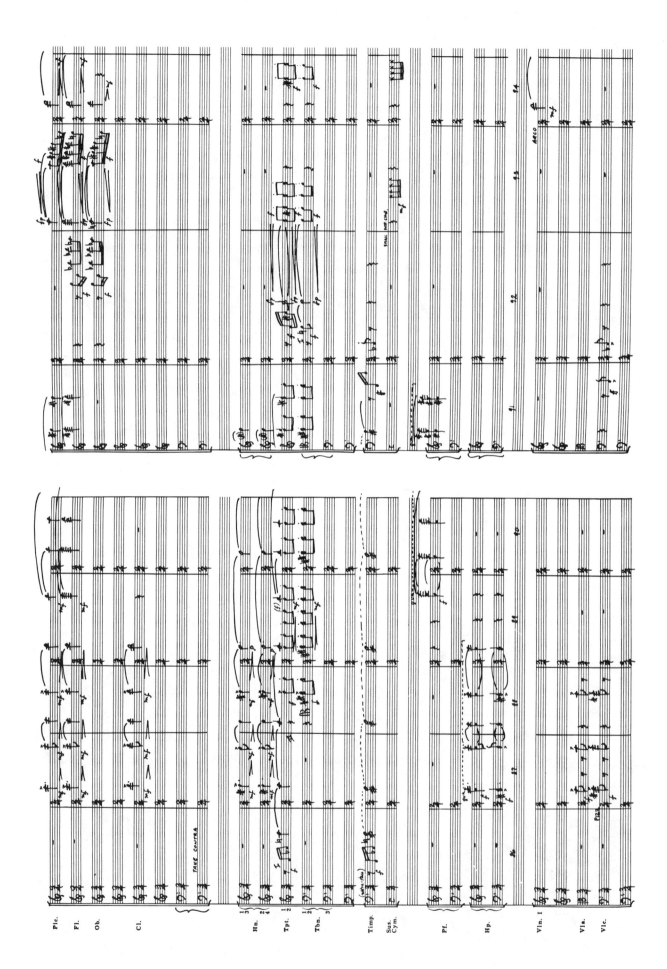

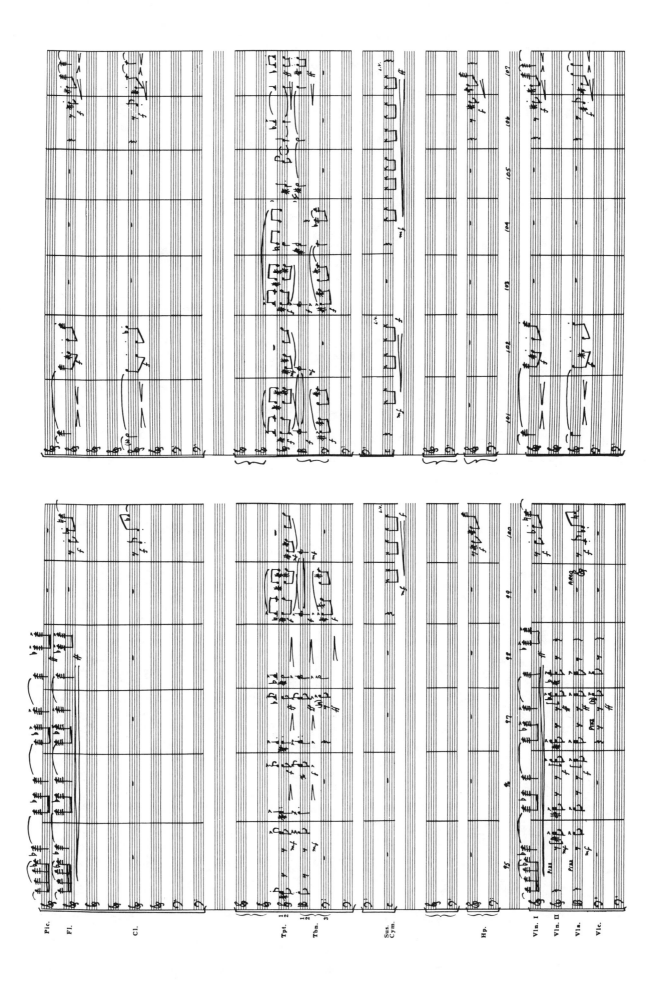

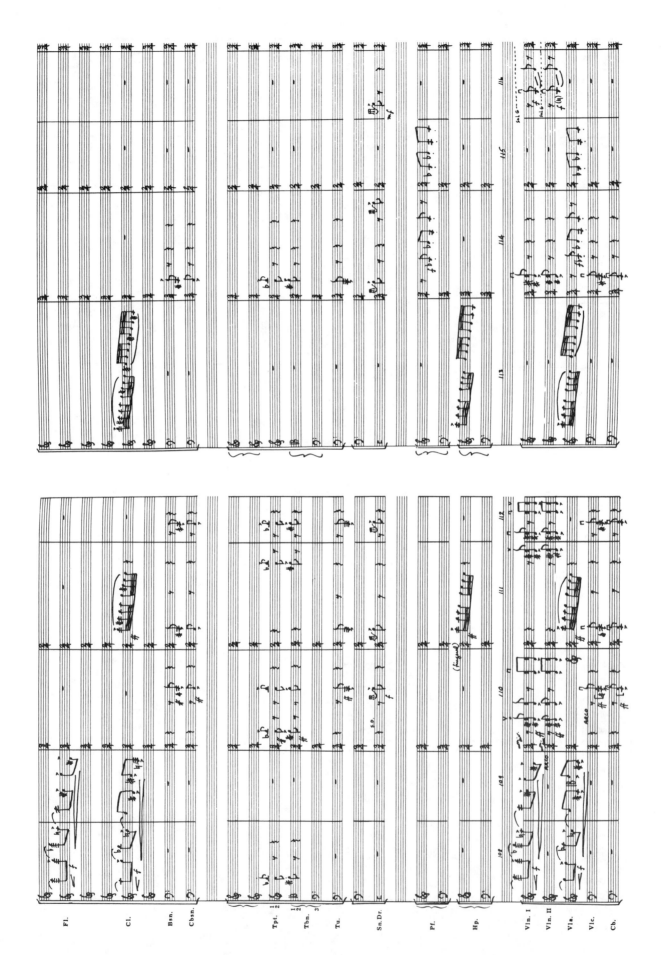

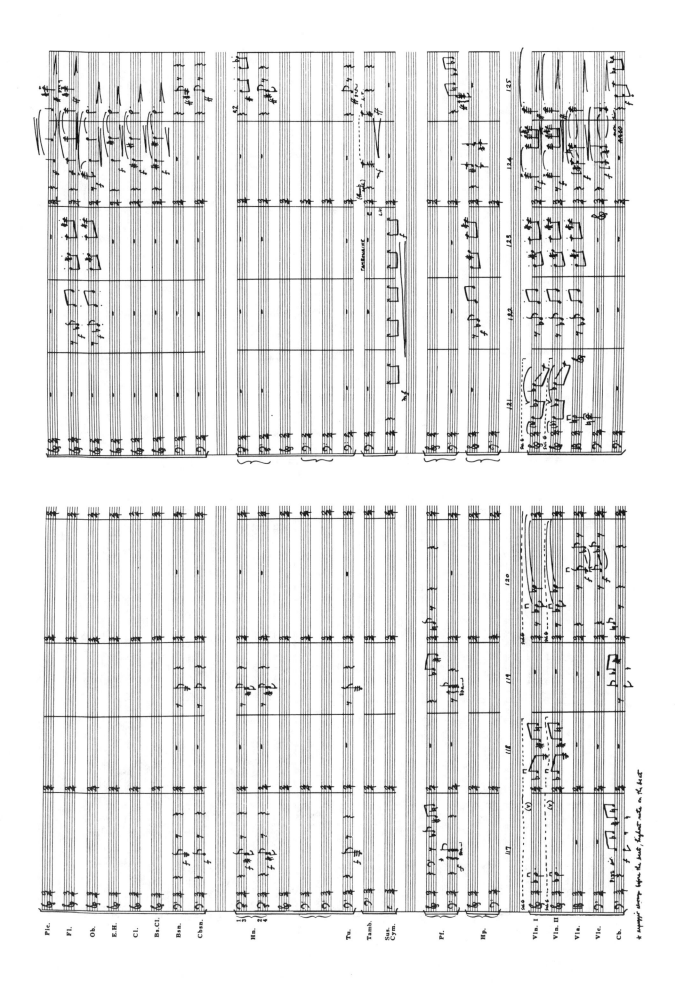

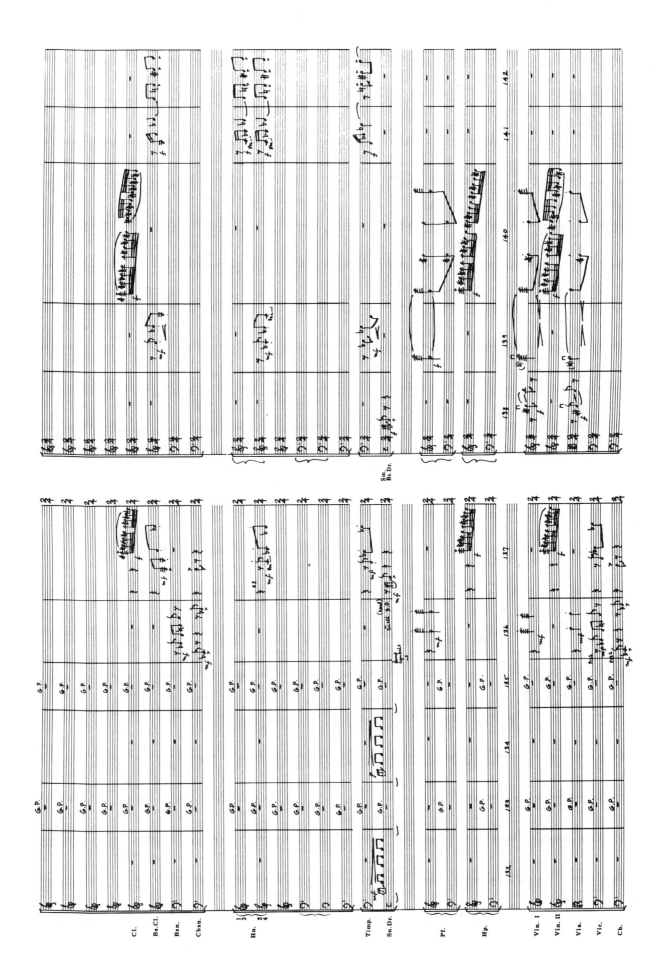

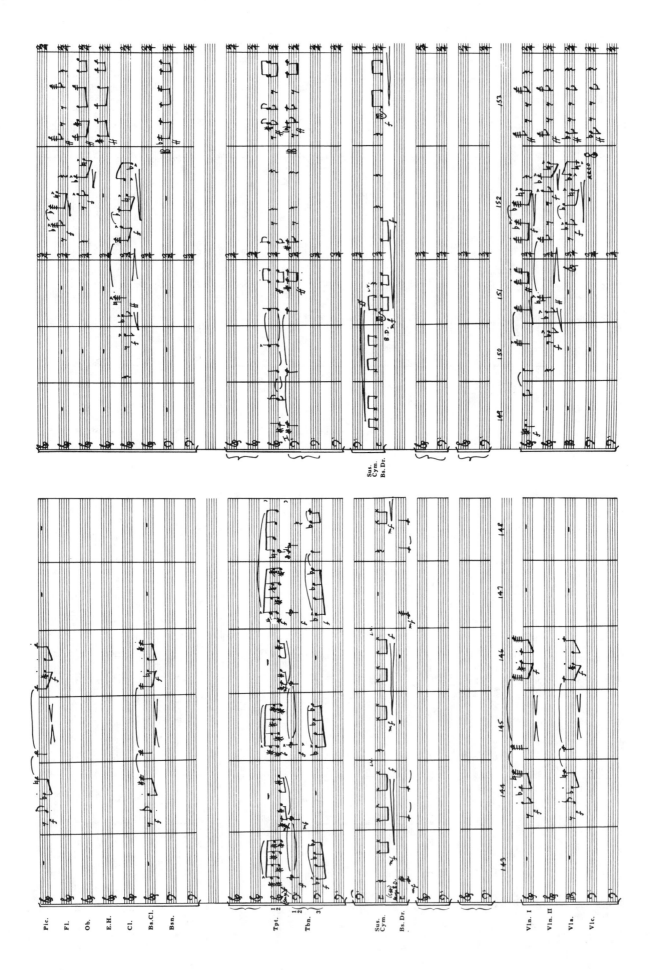

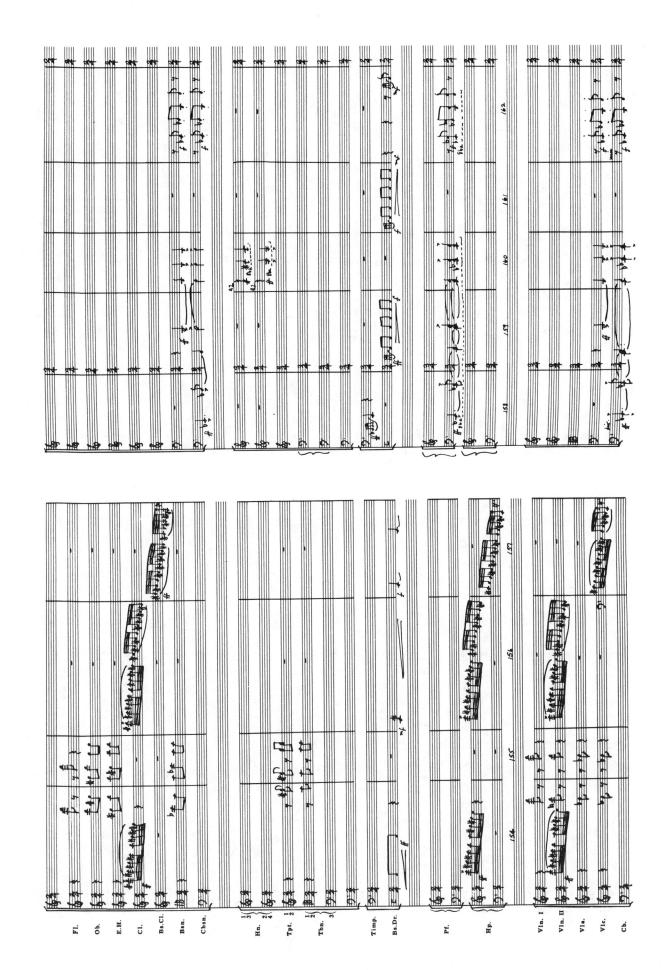

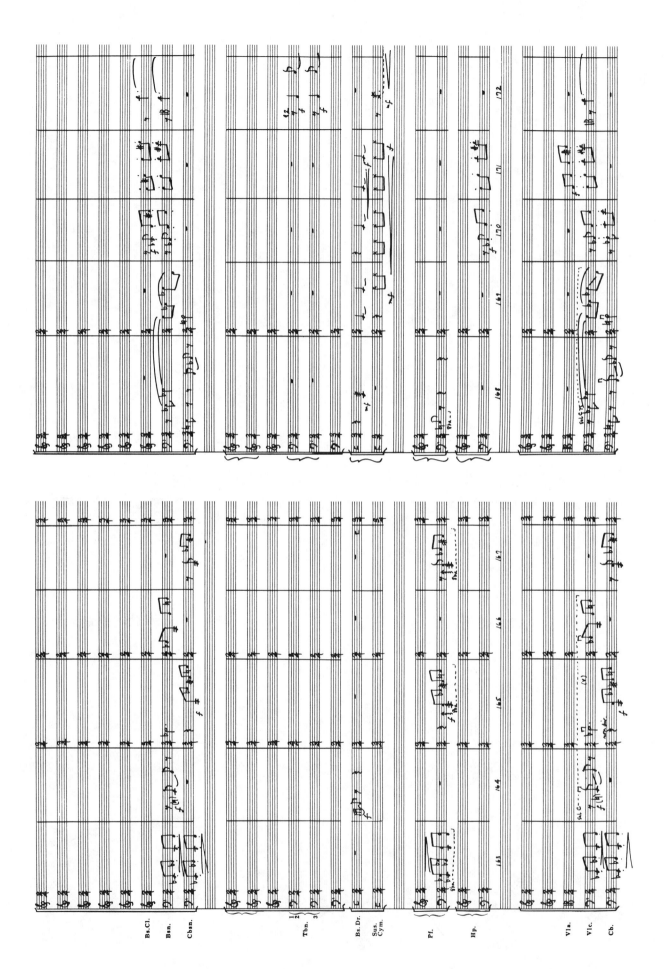

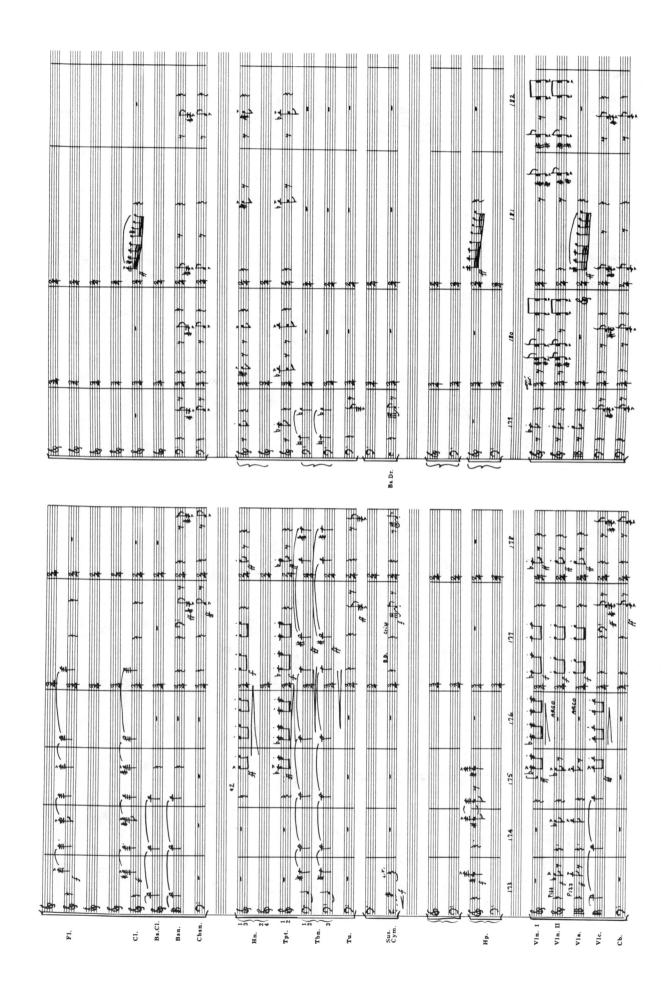

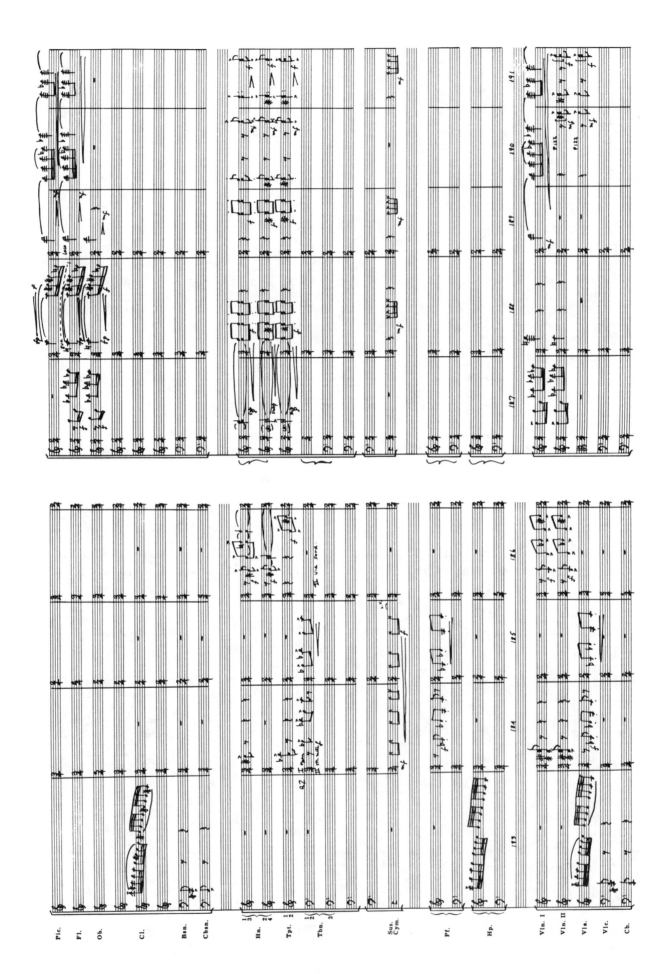

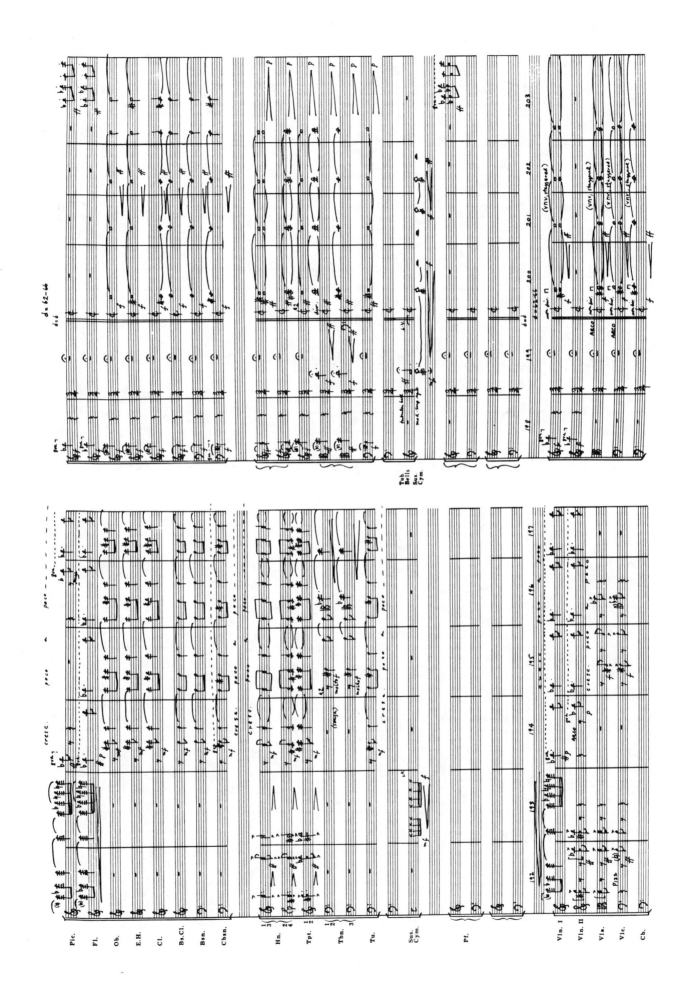

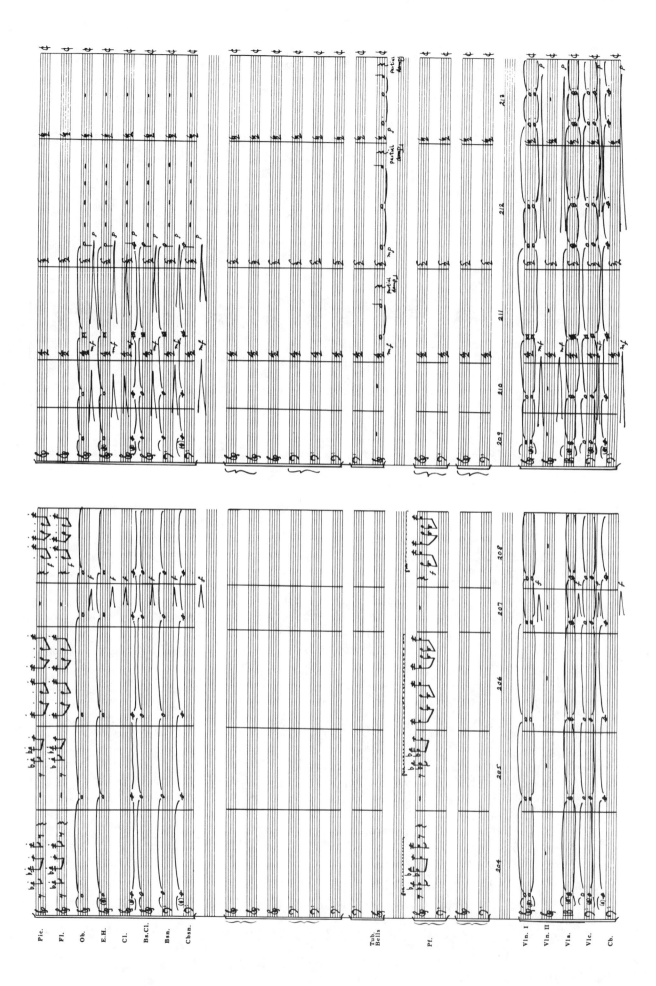

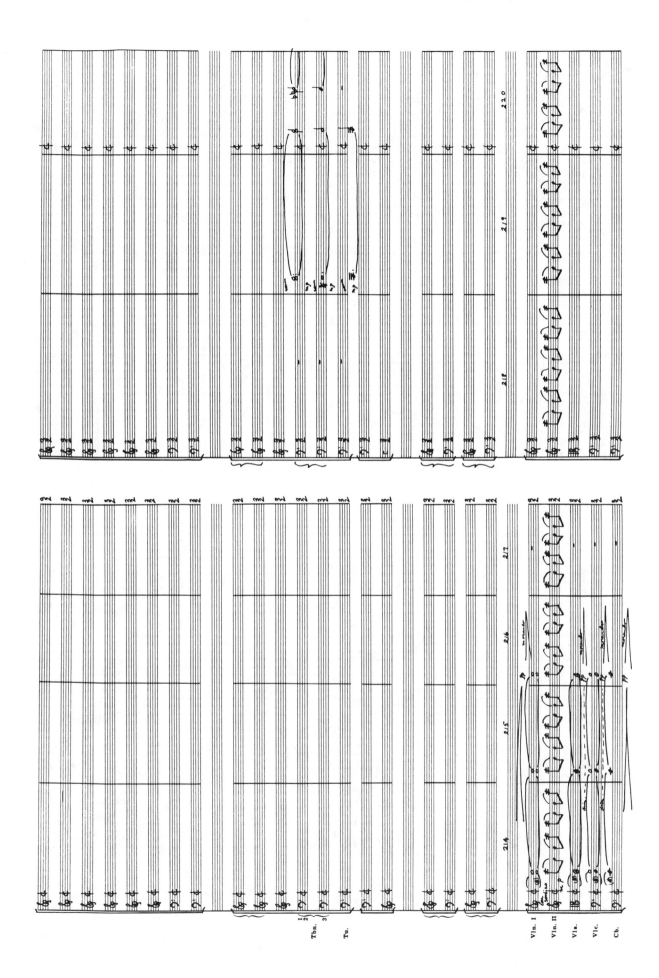

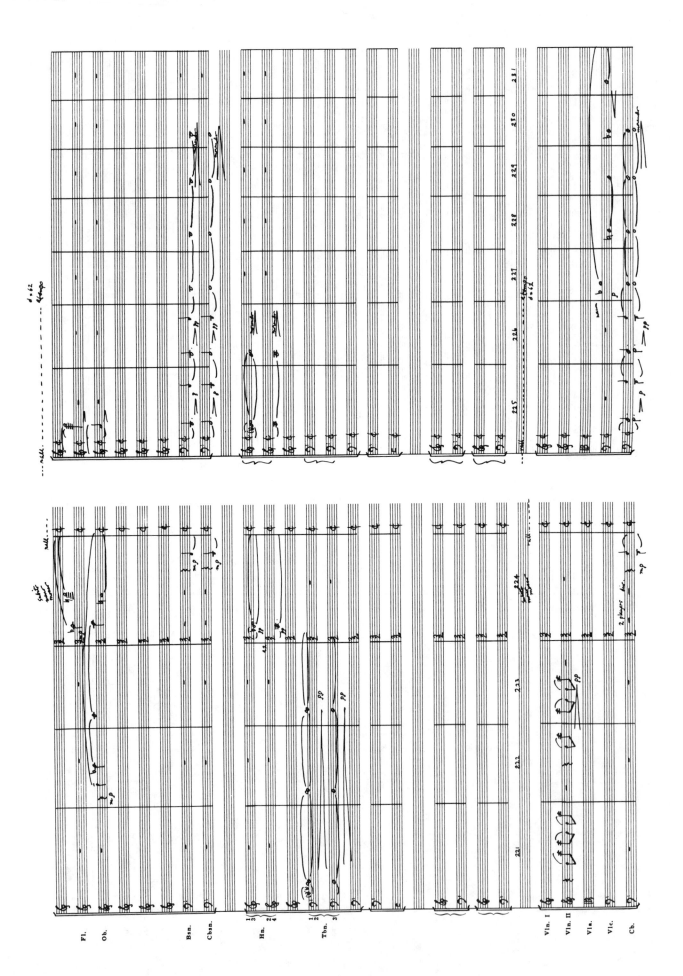

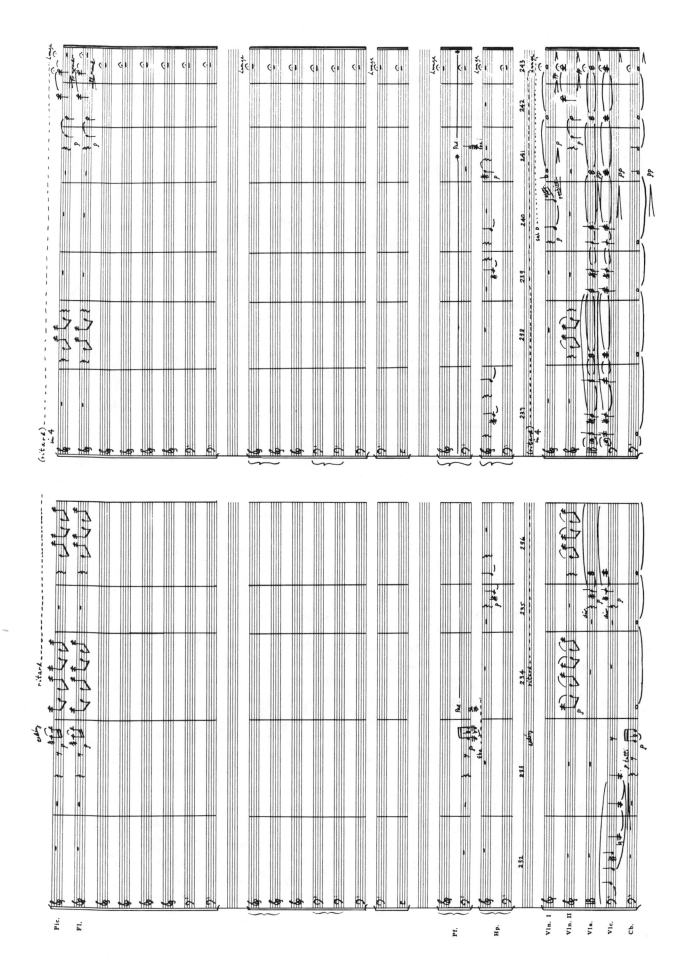

Contributors

Jane P. Ambrose	University of Vermont
Jane A. Bernstein	Tufts University
Adrienne Fried Block	Hunter College
Edith Borroff	State University of New York at Binghamton
Jane Bowers	University of Wisconsin—Milwaukee
James R. Briscoe	Butler University
Austin B. Caswell	Indiana University
Marcia J. Citron	Rice University
Susan E. Erickson	New South Wales Conservatorium
Beverly J. Evans	State University of New York College at Geneseo
Nancy Fierro, CSJ	Los Angeles, California
Susan M. Filler	Chicago, Illinois
Vivian Fine	Bennington College
Bea Friedland	Da Capo Press
Mildred Denby Green	Le Moyne-Owen College
Barbara Garvey Jackson	University of Arkansas
Barbara Jean Jeskalian	San Jose State University
Karin Pendle	University of Cincinnati
Beatrice Pescerelli	University of Bologna
Barbara A. Petersen	Broadcast Music, Inc.
Carolyn Raney	Schiller International University, Heidelberg
Nancy B. Reich	Hastings-on-Hudson, New York
Léonie Rosenstiel	Author Aid/Research Associates International, New York
Adrian T. Thomas	The Queen's University of Belfast
Judith Tick	Northeastern University
Diane Touliatos-Banker	University of Missouri—St. Louis
Heidi Von Gunden	University of Illinois
Robert Weber	Edmonton, Alberta
Ellen Taaffe Zwilich	New York, New York